ADDICTED TO ADULTERY

ADDICTED TO ADULTERY

How We Saved Our Marriage
How You Can Save Yours

RICHARD AND
ELIZABETH BRZECZEK
AND SHARON DE VITA

BANTAM BOOKS

NEW YORK • TORONTO • LONDON • SYDNEY • AUCKLAND

ADDICTED TO ADULTERY

A Bantam Book / October 1989

Library of congress Cataloging-in-Publication Data

Brzeczek, Richard.
    Addicted to adultery : how we saved our marriage, how you can save yours /
Richard and Elizabeth Brzeczek and Sharon De Vita.
        p.   cm.
    Bibliography: p.
    ISBN 0-553-05397-3
    1. Brzeczek, Richard--Mental health. 2. Relationship addiction--Patients--
United States--Biography. 3. Adultery--United States--Personal narratives.
I. Brzeczek, Elizabeth. II. De Vita, Sharon. III. Title.
    RC552.R44B79   1989
    306.73'6'092--dc20
    [B]
                                                                    89-7020
                                                                    CIP

Published simultaneously in the United States and Canada

Bantam Books are published by Bantam Books, a division of Bantam Doubleday Dell
Publishing Group, Inc. Its trademark, consisting of the words "Bantam Books" and
the portrayal of a rooster, is Registered in U.S. Patent and Trademark Office and in
other countries. Marca Registrada. Bantam Books, 666 Fifth Avenue, New York,
New York 10103.

PRINTED IN THE UNITED STATES OF AMERICA

RRD   0 9 8 7 6 5 4 3 2 1

C-1

Dedication

This book is the product of faith in God, hope for the future, and the love of many people who suffered with us through tough times and had the courage and perseverance to "hang in there" for our sake.

We owe a debt of gratitude to the mental health professionals who, with compassion and understanding, helped us work our way back to sanity through therapy. From Betty Lechner, M.A., through Marvin Pitluck, Ph.D., Sara Pitluck, M.A., and Jerome Katz, M.D., to Doris Wineman, M.A., and Jan Fawcett, M.D.

To the Reverend Lawrence Biondi, S.J., president of St. Louis University, and the Reverend Thomas R. Nangle, chaplain, Chicago Police Department, both of whom transcended the role of clergyman to assume the role of intimate friends, being there in crisis to help, share, and pray.

To Tessie Johnson for her willingness to get involved and for sending Liz the original copy of *Love Must Be Tough*.

To Florence Gerzon for her strength, friendship, and support.

To Bill Hanhardt, Russell DiTusa, and Donald De Franza: tough cops but gentle men for supporting us throughout this ordeal.

To Rita and Joe Ritrovato, who were always there for us and who almost sacrificed their own great relationship to keep ours going.

To our parents, Mom and Dad Brzeczek and Mom and Dad Weszely, who prayed, counseled, and even scolded us, but never gave up. They suffered with us and made sure that good and right prevailed.

To our children, Natalie Ann Brzeczek Loria, Mark Douglas Brzeczek, Kevin Martin Brzeczek, and Holly Lynn Brzeczek. They didn't deserve to be born into a world that heaped pain and sorrow upon their young and tender lives, but showed the strength of their convictions. They are our source of love, hope, joy, and inspiration.

Last, we dedicate this book to the present and future members of WESOM, Inc. Without their wanting to save their marriages from the tragedy of adultery, there would be no story to tell. From pain and despair they have been able to find peace and strength. With God's guidance they grow in love and happiness.

God may work in strange ways, for He is the original Rube Goldberg. He has answered our prayers and given us guidance and direction. He has saved our marriage.

—Richard and Elizabeth Brzeczek

Author's
Acknowledgments

In the course of researching and writing this book, many people have assisted me by giving unselfishly of their time. I would personally like to thank:

Dr. Jan Fawcett, Professor of Psychiatry, Rush Presbyterian—St. Luke's Medical Center, Chicago, Illinois, for his medical expertise.

Richard F. Pellegrino and Margaret Higgins Pellegrino, my Chicago attorneys, for initially bringing the Brzeczeks and me together, and for their legal assistance and expertise during the course of this project.

The Reverend Frank De Vita, Deacon Associate, Divine Providence Parish, Westchester, Illinois, for his theological expertise.

Martha Jean Powers, who helped critique the manuscript in various stages and kept me on track throughout the year and a half it took to complete this project.

The four Brzeczek children: Natalie, Mark, Kevin, and Holly, for allowing me to delve into a very private and painful part of their lives.

Dick and Liz Brzeczek, for their courage.

To the couples and individuals of WESOM, Inc., who cannot be recognized publicly in order to protect their privacy, but who willingly shared their stories and their pain in order to help others.

Barbara Alpert, Stephen Rubin, and the rest of the Bantam crew for their enthusiastic support of this project.

Finally, I'd like to thank my husband and business manager, Anthony De Vita, who encouraged me to write this book and supported me throughout the long, arduous task of bringing it to fruition. His unfailing confidence and support over the past twenty years has allowed me to realize many dreams. This book was one of them. His help was invaluable, and I could not have completed this project without it. I had the eyes; he had the vision.

Thank you,
Sharon De Vita
September 1988

Contents

PART
ONE

Foreword

Adultery is a subject most politicians and their wives refuse to discuss, let alone admit in front of millions of viewers on a nationally syndicated talk show.

In July 1987, Dick Brzeczek (pronounced Bree-zek), the former superintendent of the Chicago Police Department, and his wife, Liz, appeared on *The Phil Donahue Show* and shocked the audience when they calmly told the story of how Dick's three-year adulterous affair nearly destroyed their lives.

As Chicago's police superintendent, Dick Brzeczek was one of the foremost law enforcement officers in the country. Politically astute and intellectually imposing, Dick was well on his way to national prominence. His image was squeaky clean, his marriage long and happy, and his credentials impeccable. It was rumored that he would be the man to succeed William Webster as head of the FBI.

Married young, the Brzeczeks had worked hard to pull themselves up from poverty to prominence. Their four children attended exclusive private schools, and Dick and Liz had been welcomed into the most elite circles of society: from the White House in Washington to the governor's mansion in Illinois, to the mayor's residence in Taipei.

The Brzeczeks had it all: power, prominence, and a brilliant political future. But the couple's storybook life suddenly took a detour into hell.

As Dick's prominence grew, so did his ego. Shortly after he had been appointed Chicago's police superintendent, this once happily married man became involved with another woman. This was not just a casual fling or a one-night stand, but an obsessive-addictive relationship that not only destroyed Dick's brilliant political career and his marriage, but almost ended his life.

This is the true story of how Dick and Liz Brzeczek picked up the pieces and slowly put their shattered marriage back together. Using their own personal experience, the couple went on to form WESOM (We Saved Our Marriage), the first support group in the country for couples and individuals whose lives and marriages had also been shattered by adultery.

3

With the formation of this unique self-help group, for the first time adultery and its devastating effects were finally out of the closet. *ADDICTED TO ADULTERY* is the true story of this couple's very private tragedy and their personal triumph.

Prologue

On November 7, 1984, a bitterly cold Chicago morning, Liz Brzeczek quietly slipped into a back pew of Queen of All Saints Church.

A soft-spoken willowy brunette with intense green eyes, Liz Brzeczek looked like a woman who had everything. On the outside, she appeared to be the perfect wife for one of Illinois' brightest politicians. But on the inside Liz Brzeczek was falling apart.

For more than a year she had been living a lie—a lie that had broken her heart and nearly broken her spirit.

Liz had supported her husband both publicly and privately in spite of the fact that he was involved in an adulterous affair.

Liz had kept waiting, hanging on to a thin thread of hope born out of desperation. But on this bitterly cold morning Liz knew there was no hope—not for her or for her marriage.

When her husband had finally confessed that he was indeed involved with another woman, he had been at the beginning of a bitter political campaign.

Liz had kept her husband's secret, enduring her private hell in silence. She had agreed to wait until after the election before making a decision about their marriage.

But now the election was over. Last night her husband had lost his bid to become the new state's attorney of Cook County. Liz had stood beside her husband as he gave his concession speech, knowing the campaign wasn't the only thing that was over; her marriage was over as well.

This morning, as Liz sat in church, her attorney was downtown filing the papers that would put an end to what had once been a storybook marriage.

Divorce was not a word that came easily to Liz, a devout Catholic who began nearly every morning with Mass. Liz's faith had been the cornerstone of her life, a quiet anchor through all of life's storms. But on this, the darkest morning of her life, Liz's faith seemed to have deserted her. There were no words of comfort this morning, no prayers of solace, just a deep, aching sadness.

5

Adultery? Liz Brzeczek had *never* thought it could happen to her. Adultery was something that happened to other people.

But it *had* happened to her.

After all the years of struggling, after all they had achieved, it still wasn't enough. Dick wasn't satisfied. He wanted more. He wanted another woman.

Their marriage vows had been sacred. A solemn promise made before God. How could this have happened? *How had God let it happen?*

The Reverend H. Robert Clark, pastor of Queen of All Saints Church, approached Liz and hesitantly touched her shoulder. "Liz, are you all right?"

Liz bowed her head as tears filled her eyes.

"Whatever it is, Liz, whatever the problem, trust in God. He will help you."

The woman whose faith had carried her through every crisis in her life slowly lifted her head.

"Father," she said softly. "There is no God."

Chapter One

The Beginning of the End

Liz Brzeczek's marital troubles began almost three years before that desolate day in church. Shortly after her husband had been appointed superintendent of the Chicago Police Department, Liz realized there was something wrong with her once loving husband, and with her marriage.

Dick's appointment as superintendent had been the culmination of the couple's dreams; it had been a long, arduous journey that had taken them nearly sixteen years.

Before Dick even entered the police academy, he had decided that someday he would be superintendent of the department. Liz had never doubted him. Even as a young man Dick Brzeczek knew exactly where he was going—to the top.

Born in the Humboldt Park area of Chicago, Dick was the oldest of three children and the only son. An overly obedient child, Dick was emotionally attached to his rather strict parents; he would never dream of doing anything to defy or disappoint them. He was sixteen years old before he went on his first date, and his parents went along to chaperon. Up until the age of twenty-two, in spite of the fact that Dick was a full-time police officer, he had a midnight curfew.

Growing up, Dick was always striving for some measure of approval, some measure of acceptance. When that approval or acceptance didn't come, Dick became extremely competitive. He learned how to hide and control his emotions, developing an "I'll show *you*" attitude. He was determined to excel at everything he attempted. Being good simply wasn't good enough; Dick Brzeczek had to be the best.

While still in high school, Dick took a part-time job at St. Mary's Hospital in order to earn money to help out his family. After graduation, Dick continued working at St. Mary's in order to put himself through college.

Liz Weszely was a shy, eightteen-year-old nursing student at St. Mary's when she met Dick. He had matured into an arrogant, intimidating man who valued control. Liz disliked him on sight.

But the night she met Dick, Liz had a dream that she married him. She quickly dismissed her dream because she really couldn't stand the man. She was certain nothing would come of their meeting.

But Dick was persistent in his pursuit of Liz, and before long they began dating. Liz's natural warmth quickly melted Dick's arrogant facade. She soon realized that beneath Dick's pompous airs was a strong, honest man with a great deal of integrity. Dick was also ambitious and aggressive; he was a man who had confidence in himself and his abilities. In Dick, Liz saw a man who possessed all the qualities she lacked.

The only daughter in an extremely close, affectionate family, Liz had spent her childhood in painful self-doubt. Her loving home served as a buffer for all the ridicule she endured. An unattractive child who wore braces, thick eyeglasses, and plain clothing, Liz suffered the taunts and cruelty of other children because of her appearance. As a result, Liz grew up with little confidence in herself and her abilities.

Shy Liz Weszely, who had endured such cruelty as a child, soon found herself admiring the brash young man with the high hopes and dreams. Dick was bright, eager, and extremely articulate. He had a passion for learning and knowledge. Dick idolized Vince Lombardi and his credo for winning, and he believed he was born—*destined*—to be a winner.

The more Liz got to know him, the more she realized Dick possessed all the qualities she wanted in a husband. To her, Dick was the ideal man.

As time wore on, the couple fell deeply in love and wanted to get married. Dick was still in college, Liz still in nursing school. But Dick finally worked up the courage to broach the subject of marriage with his parents. Their veto was swift and final. Dick was too young, didn't have a steady job, and couldn't support a wife and still continue his education. Dick's parents' objections went on and on, until Dick finally dropped the subject, not wanting to disobey his parents or incur their disapproval.

Although Dick had long held the dream of becoming a doctor, he also wanted to marry Liz. Dick realized that unless he had a full-time job that allowed him to support a wife yet continue his education, he would never get his parents' permission to marry Liz.

After seriously considering the problem, Dick decided to join the police department. It seemed the perfect solution. He could work full-time as a police officer at night and continue going to school full-time during the day. He was certain that if he and Liz combined their salaries they could make it work. Becoming a police officer would mean giving up his lifelong dream of becoming a doctor, but it would allow him to realize another dream—marrying Liz.

Dick knew that if his plan worked, his parents would have to let him get married. Even at twenty-two, Dick still felt the need for his parents' approval. He talked his idea over with Liz, who told him she'd stand by any decision he made. If Dick wanted to be a cop, she'd be a cop's wife. But Dick didn't want to be just a cop; he told Liz he wanted someday to be superintendent of the department.

On June 8, 1964 Dick entered the police academy after ranking ninth on the patrolman's exam. Dick found that he loved police work; he took to the job like a man born to it. He worked the 6:00 P.M. to 2:30 A.M. shift in order to attend classes during the day.

After Liz graduated from nursing school, the couple decided they had waited long enough; they wanted to get married. They set the date, picked out a hall, and ordered rings. But there was still one obstacle: Dick had yet to mention his upcoming marriage to his parents.

With the wedding just four months away, Dick finally worked up the courage to broach the subject of marriage again. He logically countered every one of their objections until his parents finally relented and gave him their blessings. Dick and Liz were married on January 16, 1965.

Everyone agreed that the young couple seemed an ideal match. In Liz, Dick found the warmth and affection he craved. In Dick, Liz found the confidence and security she needed.

The marriage was happy and very traditional. Dick was the more dominant spouse; Liz was more passive. She was docile, devoted, and totally dependent on her husband. Dick set the course for their life together and Liz obediently followed. Dick's dreams became her dreams; his goals became her goals.

In the past, Dick often had a difficult time letting anyone get close to him. Controlling and hiding his emotions had become second nature to him. But he no longer had to hide or control his emotions. He found that with Liz, he could be himself.

Liz was not just his wife but his best friend. They talked to each other about almost everything, including their innermost hopes and dreams. Liz proved to be a wonderful sounding board for Dick. He valued her instincts and trusted her opinions. She became his most trusted confidant. Liz understood Dick, encouraged him, and supported him. More important, Liz *believed* in him.

All his life Dick had been striving for approval and acceptance, but with Liz he didn't have to strive, for she gave her acceptance willingly and without hesitation. In spite of their tight finances, Dick and Liz were blissfully happy.

The only cloud in the couple's marriage was Dick's occasional temper and his competitiveness. Dick set high goals for himself and for everyone around him. He then worked diligently to achieve those goals and expected others to do the same. Whenever Dick failed to attain a goal or accomplish an objective, he became very angry with himself and the world. His "I'll show them" attitude grew even stronger.

Driven and ambitious, Dick was a classic overachiever. He was compulsive in his expectations of excellence; mediocrity was not tolerated, even from his wife.

Aware of all the pressure her husband was under trying to continue his education and work full-time, Liz tried to make Dick's life run smoothly. Pleasing her husband was of the utmost importance to her. She wanted to be the kind of wife she felt Dick deserved.

Occasionally, when Liz fell short of Dick's expectations, he became even more demanding, compulsive, and intimidating, causing Liz to wonder if she would *ever* be able to live up to all her husband's expectations. Because she was naturally obliging and eager to please, whenever Dick expressed dismay or disappointment in her, Liz responded by trying harder.

"I didn't do anything any other wife wouldn't do," Liz said. "I loved Dick and it was only natural for me to want to please him."

During the couple's sixteen-year journey to the top of the mountain, they endured many financial hardships. Their four children came quickly. Dick frequently had to work two jobs in order to support his growing family and continue his education. In addition to working nights as a patrolman, during the lean years Dick also taught school during the day and frequently worked as a consultant and trainer for the University of Chicago's security department.

After college Dick went on to receive his master's degree. He knew he had come far, but not far enough. Despite the obstacles, Dick wanted to attend law school. Financially, it seemed impossible. But that didn't stop Dick from going, or Liz from encouraging him. If Dick wanted to become an attorney, Liz would support his decision. She knew that somehow, some way, they'd manage.

They had no idea how they would pay Dick's first semester tuition, so the couple finally went to Dick's father and borrowed the money.

Despite the intense pressure he was under, Dick's competitive edge never diminished. At the end of his freshman year in law school Dick ranked near the top of his class. On two out of the three police promotional exams, he ranked number one.

While Dick was dedicated to the advancement of his education and career, Liz was dedicated to Dick. As the nondriving mother of four small children, it was impossible for Liz to return to her nursing career, so she sold Avon door to door, and baby-sat at home in order to earn extra money. Each night, no matter what time Dick got home, Liz was up waiting for him with a hot meal and a sympathetic ear.

Despite all the hardships, the Brzeczeks' marriage flourished. All the adversity served to draw them closer. What precious free time Dick had was spent lavishing love, attention, and affection on his wife and children.

Aware of the young couple's financial difficulties, both sets of parents tried to help with gifts of food and cash.

Dick's father continued to help the couple with Dick's law school tuition, while Liz's father, a retired butcher, frequently brought over bags of pork bones and chicken necks so the young family could eat. Liz would scrape the meat off the pork bones to make patties and boil the chicken necks for soup. At times, it was all they had to eat.

Professionally, Dick was quickly establishing himself as a leader. There weren't many cops who had a master's degree patroling the streets of Chicago. Dick began getting invitations to lecture at colleges and universities. By the time Dick graduated from law school he had a long list of credentials. He was a member of the Gavel Society, an American Bar Association Silver Key Award winner, listed in *Who's Who,* and the recipient of the Outstanding Member of the Phi Alpha Delta International Law Fraternity.

When Dick received his law degree from John Marshall Law School, Liz too received a degree from John Marshall; it was a P.H.T. degree, which was given to all the wives of law students for "Putting Hubby Through." Liz was extremely proud to have made a contribution to Dick's education and career. They were a team, working toward one common goal: Dick's success.

Dick's star was rising quickly both in Chicago and nationally. He was one of only twenty-five Chicago police officers who had two advanced degrees. He loved the law, but police work was in his blood. Shortly after passing the bar exam, Dick was appointed to the position of legal counsel to the police superintendent. Dick was the first cop-attorney ever to hold the position.

On January 11, 1980, Dick fulfilled the promise he had made to Liz so many years earlier. On that January night Mayor Jane Byrne announced Dick Brzeczek's appointment as the new superintendent of the fourteen-thousand-man Chicago Police Department. At thirty-seven, Dick was the youngest superintendent in the history of the city.

After sixteen years, the long haul of stress and economic hardship was finally over. *They had made it.* They had finally achieved what they had worked so hard and long for; now they could sit back and relax. It was time to enjoy the fruits of their hard labor.

Dick and Liz were ecstatic. Dick was well on his way to a satisfying and successful career; and Liz had everything she had ever dreamed of: a beautiful family, good friends, and a warm, loving husband who was totally devoted to her and their children. They had finally reached the top of the mountain.

Within hours of the mayor's announcement, every facet of Dick and Liz's life became front page news. The press began clamoring for every scrap of information about the new superintendent and his family. Accolades for Dick began to pour in from across the country. Well educated and well known for his tough law-and-order stance, Dick Brzeczek had all the qualifications necessary to impress even the hardened Chicago press corps. A self-made man with impeccable credentials, Dick was called the most competent, qualified superintendent in the history of Chicago. Optimism ran high that Dick would finally be the man to improve the police department's somewhat murky reputation.

Not everyone, however, was pleased with the mayor's choice. The morning after Dick's appointment was announced, the Reverend Jesse Jackson, head of Operation Push, led a protest march in front of police headquarters, objecting to Dick's appointment.

In Chicago, although the final appointment of police superintendent is made by the mayor, the selection process is handled by a nine-member panel Civilian Police Board. In 1980, the board, headed by Wilbur N.

Daniel, a black Baptist minister, interviewed qualified candidates from Chicago as well as across the country. After the board completed its interviews, the members narrowed the field down to three candidates, then passed along the names of the finalists to the mayor for a decision.

The three finalists were: Lee Brown, director of public safety in Atlanta, Georgia; Raleigh Mathis, a lieutenant in the Chicago Police Department; and Richard J. Brzeczek, assistant deputy superintendent, lawyer, and a captain in the department.

The other two finalists, Lee Brown and Raleigh Mathis, were both black. The Reverend Jackson protested Dick's appointment because he claimed it was based on race. Jackson claimed that Dick's only qualification was his color—or rather, his lack of it.

It was to be the first of many shots fired at Dick Brzeczek. But he had trained all his life to be King of the Mountain, and he wasn't about to let anything or anyone stand in his way.

The Brzeczeks' dream had been a long time coming. The night after Dick's appointment, the couple went out to celebrate. When they returned, they found their home had been burglarized. Even Chicago's top cop wasn't immune to crime. The burglary frightened Liz. Her home, her privacy, and her life had suddenly been invaded. Was this simply a random act by thieves? Or had the Brzeczeks deliberately been targets? At the time, Liz didn't know, but later she would wonder if perhaps the burglary was an omen.

Dick's confirmation by the Chicago City Council was attended by the couple's entire family. Dick was a role model, living proof that the American Dream wasn't just for the rich and privileged, but for *everyone*, even the son of a Chicago Transit Authority motor man. If you worked hard, anything was possible; Dick had proved that.

With Dick's appointment the couple's life changed overnight. Almost from the beginning Dick was under incredible pressure. The position of superintendent was not a nine-to-five job but a way of life. Dick had to be available twenty-four hours a day, seven days a week. A scanner, police radio, and beeper were placed in the couple's bedroom. Not a night went by that Dick and Liz weren't awakened by some police emergency. Once a week a technician from the police department came to inspect their home and electronically sweep their telephones for bugging devices.

As superintendent, Dick was responsible not only for protecting the citizens of Chicago but for running the fourteen-thousand-man police department—the second largest in the nation—as well as for providing security for the political leaders of Chicago and all visiting dignitaries, whether they were national leaders, celebrities, or foreign heads of state.

During the first year of Dick's term several major crises developed. Within the first month, four thousand Chicago firefighters went on strike. It was Dick's responsibility as superintendent of police to protect not only the abandoned firehouses but those firefighters who chose to cross the picket lines and continue to work. Tensions between the police and fire department ran high.

Shortly after the strike ended, three white police officers were accused of beating an elderly black man to death on an elevated train. Dick and other community leaders were outraged at the act of violence. Dick promised that as long as he was superintendent, police brutality would not be tolerated. The officers involved were suspended immediately. Despite Dick's assurances that a full-scale investigation would take place, the Reverend Jesse Jackson again called for Dick's resignation, claiming he was insensitive to police brutality. Race once again seemed to be an issue. But cops, black civic leaders, and even the press rallied around Dick, applauding his prompt handling of the situation. (Two of the officers were later convicted of manslaughter. One was acquitted.)

The story remained front page news for days, until the mayor created a special commission to deal with the issue of the public's perception of police brutality. The city seemed polarized by the race issue.

One problem after another seemed to crop up. Cabrini-Green, one of the most infamous and dangerous housing projects in the country, erupted in gang violence. The climate at the project became so tense, and the public outcry so loud, that Mayor Byrne decided to move into Cabrini-Green to help rid the housing project of the crime and the gangs that controlled the buildings. Her announcement made headlines across the country.

The nation was watching; protecting the mayor was of the utmost importance, and the pressure on Dick increased. He assigned a contingent of police officers to protect the mayor and to patrol the hallways and corridors of the housing project. Officers made several sweeps of the building, confiscating guns, drugs, and other illegal paraphernalia. Dick knew that if anything happened to the mayor while she was a resident of the project, it would be his responsibility.

Dick also had the responsibility of protecting President Ronald Reagan on his first trip out of Washington after the assassination attempt. Dick and the department spent several intensive weeks preparing for the president's visit. Security was particularly tight because of the previous attempt on the president's life.

But despite the enormous problems Dick inherited, his reputation as a law enforcement officer continued to grow. Always in demand as a speaker and teacher, Dick traveled all over the country on behalf of the department. He became more and more involved in national law enforcement issues. He was invited to lecture at Harvard University, at the John F. Kennedy School of Government, and at the FBI Academy in Quantico, Virginia. He was also occasionally summoned to the White House to discuss matters of national security such as terrorism and drug running.

During this time, Dick found himself facing some tough issues at home. He wanted to establish himself as his own man and as a superintendent Chicago could be proud of. Despite the fact that he was both an attorney and the superintendent, Dick Brzeczek was first and foremost a cop.

There were quite a few ruffled feathers in the upper echelons of the police force when Dick announced that there would no longer be two sets of rules for the department, one for the bosses and another for the troops. Under Dick Brzeczek, everyone from the top cop on down would be treated equally. With Dick at the helm, it was quite clearly no longer business as usual in the department. Dick wanted to run the department his way—in a professional, businesslike manner. He felt an enormous responsibility not only to the people of Chicago but to the cops who were out there putting their lives on the line every day.

One of the first major tasks Dick undertook was to order an audit of the Office of Professional Standards. The OPS handles citizens' complaints concerning police. Many are alleged cases of police brutality. It was the first time any superintendent had ever ordered an *investigation of the investigators*.

Dick also ordered an investigation of all Chicago citizens who were assigned a police bodyguard and car. Far too many people in the city had been given preferential treatment based on their political contacts, rather than on need or merit. For too long the police department had been run, and favors granted, not on the basis of who you were but who you *knew*. Dick wanted to put an end to this policy. There were prominent people in the city who needed protection, who had a legitimate reason for a car and bodyguard, but Dick's investigation proved there were many more who had the privilege but not the need.

Dick ended up rescinding the bodyguard/car privileges of a great many people, including the Reverend Jesse Jackson. Jackson had been assigned a car and a full-time bodyguard by the city of Chicago, despite the fact that he had never held or run for any public office. There didn't appear to be any justification for the police department to provide Jackson—a private citizen—with a full-time bodyguard and police department car. Dick felt certain that Jackson would be just as safe in a car he paid for himself as in a car paid for by the department. Dick's actions didn't endear him to the Reverend Jackson.

While Dick's position brought enormous pressures and responsibilities, it also brought a number of perks: power and prominence, as well as influence and celebrity status. Next to the mayor, Dick was the second most visible person in the city.

Dick and Liz quickly got a taste of what life would be like in the public, very political eye of Chicago. Almost every evening there was a social function that required the couple's attendance. Dick and Liz found themselves socializing with President Ronald Reagan, former President Jimmy Carter, Senator Charles Percy, Governor James Thompson, Mrs. Anwar Sadat, and other national and international dignitaries. During Dick's first year as superintendent the couple also traveled to Europe, Japan, and the Republic of China.

Liz, once the ugly duckling, had grown into a graceful swan. Her thick eyeglasses were replaced by contacts. Her simple clothing had been replaced by elegant silk gowns that fit her slender size-six figure to perfection. The woman who at one time had scraped pork bones to feed her family was now socializing with the world's elite.

As Dick's prominence grew, so did his ego. The air of arrogance and superiority he projected was often offensive, even to Liz. She worried that her husband's attitude was a liability and would be detrimental to his career.

As Dick's second year as superintendent began, the pressure on him grew. Then, shortly after Dick and Liz returned from China, tragedy struck.

Dick was at home having dinner when he received a call informing him that an officer had been shot. As was customary whenever a cop was injured in the line of duty, Dick rushed to the hospital and was shocked to learn that the officer who had been shot was James Riordan, his first deputy superintendent.

James Riordan wasn't just Dick's assistant. Riordan and his wife, Loretta, had been friends of the Brzeczeks for many years.

Carefully hiding his emotions, Dick called Liz and told her what happened. By the tone of his voice, Liz knew that Dick was deeply troubled, but he kept himself firmly in control. Dick refused to let anyone, even Liz, see his grief.

Riordan, a thirty-three-year veteran of the department, was the highest-ranking police officer in the history of the city ever to be killed. Off duty at the time, Riordan had attempted to mediate a dispute between a man and a woman in a restaurant. While escorting the man outside to cool off, the man had pulled a gun and shot Riordan three times at point-blank range.

After calling Liz, Dick sent a car for Riordan's wife, Loretta, and tried to fend off the press, who smelled a big, breaking story. The police chaplain arrived, but Dick decided to break the news to Loretta Riordan himself. It was one of the hardest things Dick ever had to do. Loretta's husband wasn't the only member of her family who was a cop; three of her sons were also Chicago police officers.

Once Mrs. Riordan had been informed, the press broke the story. For the first time in his career, Dick refused to talk to the press. It was totally out of character for him. But this situation was too raw, too personal, the pain too deep.

Dick chose to stay at the hospital and personally direct the investigation of the shooting. Dick spent a tension-filled night, doing a lot of the leg work himself. A suspect was finally arrested and convicted of Riordan's death. It was ironic that the man who killed Riordan turned out to be a former Iowa police officer.

Eleven hundred mourners attended the slain officer's funeral. Liz knew that Dick was hurting deeply, but he refused to talk about the situation. He was morose and withdrawn, clearly not himself. And Dick still refused to talk to the press, which only increased their curiosity. Dick was known for being up front and honest with the press. He never ducked a problem, but met it head-on, then handled it. This was clearly a problem he couldn't handle.

Dick was asked to present Loretta Riordan with the flag that had draped her husband's coffin. He still remembers it painfully. Her husband had given not only thirty-three years to the department, but his life as well. Presenting her with the flag seemed an empty, hollow gesture after all her husband had been to the department.

A few days after Riordan's funeral, the police photographer brought in some official photographs for Dick's approval before releasing them to the press. On the bottom of the stack was a picture of Riordan's casket, and one lone mourner standing silently, weeping. Dick took the picture and put it in his top desk drawer, where it remained during his entire tenure as superintendent. It would be a haunting, daily reminder of Dick's own mortality.

Despite Riordan's death, it was business as usual in the department. But Liz continued to worry about Dick. He had never openly expressed his grief about his friend's death, and Liz knew it wasn't good for Dick to keep all of his emotions inside.

Shortly after Riordan's death, Curtis Sliwa, leader of the Guardian Angels, came to Chicago. From the moment he arrived, disagreements between the Angels and the police department erupted. Sliwa wanted the department to recognize the Angels as a group. Dick refused. His reasons were principally legal ones; the Guardian Angels had no liability insurance. If the police department or the mayor sanctioned their activities, and either a citizen or one of the Angels were injured during one of their patrols, they could technically hold Dick, the city, and the department liable.

Sliwa and Dick had a running verbal battle that was picked up by the national press. *Good Morning America* called Dick and asked if he would appear with Sliwa and debate his position. Dick agreed.

Shortly after Dick returned from his appearance on *Good Morning America,* Liz noticed a change in his behavior. Dick's sense of humor seemed to have evaporated. He became cool and aloof even with her. Dick also began drinking. While he had been a social drinker in the past, he now drank as more than a social indulgence.

Concerned, Liz tried to get Dick to talk about what was bothering him, but he denied that anything was wrong.

"I knew Dick better than anyone in the world," Liz recalled. "We were as close as two people could be, and I knew something was wrong. At first I thought it was just the intense pressure he was under. In addition to his normal duties, Dick continued to travel around the country on behalf of the department. The demands on his time were incredible. At this point, I think he was receiving about ten to fifteen requests a week for outside speaking engagements."

The more Liz tried to get Dick to talk about what was bothering him, the more withdrawn and angry he became. Dick shut her out of his life, and their once idyllic relationship began to deteriorate. All the closeness and intimacy the couple had shared for so many years seemed to dissolve.

"Dick and I had always been able to talk about everything," Liz said. "We'd always been a team, helping each other, sharing and working toward common goals. Dick and I were partners, so this sudden change was totally unlike him. It was very alarming."

Dick became extremely critical of Liz and everything she did. He didn't like her hair, her clothes, or even the way she made his toast. The harder she tried to please him, the more critical he became.

"I was so confused," Liz admitted. "In spite of Dick's arrogance he had always been a kind, caring man. But now it seemed as if he was deliberately trying to be cruel and vicious. The least little thing set off his temper. I couldn't seem to do anything right. Even minor things would become major issues, erupting into screaming battles that usually left me in tears."

Dick's constant complaints and criticism rekindled all the insecurities Liz had suffered as a child. Once again she felt inadequate; Liz was convinced that she was a failure.

"Every woman needs to feel the man she loves approves of her. When Dick's approval was suddenly withdrawn, I felt exposed and very vulnerable."

Liz repeatedly asked her husband what was wrong; she pleaded with Dick to talk to her, assuring him that whatever the problem was, they could work it out together just as they always had. He refused to admit that anything was wrong.

Liz was baffled. Dick had always confronted every problem directly, then went about solving it. But this problem he refused even to acknowledge, let alone discuss.

Over the months Dick became so verbally and emotionally abusive to Liz that even their family and friends began to notice. Dick's sister Rita recalled:

"For almost twenty years my brother and Liz had an ideal marriage. They were very much in love, and very devoted to each other. When Dick began acting strangely, we knew something was wrong, but we didn't know what. I love Liz as much as I love my brother. It was very painful to watch their marriage disintegrate, particularly since we had no idea why. I idolized my brother. He was my hero. He had worked so hard and achieved so much, to watch him change from a warm, loving man, into this . . . stranger was very difficult. My husband, Joe, is one of Dick's closest friends, and even Joe didn't know what was the matter. Dick wouldn't tell him.

"We felt sorry for Dick, Liz, and their kids, but we didn't know what to do to help them. We refused to take sides. We just tried to be there for both of them. It was very difficult, not only for my husband and me, but for my parents as well. Dick and Liz's marital problems became the focus of the entire family's attention. We had reveled in their success, and now grieved with them through their pain.

"Every morning my mother went to church to pray and light candles for Dick and Liz. We all wanted to help, but none of us knew what to do. I thought about talking to my brother but I was afraid to approach him. Dick's temper was extremely volatile at this time."

While most communication between the couple dissolved, their sex life remained very active. Sex was about the only thing they shared, the one link that still held them together. For Liz, making love now served as a false intimacy, an unspoken validation of Dick's acceptance and love.

Slowly Dick began to withdraw from everyone: his parents, his family, even his children. It was as if he wanted to put distance between himself and the people he loved.

Natalie, the Brzeczeks' oldest child, was fourteen and a sophomore in high school when her parents' marriage began to fall apart.

"I didn't know what was going on with my parents. My father was constantly yelling, and my mother was always crying. Before this, my parents had always had a pretty good relationship. Our home life had been stable and secure. But the situation at home got to the point where we didn't even want to come home if my father was there. He was drinking a lot, and the tension in our house—between my mother and father—was unbearable. It was very scary."

Despite the couple's personal problems, Dick went to work every day and continued to travel on behalf of the department. He never let his drinking or his personal problems interfere with his duties as superintendent.

On the outside, he still appeared to be the consummate professional; a man in total control. But inside, Dick was in the eye of a hurricane about to blow out of control.

Because of her husband's sensitive political position, Liz was determined to keep their marital problems private. She was certain this was just a temporary situation, so she continued to accompany Dick to all official social functions.

"There were times when I would spend the day in tears because of

Dick's verbal attacks. Then that night he expected me to accompany him, regardless of how I was feeling. It wouldn't look right for Dick to start showing up at functions without me. We were known as the ideal couple because of the longevity and happiness of our marriage. Only Dick and I knew that our marriage was now just a sham. Those evenings were extremely difficult for me. From Dick's behavior I knew he could barely stand to be in the same room with me. I held back the tears and kept on smiling. But it's hard to keep smiling when you're dying inside."

After months of her husband's abusive treatment, Liz was emotionally battered. Why did she continue to accompany Dick and support him?

"Dick was my life," Liz admitted. "He was my security blanket. We had spent so many years together—good years—that the thought of leaving him now simply never occurred to me. I was certain we could weather this storm. Besides, I'm a devout Catholic, and divorce was not a viable option. I loved Dick and was determined to fix whatever had gone wrong in our marriage. I was confident that once Dick opened up and confided in me, we could work through whatever was bothering him."

But when Dick finally told Liz what the problem was, she was dumbfounded.

"Dick claimed *I* was the problem. He said I was no longer the woman he had married; *I had changed*. Of course I had changed! As our relationship continued to go downhill, I kept changing in an effort to please him. I loved and trusted Dick. If he said I was the problem, that something was wrong with *me*, then obviously *I must be the problem*."

Continually appraising herself, Liz kept looking for ways to improve and regain her husband's respect and love. It was a painful cycle of fear and self-doubt, fed by Dick's constant diet of criticism. Her husband's psychological abuse gradually robbed Liz of all her hard-earned self-confidence.

The more Dick drank, the more abusive he became. In an effort to control Dick's drinking, Liz began hiding the liquor bottles. But this only infuriated Dick. He would search the house for the liquor, and then drink even more.

Uncertain about what to do, Liz finally sought advice from the Reverend Thomas R. Nangle, the police chaplain. Father Nangle had been a longtime friend and was well aware of the couple's problems, having witnessed Dick's bizarre behavior on several occasions. The chaplain suggested the couple seek counseling and even offered to recommend someone.

Liz had thought about counseling more than once, but it wasn't as if they could go see just anyone. Dick was a prominent public figure in Chicago, recognized wherever he went. However, though Liz was concerned about their personal problems becoming public and perhaps hurting Dick's career, she was more concerned about her husband and saving her marriage.

When Liz first broached the subject of counseling, Dick was reluctant, but finally he agreed.

"During the first session the marriage counselor sat with us for a long time, asking questions, and just listening. Every time she asked me a question, Dick would answer for me. I was accustomed to it. Dick frequently talked for me. I'm naturally quiet, even more so in Dick's presence. His personality is so strong, so forceful, I was used to his being the center of attention. It never really bothered me, but it bothered the marriage counselor."

After listening to Dick, the counselor wanted to hear Liz's side of the story. The counselor admonished Dick to let his wife answer for herself. Liz slowly began explaining what had happened to their marriage and their once happy life. All the hurt and confusion she had suffered over the past few months came pouring out. The counselor listened, then turned her attention back to Dick.

But he still refused to admit that anything was wrong. Dick vehemently denied he had a drinking problem and attributed Liz's complaints about it to exaggeration.

After more questioning, Dick finally admitted that Liz was the problem. He told the counselor that Liz was not the same woman he had married, that Liz had changed, and *that* was what was wrong with their marriage.

Mortified and humiliated, Liz sat there listening to her husband lie about their life together. Dick went on to tell the counselor that ten years earlier he had taken his first vacation in years and Liz had chosen that particular time to rip down some wallpaper. He insisted that Liz had deliberately ruined his vacation, and *that* was what had gone wrong with their marriage.

"I was stunned," Liz recalled. "My life had been turned into a living hell because of something I had done nearly ten years ago? I couldn't understand why Dick had waited all this time to bring this up. Why hadn't he told me this sooner?"

When the session was over and the couple was ready to leave, the marriage counselor leaned over and touched Liz's arm.

"Liz," she said softly. "Just remember, this isn't your fault. I've never seen a man behave this way unless he's involved with another woman."

Chapter Two

Facing Reality

Liz was stunned. Another woman? The idea had never occurred to her. She knew Dick better than anyone in the world; she knew his strengths and his weaknesses. While Dick was supremely confident in every other area of his life, he had a terrible fear of rejection. Liz was sure that Dick would never approach another woman, thus risking what he feared most.

Liz rationalized that there was no way someone in Dick's highly visible position could conduct an affair in Chicago without the press picking up on it.

"Dick never went anywhere without me," Liz said. "Despite our floundering marriage, he was either at work or at home. The only time he ever went anywhere without me was when he traveled out of town on department business."

Like other married women faced with the possibility that their once faithful and trusted husbands had strayed, Liz refused even to acknowledge the possibility of another woman. *Not her husband.* They might have been having marital problems, but Dick was not a cheater. They had been through too much over the years; they had been too happy. Adultery was something that happened to other couples, not to *them.*

But the marriage counselor wasn't the first person to hint that another woman might be the cause of the Brzeczeks' marital woes. Liz's mother, Betty Weszely, had brought up the subject shortly after the couple's problems began.

"I told my daughter right from the beginning that I thought Dick had another woman," her mother said. "He had been a devoted husband and family man for almost twenty years. What else would cause a man who had been so happy to begin acting so strangely?"

Liz didn't believe her mother any more than she had believed the marriage counselor. But she decided to confront Dick, to ask him directly if there was someone else. In all their years together Dick had never lied to her. Liz had no reason to believe he would do so now. When she asked Dick if he was involved with another woman, he vehemently denied it. In fact, Dick acted as if Liz was crazy for even suggesting such a thing. She believed him.

"Despite our troubles, I trusted Dick implicitly. Faithfulness was not something we ever discussed, it was just taken for granted. Our marriage vows were sacred to both of us. We had made a solemn promise before God. I never thought he would break those vows."

Although the couple continued counseling, their relationship did not improve. In fact, it continued to decline. Liz was so concerned that she finally persuaded Dick to seek additional help. They began seeing both a psychiatrist and a psychologist, in addition to the marriage counselor.

It was difficult for the doctors to get a clear perspective on the couple's problems. Dick was accustomed to hiding and controlling his emotions. He appeared charming, convincing, and totally intimidating. Dick was the perfect portrait of a man in complete control. He never let on that there was anything wrong with his life or his marriage.

For a while the so-called experts convinced Liz that *she* was the one with the problem. They claimed that her total abstinence from alcohol made her judge Dick's drinking as excessive.

"When I realized the doctors thought I was the one with the problem, my self-esteem shattered," Liz admitted. "You have to remember, *everyone* was intimidated by Dick. He has a strong, forceful, imposing personality. This was a man who was constantly in the news or on television. Of course the doctors were intimidated. If a man in Dick's position was telling them there was no problem, then there must not be a problem. Obviously I was just a hysterical wife who was overreacting."

The question of another woman came up frequently, but Dick continued to deny any involvement, both to Liz and the therapists.

As the months passed, Dick's behavior began to fluctuate wildly. His drinking escalated and he began having acute mood swings. Dick would either be extremely lethargic with barely enough energy to get out of bed, or he would have so much energy that Liz got tired just watching him.

As a registered nurse, Liz recognized her husband's symptoms as depression. What she didn't know was whether the depression was caused by his drinking or by something else.

After months of counseling with no improvement, the doctors suggested it might be beneficial for Dick and Liz to get away from each other for a while. They suggested the couple take separate vacations. Perhaps time and distance would help their situation.

Dick's emotional abuse and unpredictable behavior had left Liz physically and emotionally drained. She had to get away from Dick. For the first time in her adult life, Liz didn't ask for Dick's consent or wait for his approval. She simply packed her bags and went to Arizona to visit her aunt.

"Our life had turned into a battle zone. Living with Dick on a day-to-day basis had become nearly impossible. He drank and I cried. We fought about everything.

"Unless you knew Dick you couldn't see the changes in his behavior or appearance. But all someone had to do was look at me to see the toll our personal problems had taken. I had lost weight, and I was confused and upset. Emotionally, I was a basket case. My world was falling apart and I had no idea why."

The separation did little to improve the Brzeczeks' marriage. When Liz returned, she noticed that Dick's erratic behavior was beginning to affect his job performance.

In the summer of 1982 Mayor Jane Byrne announced that she was running for reelection. Harold Washington, a black congressman, also announced he would be making a bid for mayor, as would the incumbent state's attorney of Cook County, Richie Daley, son of the late Mayor Richard J. Daley.

Dick was approached by a member of Mayor Byrne's reelection committee to make a commercial endorsing the mayor. Dick agreed, much to Liz's and everyone else's surprise. The superintendent of police was an appointed position and supposed to be nonpolitical. Even though Jane Byrne had appointed him, Dick was not supposed to use his position to endorse any political candidates, not even his boss.

"I was shocked when Dick made that commercial," Liz said. "I knew he would never have agreed to do it if his judgment had not been affected."

Little did Dick know that his commercial would become the hottest issue of the already heated mayoral campaign. Candidate Harold Washington denounced Dick for endorsing Byrne. During a televised debate between the three mayoral candidates, Washington vowed his first act as mayor would be to fire Dick.

Dick verbally counterattacked and the situation between the two men escalated into a full-scale verbal war that was played out on the front pages of the Chicago newspapers. Dick announced that if Washington was elected, he would resign rather than be fired. Dick went on to say that he had dedicated his life to law enforcement and could not possibly work for a man with a criminal record.

(Harold Washington had been indicted for failure to file federal income taxes for the years 1964, 1965, 1967, and 1969. Washington had ended up paying a fine and serving thirty-six days in jail. Previous to his conviction, Washington had also had his law license suspended by the Illinois Supreme Court for mishandling clients' funds.)

Dick also claimed that the city of Chicago would not be safe with Harold Washington as mayor.

Harold Washington countered that Dick was hysterical and should see a doctor. For a man who valued control, it was clear that Dick Brzeczek was out of control.

Dick never thought Jane Byrne would lose the mayoral primary. But she did. Byrne's loss stunned Dick. In addition to everything that was happening in his personal life, Dick's professional life now seemed to be unraveling. Harold Washington won the primary, thereby sealing Dick's fate. After almost nineteen years, Dick would have to leave the police department and the job he had worked nearly his whole adult life to achieve. There was no way he could continue as police superintendent after the things he had said about Harold Washington. It was a foregone conclusion that Washington would be the next mayor of Chicago. Chicago is a Democratic stronghold. A Republican hadn't been elected mayor in more than sixty years.

Liz tried to be supportive of her husband during this time, just as she always had. But she, too, was now suffering from depression. Their marital problems had been going on for almost two long years and the struggle had taken its toll.

In an effort to get some relief from the stress of her daily life, Liz finally asked their psychiatrist to prescribe something for her depression. The medication did nothing but make Liz drowsy, so she discontinued taking it. Medication wasn't the answer to her problems. Liz knew she had to find some strength and solace within herself.

Something had to change. Their *life* had to change. Liz felt she couldn't go on much longer. She loved Dick, but every day was a constant battle of emotional abuse. She was still trying to please Dick, still trying to get him to open up to her and tell her what was bothering him, still trying to understand what had gone wrong with her marriage. Liz also kept hoping that Dick would finally admit he had a drinking problem. But he refused.

Liz finally realized that Dick was not going to change. *She* was going to have to do something on her own in order to cope with the insanity of their life.

Liz enrolled in a Dale Carnegie course in the hopes of learning to become more assertive. It wasn't a cure, but it was a start. Slowly, she began to regain some confidence. It was almost as if Liz began to gain strength as Dick fell apart.

Liz tried to shield her children from what was happening, but it was almost impossible. The kids were very aware that there were problems between their parents.

"My father was a wreck," Natalie says. "We felt sorry for him, but we were also very angry with him. We didn't understand why he was doing this. It just never stopped. They were constantly fighting, and my father was drinking very heavily. My mom kept trying to help him, but he didn't seem to want anyone's help. We didn't know what was going on or why, but we knew we wanted it to end. We just wanted our family happy again."

Liz kept hoping that once Dick was out of office their life would return to normal. Perhaps if Dick was out of the spotlight and out from under all the pressure, he would revert to the man he had once been.

When it became clear that Dick's days as police superintendent were numbered, offers began pouring in from prestigious law firms eager to have the politically powerful former superintendent on their staffs. Dick finally agreed to join the LaSalle Street law firm of Levy and Erens. It was corporate law and the last thing anyone expected Dick to do.

His brother-in-law Joe was baffled. "I couldn't believe it when Dick chose corporate law. It's stuffy and boring. Even though Dick was the superintendent, he was used to being in the thick of things. But by this time it was so clear that Dick was sick, we all thought he just wanted a slower pace. A chance to catch his breath. He was clearly suffering. But he had shut us all out. He wouldn't tell anyone what the problem was. I never pressed Dick about his job or his marital problems because I felt if he wanted me to know he would have told me. I just figured it was something he had to deal with on his own."

As the date for Dick's resignation drew closer, he grew increasingly morose and withdrawn; his depression seemed to escalate. Dick would lie around the house wallowing in his misery, drinking to drown his sorrows.

Saying goodbye to the police department was overwhelming for Dick; he took his impending departure very hard. But, as with everything else, Dick refused to discuss it with Liz. He hid his feelings by pretending not to care.

Dick's resignation was extremely painful for Liz also. She couldn't help but remember all the sacrifices they had made, all the years that had been spent working toward Dick's goal of becoming superintendent. But they had never really had a chance to enjoy what they'd achieved, because their marriage had started disintegrating so soon after Dick's appointment.

Everyone had expected Dick to hold off his resignation until Harold Washington was officially elected mayor. But on April 5, 1983, one week *before* the mayoral election, Dick took everyone by surprise by officially announcing his resignation.

Dick resigned before the election because he knew that if he waited, the first thing the new mayor would do was fire him. Dick still had too much pride to give Harold Washington the pleasure of firing him.

One week after Dick's resignation, Harold Washington was elected mayor—the first black mayor in the history of Chicago.

In spite of Dick's personal and emotional problems, he had been an extremely popular, well-respected superintendent. The city decided to throw a farewell party for him. Three thousand people came to bid Dick farewell, including Mayor Washington.

That evening Liz sat by her husband's side, listening as dignitaries and celebrities heralded Dick as a great superintendent and a loving husband and father. Liz couldn't help thinking: *If they only knew the truth.* But of course no one did. Liz had kept her personal anguish private for the sake of Dick's career.

For almost two years the couple had managed to conceal their marital strife from everyone but their families and close friends. But on the night of Dick's farewell party it was clear that something was wrong. Dick drank heavily and seemed even more despondent than usual. Surrounded by his friends and family, he sat with his head in his hands, crying, for most of the evening.

Liz ached for her husband. She couldn't help remembering something Dick had told her on the day of his appointment: "I want you to be as happy on the day of my resignation as you are on the day of my appointment." It had been only three short years since Dick's appointment, yet to Liz it seemed a lifetime ago. She wondered if they would ever be happy again.

Dick's resignation from the police force came after nineteen years of service. He was only forty years old—ten years short of being eligible to collect a pension. When Dick resigned, he received sixty days' vacation and sick pay. He took his vacation pay and bought *two* new cars—and paid cash.

Liz was shocked. With the couple's medical bills mounting due to the ongoing counseling sessions, Liz knew the money could have been better spent. Even though Dick had to give up his police department car and driver after his resignation, they certainly didn't need two brand-new cars.

From the very beginning of their marriage, money had occasionally been a sore point between the couple. Liz was a saver and tended to be more cautious and careful with money. Dick was not extravagant, but he did believe it was necessary to spend money to preserve his position.

Although Dick's salary at Levy and Erens would be well into six figures, Liz felt that the severance money should have been put toward something more practical than two new cars. It was another source of painful arguments between them.

As Dick settled in to practice corporate law at Levy and Erens, it became clear that he was desperately unhappy. He was now in the throes of a deep depression, complicated by alcohol abuse.

Then, a few months after Dick's return to private life, he began getting calls from local Republican leaders. There were rumors around that Dick was going to be asked to switch political parties and run as a Republican to try to unseat the incumbent state's attorney of Cook County, Richie Daley, son of the late mayor Richard J. Daley.

"I didn't feel Dick was in any condition to even consider entering public office again," Liz said. "Couldn't anyone see how sick he was? It would have been impossible not to notice the dramatic physical changes in Dick. He wasn't eating or sleeping properly, and he was still drinking heavily. Half the time he was so despondent it was an effort for him to just get out of bed and go to the office. At times he was like a walking zombie, he was so morose and withdrawn. Considering the precarious condition of his physical and emotional health, I thought the question of his mounting a political campaign was ridiculous.

"And I wasn't certain *I* wanted to be in the glare of the public eye again, considering what was going on in our personal life. We had managed to hide the deterioration of our marriage and Dick's declining emotional health for over two years. How could we continue to do so if Dick jumped back into the political arena, with all the media attention he was certain to receive?"

Liz was concerned not just with the welfare of her marriage but with Dick's health. While Dick had been able to fool the doctors, he did not fool Liz. She knew there was something desperately wrong with her husband.

"I told Dick I thought he was too sick to run for office. But my comments simply infuriated him. He claimed there wasn't anything wrong with him. For the sake of peace I decided to let Dick make his own decisions. I told him if he decided to run I would support him just as I always had throughout our marriage."

Liz wasn't the only one who didn't want Dick to jump back into the political arena. The couple's four children were equally opposed to the idea.

"I was only thirteen when my father became superintendent," Natalie recalled. "All four of us kids were sick of the reporters and photographers. The press would camp on our front door, then follow us around asking stupid questions and taking our pictures. We hated it. We were sick of all the publicity. We didn't want our dad to be in politics anymore. We just wanted our father to have a regular job and be a normal father again."

But the pressure on Dick kept mounting. Unaware of his marital and emotional problems, Frank Fahrenkopf, chairman of the Republican National Committee, personally encouraged Dick to run. The Republicans were certain that with Dick's immense popularity and name recognition he would be the man to finally unseat Richie Daley. Even though the polls showed Dick with a wide margin over Daley, Dick kept turning down the Republican leaders, saying he was happy in the private sector.

Finally, the local Republican leaders went to Dick's partners at Levy and Erens, hoping they could persuade them to exert pressure on Dick to run. Dick was called in to his partners' office and told that the firm wished he would reconsider. They promised Dick that if he ran, regardless of the outcome, his job would be waiting. They even offered to keep him on full salary during the entire campaign.

The morning the Republicans were scheduled to announce their slate of candidates, Dick assured Liz that he was not going to run. An hour later he telephoned Liz at home and told her he had changed his mind. He had decided to run for Cook County state's attorney against the incumbent

Richie Daley. He had called to let Liz know he was on his way over to make the official announcement.

Liz wasn't surprised. Nothing about Dick's bizarre behavior surprised her any longer. She had no idea how he was going to tackle such a monumental task. Dick could barely function on a day-to-day basis. How on earth would he be able to stand the rigors of what was certain to become a long and bitter campaign?

That morning Dick held a press conference to announce his candidacy. The race was on, and once again the couple was thrust into the political spotlight of Chicago.

Shortly after Dick announced his candidacy, in keeping with her promise to support her husband, Liz and their four children attended a fund-raiser for Dick. There were over two thousand people in attendance, people who believed in Dick and supported him. Dick had been an immensely popular figure in Chicago: a self-made man from humble beginnings with whom everyone could identify.

But the man who appeared at the political fund-raiser that night was not the Dick Brzeczek the public had come to love and respect. The man who appeared was a stranger. Totally despondent, Dick sat at a table drinking all evening.

Liz and the four Brzeczek children sat and watched Dick with growing apprehension. Liz tried to caution Dick to slow down his drinking because he still had to give a speech. But Dick ignored her and continued to drink even more.

By the time Dick gave his speech he was drunk, and Liz was mortified. The Brzeczek kids watched their father with mounting horror.

"We were so humiliated," Natalie recalled. "My father made a public spectacle of himself. We begged our mom to let us leave. We even told her we'd walk home—anything—just so we didn't have to be in the same room with my father.

"People kept coming up to my mother and asking her how much my dad had to drink—like it was her fault! It wasn't her fault my father got drunk. My mother had been trying to get my father to stop drinking all night. We all had. But my father wouldn't listen to her, or to anyone. He just kept drinking."

That night proved a turning point in Liz's life. Watching her once-commanding husband make a fool of himself and of her, Liz knew she had to do something. She could no longer cope with Dick's drinking. It was tearing their family apart.

Liz thought long and hard about calling Alcoholics Anonymous. Her husband was in the middle of a bitter political campaign. If word leaked to the press that Liz was attending A.A. meetings, it could ruin not only Dick's chances for state's attorney but perhaps even his reputation and career. But, after two long, nightmare-filled years, Liz realized that public recognition was the least of her problems. For the sake of her children as well as her sanity, Liz knew she had to take control of the situation.

The first time Liz called A.A. she left a fictitious name. Someone from A.A. called Liz back, listened to her, then referred her to Al-Anon, which is a support group to help friends and families learn to live with an alcoholic.

Liz knew she had to learn to cope with Dick's drinking. He wasn't going to stop; Dick refused to even recognize that he had a drinking problem.

Joining Al-Anon was the beginning of Liz's self-growth and the resurrection of her badly shattered confidence. At Al-Anon, Liz found people who not only understood exactly what she had been going through but offered her support in learning how to live with and deal with Dick's problem.

For the past two years the doctors and counselors had insisted that Dick didn't have a problem. At Al-Anon, Liz finally found someone who believed *her*. It was a tremendous relief. Despite the doctors' and Dick's claims, Liz finally realized she was not the one with the problem. *She* was not responsible for her husband's drinking. Liz finally had to face the fact that her brilliant, successful husband was an alcoholic.

At Al-Anon, Liz learned how to live with an alcoholic. By hiding the liquor bottles, cautioning Dick to watch his drinking, and trying to protect Dick from himself, she had been hurting him, not helping him.

Until Dick faced up to his own actions, until he was ready to admit that he had a problem, there wasn't anything Liz could do for him, except learn how to live with an alcoholic.

Al-Anon gave Liz back some of the self-respect Dick's abuse had stolen from her. Liz learned to accept what she had denied for so long: *she could not make Dick stop drinking*. He had to do it on his own. Until Dick realized and admitted he had a problem, there was nothing Liz could do for him.

Al-Anon also showed Liz, through its Twelve Step program[1], how she could take control of her own life. For Dick's sake, Liz had to let her husband sink or swim on his own. Until Dick hit rock bottom, until he realized his drinking and his life were out of control, no one could help him. Not even Liz.

Because of Liz's tremendous love for Dick, or for the man he had once been, Liz knew she had to let go of her husband and let him hit bottom, no matter how painful it was for her.

Joining Al-Anon was just another source of tension between the troubled couple. Dick deeply resented the fact that his wife had sought outside help. Liz's attendance at Al-Anon fostered Dick's verbal abuse. While Liz went to the meetings, Dick stayed home and drank.

Three days after Dick announced his candidacy for state's attorney, he was sitting in the living room with his head in his hands. He had been drinking heavily and was so clearly distraught that Liz's heart went out to him. She decided to try to talk to him one more time, hoping he would confide in her, tell her what the problem was that had escalated his drinking and led to his deep despair.

She called Dick in to dinner. He walked into the kitchen and sat down. He was so dejected that Liz put her arms around him and asked him once again what was wrong.

"Dick looked up at me, and I could see the sadness in his eyes," Liz remembered. "I finally just said, 'Please, honey, tell me what it is. Whatever the problem, we can work it out.'"

Dick just looked at her. He didn't say anything for a long time.

"Is it another woman?" Liz prompted for the hundredth time.

"Yes," Dick admitted. "There is another woman. And there has been for over two years."

What Dick didn't tell his wife was that there wasn't just one woman but two.

Chapter Three

Dick's Story: Part 1

*Following is Dick's account of the incidents that
led to his personal and professional crises.*

To this day, I still don't know why I chose that particular night to tell
Liz. I really hadn't planned it. It just sort of happened. For more than two
years I had been living a double life—a life of secrets and lies.

When you work with cops every day, you know the ones who play
around. It's almost like an occupational hazard. I always had a disdain for
those men. I was a homing pigeon. My wife and my family were
everything. Liz and I had always been a team. We did everything together.
I went to work and came home, that was it. I couldn't understand how
other men could have affairs. I guess I perceived it as some kind of a
weakness or character flaw. How could they do it? I never understood it,
until it happened to me.

I never planned to get involved with another woman. I didn't wake up
one morning and say, "Today I'm going to look for a woman and have an
affair." That wasn't how it happened.

I was on my way to appear on a segment of *Good Morning America*
when I met Diane. [Her name has been changed to protect her privacy.]
When I boarded that plane, it was with a full briefcase and a full mind. I
planned to work the whole trip. Diane was seated next to me. Because of
the air traffic controllers' strike we were stranded at O'Hare airport for
nearly three hours.

Diane started talking to me, and, as I usually did, I told her all about
Liz and the kids. My family was my whole life. I've loved Liz since the
day I met her. She has a gentleness, a kindness, and genuine warmth that
I've found in very few people.

When we first met, Liz was kind of shy and insecure. But as the years passed, particularly after I became superintendent, Liz really came into her own. She really was an asset to me, both personally and professionally.

So why did I have an affair?

I wish I knew. I know *how* it happened, but not why. Diane was a flight attendant, but she also conducted business seminars. I was always concerned about the image of my executives and thought it might be beneficial to have her give her seminars to some of the top people in the police department.

Like many other long-married, middle-aged men, I had never even contemplated having an affair. I would never have just approached a woman. It wasn't my style. Although, in my position, I had been approached many times, I just wasn't interested. I don't know why it was different with Diane. Perhaps I was intrigued by the chemistry between us.

From the moment Diane sat down next to me, there were certain silent messages between us. There was an electricity between us, a physical enticement that was new, exciting, and very stimulating.

A lot of people think men who have affairs are having sexual problems at home. But that's not always the case. Sex was never a problem between Liz and me. We've always had a very satisfying and fulfilling love life. So it wasn't just sex.

It wasn't like I was out looking for another woman. I wasn't. Even though I didn't make the first move, I accept full responsibility. I could just as easily have discouraged Diane, but I didn't. Perhaps if that instant, mutual attraction hadn't been there, nothing would have come of the relationship.

When the plane landed in New York, Diane and I exchanged business cards. I told her to give me a call if she ever came to Chicago and we could discuss her seminars. Diane lived in Minnesota, so it seemed like an innocuous invitation at the time.

Being the superintendent of the Chicago Police Department was a goal I had set for myself years ago. I had finally achieved it. I was on top of the mountain. People were suddenly telling me how wonderful I was. I started believing them. In a way, my position *did* go to my head.

I was thirty-eight years old and at the pinnacle of my career. I traveled all over the country giving lectures at prestigious universities and law schools. I taught the special agents in charge of field offices at the FBI

Academy. Liz and I were suddenly socializing with the president of the United States, governors, senators, and other celebrities.

There were even rumors circulating in law enforcement circles that I was going to be the one to follow in William Webster's footsteps as head of the FBI. I've got to admit, it was pretty heady stuff.

I loved my job, but I never anticipated the extreme amount of pressure I'd be under. From the day of my appointment it seemed as if every day brought another crisis, another problem. No matter what, somehow, some way, all the problems seemed to lead directly back to my office. If it wasn't Jesse Jackson screaming for my resignation, it was gang activity at Cabrini-Green, or the Tylenol murders. Cops were getting shot left and right, and I took each and every one personally. Those guys were out on the streets doing their job and trying to make me look good, and I felt responsible for them.

In spite of all the problems and the pressure, I loved what I was doing. I was *born* to be a cop. And I loved being superintendent. The power, the prominence—I loved it all.

A week after I met Diane she called me. I was a little brusque with her on the phone because she happened to catch me at a very bad time.

A week after Diane's first call, she called again. I was out of the office at a meeting. During a short break, I went to a pay phone to call her back. Diane wanted to get together for lunch, and I agreed. I wanted to see her again.

The following week Diane called again and we set up a time to meet. She was flying into Chicago, and I had someone from my office pick her up. When I went to meet her for lunch, I brought along an assistant. I didn't want our lunch to be misconstrued in any way. I didn't want to be seen dining alone in the company of another woman. When I saw Diane again, it only confirmed my growing attraction to her.

I didn't hear from Diane for a few weeks, and then a few days before my birthday she flew down to Chicago unannounced and brought me a birthday present. We had lunch, and I finally had to admit that I had just been kidding myself. This was more than a business relationship. But I didn't do anything to discourage Diane or what was developing between us.

I tried to deny what I was feeling. I felt guilty as hell. I was happy with my wife, my kids, and my job. I was happy with my *life*. But when I was with Diane I felt like a seventeen-year-old kid again; she made me feel an excitement I hadn't felt in years.

After years of struggling, Liz and I had achieved all we had set out to do in life. While we were struggling, the promise of the future seemed to sustain me. But now I had climbed all my mountains. But it wasn't enough. I just wasn't satisfied.

Maybe it was just the prospect of being with someone new and exciting. The idea of making love to Diane was stimulating both sexually and emotionally. There was a strong physical attraction between us that was nearly overwhelming.

I had a comfortable life with a familiar wife and familiar sex, and suddenly comfortable and familiar weren't enough anymore. I wanted more. *I wanted Diane.*

I knew it was wrong. I've spent my whole life in law enforcement and know better than anyone the difference between right and wrong. But at the time, I wasn't thinking about right or wrong. I was only thinking about Diane and how she made me feel.

She stimulated my sexuality. I was a man who valued control. Yet, when it came to Diane, I had no control. I was overwhelmed with thoughts of her. I was filled with a sexual curiosity that bordered on obsession.

When Diane called me again, I suggested we have lunch. I knew that sooner or later someone would see me with this attractive woman and tongues would start wagging. I didn't want to hurt Liz. I never wanted to hurt her. I knew I had to be very careful and very discreet. I couldn't afford to let the news of this budding relationship leak. I made arrangements to rent a hotel suite for Diane and me so that we could have some privacy.

That day in the hotel suite, for the first time in my life I made love with another woman. I was certain that if I got Diane out of my system, everything would be all right again. I thought one afternoon would curb my sexual curiosity, but I was wrong. One afternoon with Diane did nothing but increase my appetite for her. In the beginning of our relationship, sex was a big part of it, but as time went on, our relationship became much more than just physical.

She dominated my thoughts. At first, the excitement of the new relationship was energizing and stimulating to me. The erotic absorption was exhilarating. I couldn't wait to see Diane again.

A week after our first encounter, I had to fly to Harvard to teach a week-long seminar. Because of our children, Liz rarely went with me. But Liz was used to my traveling. I had always traveled a great deal on behalf of the department, so she really didn't suspect anything.

When I went to Harvard, I invited Diane to go with me. She was a flight attendant for a major airline and flew free; she could easily arrange her schedule to fit mine. Her job was almost tailor-made for us, because there was no way I would have been able to carry on my affair for so long in Chicago without the press picking up on it. I think that's what kept our relationship going for so long. We didn't see each other every day, or every week, so that when we did see each other it was like a honeymoon.

The prospect of spending a whole week alone with Diane in a place where I didn't have to fear being recognized was exciting. We arrived, settled in, and then went out to dinner. We were waiting in line for a table when someone tapped me on the shoulder. I turned around to find myself face to face with a priest from a local high school in Chicago. A priest who not only knew me but Liz also.

"Aren't you Dick Brzeczek, superintendent of the Chicago Police Department?" he asked.

I admitted I was, wondering if I looked as guilty as I felt. We chatted for a few moments and then he was on his way. If I thought being superintendent put me under a lot of pressure, it was nothing compared to that moment.

After dinner Diane and I returned to the hotel for the evening. The next morning Diane announced she was going home. She didn't want to stay the whole week. She felt our relationship was progressing too fast, and bound to go nowhere. She didn't want to conduct an affair with a very prominent, very married man. She also said she had a policy of never dating married men. I later learned she had been married once, and divorced. The man she had married was already married when they met—on another flight. It was almost the same scenario of how she had met me. This guy left his wife for Diane, but their marriage didn't work out.

That morning, though, when Diane said she thought it would be better if we didn't see each other anymore, I must admit I was almost relieved. I had suffered my own conflict of conscience. I had never gone to bed with anyone other than my wife. I guess the reality of my actions hit home. I had actually betrayed Liz—something I had never thought I could do. I was overwhelmed with remorse and guilt. I loved Liz, so what the hell was I doing?

Diane flew home, but I remained in Boston. I couldn't stop thinking about her or the excitement she had brought to my life. It was as if I was obsessed with her. Being with Diane had been an idyllic interlude from the intense pressure I constantly seemed to face. She was a powerful, pleasurable antidote to the tension that filled my life.

What had started out as simply a physical attraction was now something much more. Emotionally, I felt as if I needed her. Despite my intense guilt, despite my conflict of conscience, I knew I wasn't ready to give up Diane or our relationship. I just couldn't. It was as if I was addicted to her.

It was wrong, and I knew it, but it didn't matter. The values I had held dear my whole life suddenly didn't matter. Right and wrong no longer seemed to apply to me. I thought I was above the rules. I wasn't acting or reacting with my mind or my intellect, but something else altogether.

I knew full well the risks I was taking, and the possible consequences. Hell, I was a man used to taking risks. But at the time, the risk seemed worth the consequences. I called Diane from Boston and told her I wasn't ready to give up her or our relationship. I wanted to see her again. She agreed.

I take full responsibility and full blame for what happened. It was my fault and no one else's. No one forced me to make that call. I did it because at the time I wanted to. Without really realizing what had happened, I suddenly found myself emotionally and physically in the middle of a full-blown extramarital affair.

I felt so damn guilty that I began to withdraw from Liz. I thought it would be easier if I put some distance between us. Liz knew me so well, she noticed immediately that something was wrong, not just with me but with our marriage too. Liz was used to me sharing my innermost thoughts and feelings with her. But this was one thing I couldn't share. I couldn't talk to Liz about it; I couldn't talk to *anyone* about what I was doing.

For almost nineteen years, Liz had been my best friend. You have no idea what it did to me to have to lie to Liz and betray her.

Because of my own guilt and anxiety, our marriage began to suffer. Every time Liz would ask me what was wrong, I'd tell her it was nothing. For a long time, I tried to deny that anything was wrong. But Liz knew better. The more she asked, the more I denied.

I was acting blindly. I'd had no experience cheating or lying; those things were totally foreign to me. I'd always dealt with everyone and everything from a position of honesty. This new role was difficult for me, and yet I couldn't seem to stop myself.

Liz and I began fighting—about everything. I began to criticize her and everything she did. Liz just tried harder. But the harder she tried, the angrier I got. I wasn't angry with her, I was angry with myself for what I was doing to her, and to us. I guess finding fault with Liz allowed me to justify my own actions.

Liz didn't deserve the way I treated her. Pride and honesty were values I had built my life and career around. Now, I found myself doing something deceitful and dishonest, and I didn't like myself very much.

So why didn't I break off my relationship with Diane? I couldn't. I tried. She was a compulsion with me. I couldn't go a day without talking to her on the phone. I couldn't wait to see her again, to be with her. It was like an ache in my whole body. My mind knew that what I was doing was wrong, but every other part of me craved her. I wanted and needed her in my life.

I was not accustomed to being ruled by anything but logic or reason. I'm a trained attorney. I deal with logic and reason every single day. I was used to always being in complete control of myself and every situation. I *valued* control. Yet, here I was allowing physiological responses to a woman to *control me*.

I was torn between Liz, my wife; and Diane, my obsession. I began living a secret life. I was trying to hide my affair from my wife and my friends, trying to see Diane and keep that relationship going, and yet still handle the tremendous pressure of my job. I was arrogant enough to think I could handle everything.

But I couldn't. Things started slipping, and I began drinking. The first drink seemed to blot away my troubles, but I never seemed to be able to stop at just one drink. If one made me feel better, two or three would make me feel great, and take all my problems away.

Liz doesn't drink at all as a result of a bout with hepatitis that damaged her liver. She immediately became concerned about my drinking. It was just another sore spot between us, something else to fight about. I kept insisting I didn't have a drinking problem. I could handle my liquor. I was certain of it. But Liz wasn't.

I had always been in demand as a speaker. Now I found myself having a few drinks beforehand, not because I was nervous, but just because of the self-imposed tension I was under.

As time went on, Diane began to pressure me. She wanted me to leave Liz and the kids. She felt there was no reason to continue the marriage. I always knew I would never leave my family. Never. In spite of everything, I loved Liz, and I didn't want to leave her.

In the beginning of my affair with Diane, our relationship was very warm and loving. Yes, sex was a big part of it, but that wears off very quickly. When we first started seeing each other we would frequently discuss how wonderful things would be if we were married. We talked about it in a dreamy, far-off way. I guess the only way I can describe it is when two young kids first begin a relationship. They wistfully talk about getting married—*someday*. It's something far in the future; something to think about. I never really thought about the realities of my getting a divorce, or just what it would entail: leaving Liz and the kids, packing up and moving out of state, leaving my friends and the life and career I had spent years building. I never thought about the realities of divorce, because I never really wanted a divorce.

In some ways, I think Diane was jealous of Liz. Liz was my wife, the one who was sharing in my success. Liz was the one who accompanied me to all the official functions, meeting all the celebrities and dignitaries.

Diane felt that *she* should have been the one on my arm, accompanying me to all these functions, meeting all these dignitaries. Diane was always very impressed with celebrities. She had a habit of telling me about every famous person she had ever dated.

She continued to pressure me about leaving Liz. What I didn't need was more pressure in my life. I tried to stall for time. I was lying to my wife, my mistress, my friends, and my family. To pacify Diane I finally told her I had moved out of the house and was living with my parents. But I stressed the fact that I could not divorce Liz while I was superintendent.

As for my relationship with Liz, that wasn't going much better. We started going for counseling. I only went because I thought I might be able to understand what the hell had happened to me. Somewhere along the line I realized I had lost control.

The counseling didn't help because I wasn't honest with the doctors and therapists. I certainly couldn't admit I was having an affair with another woman, while my wife was sitting right there in the room.

My whole attitude was lie and deny. It worked—for a while. I actually had the doctors convinced that I wasn't the one with the problem, but Liz was. I thought it might take some of the pressure off me. I'm not very proud of that, but it's the truth.

Liz wasn't the only one I withdrew from. I withdrew from everyone, even the friends I'd had for years. No one really knew what was wrong with me. My sense of humor, which I'd been known for, seemed to disappear. It's hard to be funny when there isn't anything in your life worth laughing about. I just didn't want to see my friends, or anyone else for that matter. I didn't want to add to the list of people I was deceiving.

I found that I didn't adapt very well to a life of deceit. I had always felt like a moral, decent man. Lying and lying and telling more lies didn't come easy to me.

I kept trying to find a way to juggle all the pressure. I continued to shut Liz out of my life. Maybe I thought that the worse I treated her, the better I'd feel. But it didn't work that way. I felt miserable. I thought I could handle the affair, my marriage and my job. I had always been able to handle anything.

My drinking increased. I guess I was trying to drown my troubles. I thought the alcohol would help, but all it did was make things worse. Alcohol enabled me not to have to face what I was doing. I was deluding myself and everyone around me. I didn't want to have to come to terms with my own actions.

I had always been a man who never ran from a problem; a man who prided himself on acknowledging every problem and then setting about solving it. But this was one problem I couldn't face and I couldn't seem to solve. I was frustrated, unhappy, and terribly sad. Drinking helped me to avoid facing these feelings. My world was narrowing until the only thing occupying my mind was my own problems.

I was struggling to maintain some semblance of sanity in my life, struggling to keep up a false front. At times it felt as if my life was blurry, slightly out of focus. It was as if I was watching someone else live my life.

In the beginning of my relationship with Diane, there was a great deal of joy and pleasure. But as time progressed, there was a lot less joy and a lot more pain. The joy wasn't worth the pain, but I still couldn't break it off. When I was with Diane, there was still some excitement, some exhilaration. When I was with her, particularly when I was in Minneapolis, I didn't have to worry about being recognized or having a microphone shoved in my face. I was not Dick Brzeczek, superintendent of police, but just an ordinary citizen. Not many people knew or recognized me up there. In some ways, I think that was part of the attraction of the relationship. Although I loved my job, sometimes I just wanted anonymity. I wanted to be able to go shopping or out to dinner or to a show without being recognized. I wanted to escape. My relationship with Diane allowed me to do that.

Diane's pressure increased as time went on. She wanted me to make a decision about our relationship. I kept stalling, hoping for some way out of the mess. I didn't like knowing that I needed Diane, but I did, and no matter how I tried to deny it, I realized that not only did I know it, but Diane knew it too.

When I met another flight attendant, Laura [her name has been changed to protect her privacy], I sure as hell didn't intend to get involved with her—or with *any* other woman. I met her on a flight to Orlando shortly before I resigned as superintendent. After I boarded the flight, Laura took my bags and put them in the overhead compartment. She later told me she checked out the nametags because I looked familiar to her. She lived in Chicago and had seen me on television.

Hell, any guy can tell when a woman is interested. I initiated that relationship, but she was very receptive. During the flight, I went back to the galley area and we talked for probably an hour. She told me she had been divorced for about three weeks, and she seemed down about it.

When we landed in Orlando, she had a two-hour layover, so I asked her if she wanted to have a drink. She was in uniform, so I knew she couldn't go into a bar, so we went into a restaurant. Laura had a Coke and I had my usual drink. We sat and talked for almost two hours. I became so involved in our conversation, I almost forgot that Diane was meeting me in Orlando. I walked Laura back to the gate, and she went in one door while Diane came out another. They missed each other by minutes.

Diane found out about Laura from another flight attendant who had seen Laura and me together. Diane hit the ceiling. She was absolutely furious, particularly when she learned that Laura worked for the same airline. She took it upon herself to call Laura and spill the beans about our relationship. But Laura and I continued to see each other, despite Diane's rage.

I honestly don't know why I started seeing Laura. Diane had me so tied up in knots emotionally, I didn't know what the hell I was doing. At the time, maybe I thought Laura could help me break free of Diane—you know, sort of a diversion. Maybe I did it to punish Diane for the control she had over me. I wasn't used to being controlled by anyone.

With Liz, I was the one who was always in control; but in my relationship with Diane, *she* was the one in control. Although Liz and Diane are physically similar, emotionally they are nothing alike. They are both tall and thin, and even dress in a similar fashion. If someone saw them standing side by side they might think they were related. But there were major differences.

Liz *always* cared what I thought of things; my opinion of her was very important. Liz always sought my approval; she would go out of her way to try to please me.

Not so with Diane. Diane didn't care what anyone thought of her. She pleased only herself; *her* opinion was the only one that mattered. I wouldn't dare criticize Diane because she would fly into a rage. With Diane, it was as if I was the one who was always seeking acceptance and approval. She controlled our relationship. If I did something to anger or annoy Diane, she would put her telephone answering machine on and leave it on for days at a time so I couldn't reach her. It made me frantic, and she knew it. Liz would never do something like that to me. Never.

I always knew Liz needed me. Diane didn't need *anyone*. Diane had also had much more exposure to the world and was very independent. Liz, on the other hand, had led a very sheltered life. Most of Liz's life experiences came through me, while Diane's life experiences came on her own.

Liz had always understood about the pressure of my job; not so with Diane. I tried to juggle my time between them. I always spent holidays with Liz and the kids, and that bothered Diane—she felt I should be spending them with her. But Liz and the kids were my family.

I tried to see Diane as much as possible, but at times it was difficult. If I didn't show up when I was supposed to, she would get angry, put her answering machine on, and we'd start that whole thing all over again. The more she tried to pull away, the more I seemed to want her.

When she pulled a stunt like that, I couldn't just jump in the car and drive over to see her. Minneapolis is a six-hour drive from Chicago, and with my schedule, it wasn't always easy to get away. Although many, many times I did just jump in the car in the morning and drive straight through, see her for a few hours, and then jump in the car and drive home again.

During our affair, I don't think Diane was seeing anyone else, although I can't swear to it. I was in Chicago, and she was in Minneapolis, or wherever else her job took her. Whenever I called her, though, whether it was late on a Saturday night or early in the morning, she was always where she was supposed to be.

Juggling my secret life, trying to please my wife and both my mistresses, and handle my job began to affect my work.

In the beginning of 1983, when Jane Byrne was running for reelection, I said some things that—well, I don't regret what I said or did. But on the other hand, had my objectivity not been clouded by personal problems, I probably would have said or done things a bit differently.

People still criticize me for making a campaign commercial endorsing Jane Byrne for reelection. To this day I don't regret it. I was never a yes-man, and Byrne put no pressure on me to do the commercial. In fact, we never even discussed the matter. David Sawyer, Byrne's media consultant, approached me about it and I agreed. I have a lot of respect for Jane Byrne. I think she was a good mayor, and good for the city. She took on the big boys and won, and I admire her for that. Jane Byrne has a lot of courage and is a genuinely nice lady. Not that we didn't have our disagreements—we did—but I still think she did a good job.

I had no idea Harold Washington was going to make me an issue during the campaign because of that commercial.

As for my comments about Washington being a convicted criminal, I said them and I meant them. I never thought I'd see the day Chicago would elect a mayor who had a criminal record. I wasn't trying to inflame the already torrid issues during the campaign or become an issue myself. I was simply stating the facts. I had always taken a law-and-order stance. For me to approve or endorse Washington with his criminal record would have been a joke.

I think part of the problem was that I was never a team player. Hell, I was a cop, not a politician. I didn't do anyone's bidding, ever. I couldn't stand all the bullshit that went on in politics. But I surely never intended to become an issue. I probably should have used better judgment, but I really wasn't thinking too clearly. I was too immersed in my own private hell. The only thing Washington said that was right on target was that I should see a doctor.

The pressure kept building. I felt as if I was falling down a deep, dark vacuum, and no matter what, I couldn't seem to get out. I felt as if I had a noose around my neck. It was particularly difficult when the Tylenol murders erupted in Chicago. There was some nut running around poisoning innocent people, and we had absolutely no leads or clues as to his or her motive. Talk about pressure! To this day, the Tylenol case remains unsolved. I didn't think the pressure would ever ease—not in my job, and certainly not in my personal life.

My lies and my secret life were almost pushing me over the brink. When Jane Byrne lost the election, I was stunned. I really expected her to win. It was clear I was going to lose my job. I sure as hell couldn't stay on as superintendent after what had gone on between Washington and me.

The thought of leaving the police department after so many years deeply distressed me. I really didn't want to leave the force. Police work was all I had ever known. Even though I had a law degree, I was first and foremost a cop.

I had been telling Diane that I would never leave Liz while I was superintendent; that had been my excuse for not making a decision about the women in my life. When it was clear that I was not going to be superintendent much longer, the pressure from Diane increased. She felt there was no reason for me to stay with Liz anymore. But in my mind, there was a reason. I still loved Liz. I knew I would never embarrass her that way. Liz had helped me and supported me for so many years, I couldn't do that to her. In spite of everything, I loved Liz.

She didn't deserve what I did to her. I never really *wanted* to leave Liz. What I wanted was my wife, *and* my mistress.

In some ways, thinking back on it now, I wonder if part of the reason I finally agreed to run for state's attorney was to buy more time for myself. I would never be able to leave Liz during a protracted political campaign without ruining my career. I don't know what I expected to happen. I was the one who couldn't make a decision. I couldn't break it off with Diane. And I knew I couldn't go on this way much longer. It was affecting my whole family—my kids, my parents, my sister, my in-laws, everyone. They all thought I was nuts.

The day I announced my resignation from the police department, I was on my way to Washington, D.C., at the request of Bill Webster, the head of the FBI. I had told Liz before I left that I was going to issue a press statement announcing my resignation. My resignation made national news and a contingent of press met my plane.

Diane was elated by my resignation. Now there was nothing standing in the way of my asking for a divorce. Except of course my wife, my kids, and Laura, my other mistress.

At this point, Diane, too, was becoming irritated with my drinking and my mood swings. She kept telling me I had a drinking problem. Hell, I wasn't an alcoholic. I went to work every day, still did all the things a man in my position was expected to do. Alcoholics were people who had some moral defect, some weakness that caused them to drink. That wasn't me. *I* could handle my liquor.

I was down in the dumps all the time, hardly a barrel of fun to be around. When I was up in Minneapolis, or when we traveled together, Diane kept telling me to snap out of it. She tried planning things for us that would improve my spirits. We went to the movies, out to dinner, and a lot of other things, but nothing seemed to help. I couldn't just "snap" out of what was bothering me. But Diane simply didn't understand. She had no sympathy for me or what I was going through.

Leaving the police department was very traumatic for me. I was forty years old and had no idea what I wanted to do with the rest of my life. The police department had been my life for nineteen years. I had a love and affection for the department that—unless you've been a cop—it's difficult to understand.

Liz tried to be encouraging and supportive during this time, but I refused to admit that leaving the force was painful. She tried to help me, but no matter what she did, I refused to admit that it was having any effect on me. I pretended I was glad it was over. No more pressure, no more spotlights.

Inside, I felt as if I were dying. I reverted back to hiding and controlling my emotions, especially with Liz. I didn't want her to be understanding and supportive. It just increased my guilt and filled me with remorse.

The night of my farewell dinner was one of the hardest things I ever had to sit through. All these people, including Mayor Washington, were parading across the stage, exalting me and my accomplishments, going on and on about what a good family man, a good husband, and a good father I was. I realized what a fraud I had become. I sat at the table with my head in my hands and cried. It was a difficult night for me in many ways.

I had accomplished a lot as superintendent. I was very proud of what I had done. But it was over now. I had worked my whole life toward this one goal, and I had let it slip through my fingers. I just couldn't believe it. Liz and I should have been enjoying this time; we had worked so hard to get there. But we never really had the chance because I had become involved with Diane so soon after my appointment.

Even before I announced my resignation, I had been contacted by a number of law firms that wanted me to join them. I finally decided to go with Levy and Erens. It was a large corporate firm that handled national banking and international corporations. I thought it might be nice to have a slower pace after the rat race I'd been in. I also thought that maybe a less pressured situation would help me to get a handle on my personal life.

Diane came to Chicago the weekend after I started at Levy and Erens. She was going to help me pick out furniture to decorate my new office. We spent the day at the Merchandise Mart and then I took her to the Cape Cod room for dinner. While we were there, Lee Philip and her husband, Bill Bell, came in. Liz and I had just spent a weekend with the Bells at their Lake Geneva, Wisconsin, home, and here I sat with my mistress. Lee and Bill commented about my retirement party and how nice it was. After they left, Walter Jacobsen, the local anchor on WBBM TV, came over. He too had been at the party, covering it for the station.

Diane said very little, but when she got back to Minneapolis, she called a girlfriend in Chicago and asked if there had been any press coverage about the party. All this time I had been telling Diane I had moved out of the house and was living with my parents. Well, when she learned that Liz and the kids were at the party, she knew I had been lying to her. She was furious. Diane screamed and raged at me for days and days about it.

Sometimes I wonder how the hell I kept all the lies straight. I was lying to Liz, to Diane, and to Laura. The stress of trying to remember what I told to whom was about to kill me. I'm surprised I didn't have a heart attack.

Shortly after I settled in at Levy and Erens I realized I *hated* corporate law. It was stuffy and boring. I missed the excitement, the challenge of police work. Even though I had been the superintendent I had still been involved on a day-to-day basis. I had still personally handled some very sensitive investigations, and I missed it.

When I was approached to run for state's attorney, I was flattered. It really fed my ego. When you've been in the spotlight so long, it's hard to stay in the shadows. I didn't have anything personal against the incumbent state's attorney, Richie Daley. I just didn't think he was particularly good at his job, but it wasn't *personal*. I always felt that Richie Daley became state's attorney because of his father's name, and not on his own merit. Because Richie's father had been mayor for so many years, a lot of people in Chicago love Richie Daley simply because he's the old man's son. He's a Daley, and everyone in Chicago loves the Daleys.

Being state's attorney wasn't a position I had ever coveted. But the state and national Republican leaders began pressuring me to run. They had already taken polls that showed I was way ahead of Daley. Everyone was certain I could easily beat him. I had a lot of name recognition from being superintendent. If a Republican could defeat a Daley—well, that would really be a coup for the party. I was very flattered that they thought I was the man who could do it.

But I still didn't want to run. I had enough problems in my life without mounting a political campaign. For the first time in my life I didn't know if I could handle the pressure.

Frank Fahrenkopf urged me to run. He was certain I could beat Daley. Fahrenkopf even went so far as to tell me that he'd have President Reagan call me if it would help sway my decision. It really fed my ego, particularly when Senator Paul Laxalt offered to come to Chicago to host a fund-raiser for me.

I knew Liz was upset about my campaign. She never said a word about it; she never told me not to run. But I knew she was worried about me. At one point she asked me if I thought I was well enough to even launch a campaign. I got furious. Of course I was well enough. There was nothing wrong with me.

I really had no intention of running, right up until the day the party was slating the candidates. Even when my bosses at Levy and Erens called me in and encouraged me to run. They were very nice about it. Running a political campaign is time consuming; it's a full-time job. They promised to keep me on the payroll, and hold my job for me no matter what the outcome of the election. I was making well into a six-figure income by that time, and it was a generous offer. Still, I refused.

I wish I knew why I decided to run. I don't. That morning, when I left the house, I told Liz I wasn't running. A few hours later I called her back and told her I was on my way to inform the committee that I would indeed be the Republican candidate for state's attorney. Despite everything that was going on, I still valued Liz's opinion. She always told me the truth. She always had the ability to see a situation clearly and advise me accordingly.

Liz promised to support me and do everything she could to help me win the election. It was just like the old days. No matter what I wanted to do, I knew that Liz was the one person in the world I could count on, the one person who would stick by my side.

By the time I announced my candidacy, it was an effort for me to function on a day-to-day basis. I was having trouble sleeping and eating. I was drinking, but drinking wasn't the problem. The problem was what was causing the drinking, and that was my relationship with Diane.

Diane was not pleased when I told her I was running for state's attorney. She knew then I wouldn't leave Liz, at least not during the campaign, and the election was nearly thirteen months away.

Shortly after I announced my candidacy, things just seemed to slowly fall apart. When Liz joined Al-Anon, I was really upset about it. I guess in her own way she was trying to make some sense out of the nightmare that had become our life. And it was a nightmare. For her, for me, and for our kids.

So why did I choose that particular night to tell Liz about Diane? I honestly don't know. I was exhausted. I was just plain tired of the whole mess. I couldn't break it off with Diane. I had tried over and over again, and yet I still kept going back to her. It was as if I were a heroin addict and needed a fix; Diane *was* my fix.

I had never faced a problem without Liz's help and support before. I had been carrying this around for two long years and it had taken its toll on all of us: my kids, my parents, everyone.

That night, when Liz asked me what was wrong, and if there was another woman, I knew that I simply couldn't lie to her anymore. Maybe I told her to ease some of my own guilt, maybe it was just to relieve some of the pressure on Liz, to let her know *she* wasn't the problem as I had been insisting. I was just plain tired of living a lie. I thought if I told her about Diane, it would force me to make a decision about my life.

As long as I live, I'll never forget the look on Liz's face when I told her. She had loved me and trusted me, and I had betrayed her in the most heinous way. When I told Liz there was someone else, I watched the sparkle go out of her eyes.

It was never my intention to hurt Liz, but that night I knew I hadn't just hurt her. I had destroyed her.

Chapter Four

Stand by Your Man

Liz Brzeczek believed in her husband as strongly as she believed in God. Nothing could have prepared her for the sense of betrayal she felt when he told her there was someone else. It was the death of her innocence.

Like other wives forced to face their worst nightmare, Liz found her security and emotional well-being blown apart. For two years she had denied the possibility; now, she could no longer deny the reality.

"All this time, I thought I was the problem. I thought there was something wrong with me," Liz recalls. "But it wasn't me, it was another woman! I felt like a stupid fool. For almost two years my husband had been lying to me. I couldn't help but wonder what else he had lied to me about. I began to wonder if the life we had built together had just been a sham.

"Dick's confession was soul-shattering. I was calm, but I felt dead inside. In that instant when Dick finally told me the truth, I think a part of me *did* die."

Liz went through all the ranges of emotions most betrayed spouses feel when they finally learn the truth. These feelings are very similar to those one experiences upon the death of a loved one: shock, physical reaction, followed by disbelief, rage, a sense of loss, and finally a strengthening of inner forces.

Once Liz knew the truth, she demanded to know who Dick's mistress was, and how he had managed to keep it a secret for so long. He told her all about Diane.

"I kept asking myself *why*? Why had he done it? If my husband had to go out and find another woman, then I must not be enough for him. I lost all the self-confidence I had regained over the past few months. I felt worthless."

The night of Dick's confession was a nightmare for Liz. She told her husband that if he loved the other woman and wanted a divorce, because of the campaign she would give him a quick, quiet one. But if he still loved her, he'd have to give up the other woman. For more than two years Liz had lived with the shadow of another woman in her life. Now that she finally knew the truth, Liz was unwilling to put up with it any longer.

"Dick told me he needed some time to think and would let me know his decision soon. This was another let-down. After all, he'd already had two years to decide who he wanted.

"I don't think I'll ever forget that night. It was Halloween, and the doorbell kept ringing. Our children were home, but downstairs in the den. The world was going on as if nothing had happened. But my world had ended. It was such an eerie feeling sitting there discussing this other woman and *my* husband's feelings for her.

"I started to cry, and I couldn't stop. I've always been able to handle any type of crisis, but this was too much even for me to handle."

Watching Liz fall apart before his eyes, Dick became very concerned. He put his arms around Liz and tried to comfort her, but she was inconsolable. The children came up to see what was going on. They asked Liz what was wrong, but she couldn't talk, couldn't answer them. She just couldn't stop crying.

"I'm sure they just thought, 'My parents are arguing, and Mother is having another one of her crying fits.' Our house had been in constant turmoil for more than two years, so I'm sure the kids didn't really think anything about my behavior. At the time, my crying didn't seem all that strange. I couldn't tell the kids the truth. I really didn't want them to know. This was just too painful. I wanted to protect my children from their father's betrayal. My kids had suffered enough. And when I realized another woman had caused all of our grief, I was furious."

The night dragged on as if in slow motion. Dick finally went to bed, leaving Liz alone to face the longest night of her life. Her mind was filled with so many thoughts; she tried to stay calm, to think, but all she could do was cry.

Her feelings and emotions were hopelessly tangled. She'd never anticipated facing this kind of problem.

Did she hate Dick? Did she love him? Did she want him to stay? Should she file for divorce, or try to work things out? Her emotions swung back and forth. Liz became very angry. Adultery was something that happened to other couples, not to them. But it *had* happened.

"I was so furious with him. After all we had been through over the years, how could he do this to me? To us? I didn't understand it. We had worked so hard, struggling and doing without, sacrificing so he could achieve his dreams—and for what? For him to take up with another woman! I felt violated in the most intimate way."

All night long, Liz wrestled with her conflicting emotions. By morning, she was drained. She couldn't do anything until Dick made his decision. In the meantime, life had to go on. She needed the normalcy of everyday life, something to cling to. She made breakfast for her children, then drove them to school. The previous afternoon, before Liz had learned of Dick's betrayal, she had invited her parents over for breakfast. Now Liz knew she would have to tell them what had happened.

When her parents arrived, they sat at her kitchen table with a pot of coffee, and Liz told them the whole story. She cried, and they cried. Her parents were surprised, but not shocked. Liz's mother had suspected it all along.

"The morning Liz told us about Dick's affair, we tried to be supportive. Her father and I never criticized Dick or condemned him. He was her husband and she loved him. He was also the father of her children. They had spent nineteen years building something together, and you don't just throw that away.

"It certainly wouldn't have done any good for us to start throwing stones. It wouldn't have helped Liz. We just sat and listened to her, telling her we'd support her no matter what she chose to do. We love our daughter. We hated to see her in so much pain.

"I'm sure a lot of mothers would have told her to divorce Dick. But I didn't. For what? What would it solve? Unless someone had stood in my daughter's shoes, gone through all that she had gone through, they couldn't begin to understand. No one could make a decision like that for her. Whatever she chose to do, her father and I would support her and stand by her. We prayed for her."

Dick phoned Liz from the office while her parents were still there. He told her he had made his decision and was going to break off his affair. He wanted to stay married to her and rebuild their life and their relationship. Liz was ecstatic. Despite everything, she still loved Dick. She wanted to forgive him; she wanted to trust him again and make her marriage work.

Liz had promised to spend her life with Dick, and her feelings and her commitment to him hadn't changed, despite what he had done. Almost everyone in the family, except for the couple's children, knew what had happened. At least it explained Dick's bizarre behavior over the past few years. Both families were delighted that Dick had broken off his affair and was going to make an attempt to put his marriage back together.

For the next month, Dick and Liz enjoyed a brief "honeymoon" period. Dick swore that his affair was over and he was going to rededicate himself to Liz and their marriage. Liz really wanted to believe him. Dick had made a mistake, and now it was time to forgive and go forward. Liz assured Dick that she forgave him and trusted him. She too wanted to get their marriage back on the right track.

Determined to help him win the election he was seeking, Liz and the children threw themselves into helping Dick campaign.

Just before Christmas, Dick had to travel to Minneapolis on business. Liz was a bit nervous about his trip because she knew Dick's mistress lived in Minneapolis. But Dick assured her that his affair was over and she had nothing to worry about.

But, over the Christmas holidays, Dick began having emotional problems again. He began drinking heavily and his moods became erratic. Soon, he was once again morose and withdrawn. Liz blamed his recurring depression on the stress of the campaign and the breakup of his affair.

Liz thought they needed to get away together and made arrangements for them to take a cruise. The night before they were to leave, Dick had to fly to Washington. He called Liz from the airport and told her that since they were leaving the next morning, he planned to stay at the airport for a few hours to discuss some things with his campaign manager.

Liz became suspicious that night. Although Dick had sworn that his relationship with Diane was over, Liz had a feeling he was lying to her. Liz called the airline Diane worked for and left a message for her. Diane never returned Liz's call. But while Dick and Liz were on their cruise, Diane did call Liz. Dick's mother was staying with the couple's children and it was she who took the call.

"My poor mother-in-law," Liz recalled. "Of course, by now everyone in our family knew about Dick's affair with Diane. But we all thought it was over. The first thing my mother-in-law said when we walked in the door is, 'That woman called.' She was so upset."

Dick became unglued at the prospect of his wife and his mistress talking. He once again swore to Liz that his relationship with Diane was over and made Liz promise not to call Diane.

Liz didn't call, but a few days later Diane again called Liz. Diane was very upset that Dick had finally told his wife about her. Dick's wife and mistress talked for nearly six hours. Diane went into a great deal of detail about her relationship with Dick. She wanted Liz to know every little aspect. She told Liz that when Dick was with her, he was happy and carefree. She insisted that they had a wonderful relationship. Diane went on to inform Liz that Dick had never broken off his affair, as he had told her. In fact, it was going on stronger than ever. When Dick flew to Minneapolis in December, he'd spent some time with Diane and presented her with a pair of diamond earrings. He had bought Liz an identical pair for Christmas. Diane also told Liz that she wasn't the only woman Dick had been seeing. Diane proceeded to tell Liz all about Laura, the other flight attendant Dick had been seeing.

Liz was livid; once again Dick had been lying to her. The more Diane talked, the more furious Liz became. While she spoke to Diane, Liz roamed the house, yanking Dick's plaques and awards off the walls. Liz was on a portable phone, and she just started packing his things. She had believed Dick when he told her his affair was over. But he had betrayed her once again. She hated Dick for what he had done to her. He had asked for—pleaded for—her trust, and Liz had blindly given it to him, only to be deceived again. Liz knew she could no longer believe anything her husband told her. His promises were worthless.

That afternoon, while his wife and mistress were talking on the phone, Dick was attending a luncheon for Illinois Senator Charles Percy. Dick had been trying to reach both Liz and Diane all day. When both lines were busy, he panicked, realizing they must be talking to each other. He raced home. When he saw that Liz had packed up all of his things, he went crazy.

She told him all about Diane's phone call and confronted him about his continuing lies. Liz told him to get out of her house and her life. She had had it with him. Dick became hysterical. He didn't want to leave Liz or his children. He collapsed on the couch, totally bereft.

"Dick kept telling me *I couldn't do this to him*, that he loved me and *only* me," Liz recalled. "We sat deadlocked for hours just arguing and arguing. I wanted him out, and Dick kept insisting he was staying."

In the end, Liz finally relented and let Dick stay. She felt sorry for him. He was so devastated when faced with the prospect of leaving her and the children that Liz felt she had no other choice. She still loved him, but she didn't love what he was doing to her.

Like most betrayed spouses in a similar situation, Liz wanted to believe Dick; she wanted to believe that this time would be different, that this time he'd finally break off his relationship.

Liz agreed to let him stay on the condition that he call Diane, in front of her, and break off the relationship immediately. Dick made the call.

Afterward, he was repentant and sad, loving and attentive. Dick kept insisting that Diane was out of his life for good. But after the glow of reconciliation faded, Dick once again fell back into the cycle of depression, drinking, and psychological abuse.

By Easter, Liz had decided she couldn't take it anymore. She suspected that Dick was still seeing Diane, but she had no proof. She finally suggested that Dick move out of the house for a while, hoping that it would help him straighten himself out. To her surprise, Dick told her he had already rented an apartment. He moved out that weekend.

The couple's families could not believe what was happening. Dick had been the shining star of the family, the one person everyone had looked up to and admired—until now. Dick's behavior was extremely disappointing and quite stressful to everyone. Liz's parents and in-laws continued to provide support for Liz and the children, trying in their own way to help her cope with what she had to face, but it was difficult. Everyone was clearly in Liz's corner.

All during this time, Dick was still involved in the campaign for state's attorney, a campaign that at times was bitter and heated. That weekend, things seemed to explode both personally and professionally for Dick.

Although Dick and Liz had managed to keep their marital problems secret from the media for almost two and a half years, the weekend Dick moved out one of the gossip columnists in Chicago got wind of their separation and reported that they were on the verge of divorce.

The newspapers also reported that Richie Daley, the incumbent state's attorney and the man Dick was running against, was investigating Dick's handling of the police contingency fund while he had been superintendent.

The news of the investigation made front page headlines all over Chicago. Although the entire police department was under investigation, it was Dick who received most of the publicity.

When Dick resigned, and Harold Washington became mayor, Washington had appointed Fred Rice, a black career police officer, to replace Dick. Shortly after Rice took over the helm of the department, an anonymous phone call was received reporting that a police official (not Dick) had been using a city car for personal use. This anonymous tip touched off a wide-scale investigation of the police department and its handling of financial matters. Initially, the investigation was handled by an internal police body, the Internal Affairs Division, but soon the department turned over its evidence to the United States Attorney's Office, which declined to prosecute. The department then turned the information over to the first assistant state's attorney.

No one knows how the news of the investigation reached the media, although it has been widely speculated that either someone in the police department, or in Richie Daley's office, leaked the information to the press in order to discredit Dick and his candidacy.

The leaks about the investigation, and about Dick's marital woes, couldn't have come at a worse time. Dick didn't appear overly concerned, but Liz was; she had no idea what the investigation was about, or what, if anything, would come of it.

Liz was drawn into the investigation, though, when Officer Irene Voight of the Chicago Police Department called her and advised her that Superintendent Fred Rice wanted her to come down to police headquarters and answer some questions regarding her husband. Liz, a bit surprised, told Officer Voight that she would be happy to answer any questions Superintendent Rice had—over the phone.

Officer Voight then proceeded to inquire if Liz had traveled to Atlanta with Dick while he was superintendent. She said no, she hadn't. (Records later showed that only one ticket had been purchased.) Next, Officer Voight asked if Liz knew of any business dealings Dick had with a Miss Diane Nary. Liz panicked. Obviously the police department and Superintendent Rice knew about Diane and Dick. How much they knew, she wasn't sure. What Liz couldn't figure out was why they were asking *her* about Diane? Unless it was an attempt to let her know that her husband was involved with another woman.

Liz didn't know what the officer was looking for, but she answered the question truthfully: she really didn't know of any *business* dealings Dick had with Diane.

When Liz hung up she was livid. All this time she had been quiet about Dick's relationship with Diane in an attempt to protect Dick. But apparently it had been to no avail—Superintendent Rice and the department obviously knew all about Diane. Who else knew? Liz wondered. And did this have anything to do with the investigation of Dick?

She confronted Dick about the phone call, and they had a heated argument. Dick was equally furious about the call. He felt the department had no business involving Liz in an investigation of his tenure as superintendent. More important, he too felt that the phone call had been made solely to let Liz know about Diane.

In order to repair some of the damage done to Dick's campaign by the rumors, Liz continued to appear with Dick socially, but information about their marital problems continued to appear in the press, which only further upset Liz and the children.

No matter what happened to her marriage, she didn't want their personal problems to be the cause of Dick's losing the election. She didn't want Dick or anyone else to be able to point a finger at her and say that Dick's defeat was her fault. So Liz continued to play the loving, doting wife in public for the sake of Dick, his career, and his image.

After Easter, their daughter Natalie was invited to a formal dance at a private school. The parents of Natalie's date wanted Dick and Liz to attend with their daughter. Although Liz was reluctant, she and Dick attended the dance with Natalie, for the sake of appearances.

That evening, Dick was warm, loving, and attentive. For Liz, Dick's affection was a temporary relief from all the pain and hurt he had caused her. Liz saw Dick's kind treatment as a silent form of approval that reinforced her hope that their marriage could somehow be salvaged. That night Liz saw a glimpse of the man Dick once had been. She ended up letting Dick spend the night with her.

The next morning, without even discussing it with her, Dick announced he was moving back home. He let his campaign manager take over the apartment, and although Liz had severe reservations about getting back together with Dick because she wasn't certain anything had been resolved or settled, including his relationship with Diane, Liz did allow him to move back home.

Throughout the campaign, Dick's physical and emotional health continued to decline. He appeared to be in a state of chronic depression. The couple was still in counseling, but Dick's physical and emotional health didn't improve. The doctors finally realized that Dick really did have a problem and prescribed an antidepressant drug for him. Dick was now mixing alcohol and prescription medication.

The medication didn't help. Functioning on a day-to-day basis was almost impossible for Dick. He was miserable, and once again moved out of the house and into his old apartment. On the day Dick moved, although he had sworn that his affair with Diane was history, Liz suspected he had been lying to her all along.

On a hunch, Liz called the airline Diane worked for and learned that Diane was on a flight bound for Chicago. Liz now understood why Dick had chosen that weekend to move out; he wanted to be free to see his mistress.

Liz drove to the airport fully expecting to find her husband with Diane. But they weren't there. Liz then called Dick's campaign manager and demanded he take her to Dick's apartment. The apartment was in a high-security building, and Liz knew she would never be able to get in without Dick's manager. The man was loyal to Dick, and adamantly refused, but eventually Liz persuaded him to take her there.

Before leaving, she called Dick's parents to come over and sit with the children. But when she told them what she was going to do, Dick's parents insisted on going with her. They wanted to be there to offer Liz emotional support.

Dick's parents waited in the lobby while Liz went upstairs. Dick refused to answer the door, until Liz threatened to scream the place down and make a scene he'd never forget. When she walked into the apartment and saw an expensive Gucci wallet on the bed, she knew her instincts had been right—Diane was there.

"Diane and I sat and talked," Liz recalled. "Dick really didn't say much; he just sat there and listened. I didn't scream or yell or lose control. I was past all of that. I was determined to keep my dignity. I told them both that they had done enough to me and my family, and that I was filing for divorce."

Diane became very agitated and upset. She didn't feel she was ready to make a commitment to Dick. Liz was past the point of caring what either of them wanted. She knew what she wanted—out. Her husband had lied to her and played her for a fool for the last time.

When Liz got home that evening, she knew the time had come to tell her children she was filing for divorce. She also knew she would have to tell them why.

The children still didn't know their father was involved with another woman. Liz had tried to shield them from their father's behavior, but she knew she could no longer protect them. She had to tell them the truth.

Liz told her three youngest children, Mark, Kevin, and Holly. Natalie was in Europe at the time, but she remembered the day clearly:

"I called home and my brother Kevin answered the phone. I asked to talk to Mom or Dad, and Kevin just blurted, 'Dad's got a girlfriend, and they're getting a divorce.' I was hysterical. I couldn't believe it! My father had a girlfriend! I was halfway across the world, and my life fell apart in one phone call. I had another week and a half left in Europe, but all I did was cry. I couldn't stop thinking about what was happening at home."

Holly was just twelve and didn't really understand what was happening between her parents. She knew something was wrong, but not the full extent of the problem. Kevin, who was fourteen, understood fully:

"I knew for a long time that something was wrong between my parents. My mom tried to shield us, but I could tell. I suspected my dad might have a girlfriend, or at least I *thought* about it. But then I would feel guilty for even thinking such a thing about my own father. He had been a great father, he was always at every one of my baseball, football, or hockey games. Until the problems began. Once my parents started arguing, and my dad started drinking, he stopped coming to any of my activities. I knew something was really wrong, but I was afraid to ask my mom about it. I guess maybe I didn't want to know. When my mom finally told us, I was really upset. I was one of the few kids in my school whose parents weren't divorced. Before this happened, our family was like *The Brady Bunch*. I never expected this to happen to our family. I was really disappointed in my father. And very hurt. I couldn't understand how he could do this to us. I remember going into the shower and running the water for a long time so no one would hear me cry."

Mark, the couple's oldest son, was sixteen at the time and seemed to take the news the hardest.

"I hated my father for what he was doing to us, and to my mother. How could he love us and do this to us? I was scared and angry. If my dad had been there when my mom told us, I think I would have decked him."

The children weren't the only ones to take the news of the couple's imminent divorce badly. When Liz told Dick's parents, Dick's father became so upset he collapsed. Liz had to call the paramedics to revive him.

The entire family seemed in shock. Dick was the last person in the world anyone ever expected to have an affair or cause the breakup of his once happy family. Dick's sister Rita was especially devastated by the news:

"I'd never turn my back on my brother, but what he was doing was affecting our whole family. Because of my brother's affair with this woman, my mother suffered a mild heart attack. She had to be hospitalized for almost a week. This problem with Dick was with us every single day; there just wasn't any relief. The stress was unbearable for all of us.

"One day Dick would swear his affair was over, and the next, he'd be on the phone with his girlfriend right in front of Liz and the kids! He was just acting crazy.

"When the kids finally learned the truth, it was a very difficult period.

Joe and I wanted to let them know that even though their parents' marriage was breaking up, the rest of the family still loved them and would always be there for them. But God, it was so hard on everyone. It got to the point where my own marriage suffered because of the situation."

The day after Liz told the kids, Mark wanted to call his father at his apartment. Liz had severe reservations, but finally she let Mark call. She could hear her son screaming at Dick. Mark was getting more hysterical by the moment. Liz finally took the phone away from her son and tried to calm him down. But Mark broke free of his mother and ran. Mark was so agitated, he hyperventilated and fell down the stairs. Mark stopped breathing for a few moments, and Liz had to give him mouth to mouth resuscitation to revive him.

Mother and son sat at the bottom of the stairs just holding each other and crying. Liz ached for her children, for what they were going through because of their father's behavior.

When Liz had dropped the phone, Dick became worried. He rushed home, contrite and apologetic. He kept insisting to his wife and son that he loved them and didn't want to leave them.

Liz was still holding Mark, trying to calm him, to be strong for his sake. Dick had told her the same lies so many times, she knew she couldn't believe him. Something snapped inside of her.

"I looked up at Dick and told him to get out," Liz remembered. "I told him I didn't need him anymore."

For the first time in all their years together, Liz finally realized she *didn't* need Dick. Not anymore. If she could handle two long years of a living nightmare, she could handle anything. She still loved Dick, but she didn't love what he was doing to her, her children, or their families. Liz told him again that she was filing for divorce and to get out of her house.

Dick begged her not to file, but Liz knew it was time to take control of her life. It was time to face reality. Her husband was an alcoholic, a liar, and a cheat. She couldn't allow him to ruin her life or her children's any longer.

Dick refused to leave. For six hours they sat in a stalemate, Liz insisting she wanted a divorce, Dick pleading with her to give him another chance. He swore that this time his affair was *really* over. He even called their parents to apologize for what he had put everyone through.

Liz desperately wanted to believe Dick and to give him one more chance. Like most betrayed spouses, Liz always held out hope that this time he'd really break it off, that this time it would really end. She finally gave in and let Dick stay.

But once again, Dick was lying. Although he denied it, Liz and the children suspected that he was still seeing Diane. Shortly after Dick moved back home, Mark, who was still having difficulty handling the situation, got Diane's phone number from Liz and called her. Mark was furious that Diane was breaking up their family and wanted to express his feelings to his father's mistress.

After Diane talked to Mark, she called Liz. Diane confirmed what Liz had suspected all along; Dick's affair was *not* over. In fact, Dick had promised to marry Diane after the election.

It was the final blow. Liz knew she had to face reality. Her marriage was over. She told Dick about Diane's call and refused to listen to anything he had to say. She told him she would begin divorce proceedings.

Finding a lawyer to represent her was a difficult task. Liz and Dick were not exactly an anonymous couple. She finally contacted a well-known Chicago divorce attorney who assured her he could be impartial and put her and the children's interests first.

Liz told the attorney the whole sordid mess. It took three and a half hours. While Liz was discussing her case with her attorney, Dick called the attorney's office, begging Liz not to sign the papers. But it was too late; Liz had already signed them. She paid the attorney one hundred dollars, with a promise to pay another thirty-five hundred before he filed the papers. The sum seemed exorbitant, but Liz had no choice.

She instructed her attorney to wait until the day after the election to file, regardless of whether Dick won or lost. Liz was going to continue to support Dick and play the dutiful wife until the election was over. After all their years together, Liz felt she owed Dick that much.

As soon as Liz signed the legal documents, she took the children and went up to Lake Geneva, Wisconsin, to stay with longtime friends, Lee Philip and her husband, Bill Bell. While she was gone, Dick moved back into the house. He kept trying to talk Liz out of filing, insisting he loved her, not Diane.

Dick was not just mentally off balance now but physically run down as well. As his drinking increased, he stopped eating and sleeping. He had dwindled to a mere shadow of his former dynamic self. His speeches were wooden, he had no energy, and he looked terribly haggard. His drinking had taken its toll, as had his depression. The antidepressant medication wasn't helping at all. In fact, one side effect Dick suffered was temporary impotence, which only added to his distress. Yet he still continued to campaign.

"I wasn't even going to vote for him," Natalie revealed. "I didn't want my dad to win; I was just so angry with him. I campaigned for him only because my mother wanted us to. During this time, my mother was the only stable thing in our lives. In spite of her own pain, she was always there for us, for my grandparents, for everyone. She was the one to comfort us, to reassure us that even though she and my dad were going to get divorced, everything was going to work out. She made us believe everything was going to be all right. After all she had been through, knowing what my father was doing, I don't know how she handled it. I only hope that if I'm ever faced with the kind of thing she was, I can handle the situation as well as she did.

"As for my father, he didn't seem to care that he was destroying our lives or our family. He didn't seem to care about anything except his girlfriend."

With Liz's help, Mark and Kevin were trying to adjust to the fact that their parents' marriage was over.

"I love my mother," Mark insisted. "She's the strongest person I've ever met. To put up with what she did—I don't know how she did it. She endured so much crap, and my father hurt her so much. I guess she really must have loved my dad to put up with what she did for so long. I admire my mother and respect her more than anyone in the world.

"As for my father, I hated him. I didn't want him to win the election, either. I campaigned for him because my mother asked me to, not because I wanted him to win. I didn't care what happened to him."

Kevin's feelings echoed his brother's: "I was pretty upset most of the time. School was very difficult for me. I was a freshman in high school when I found out my parents were getting divorced. I remember sitting in class thinking about what was happening at home. It's all I ever thought about. I would put my head in my hands so no one could see me cry. It was embarrassing, but I couldn't help it. My mother was super through this whole thing. She tried to be as supportive as she could, but I couldn't help feeling bad. The feelings just wouldn't go away. I kept hoping I would wake up and it would all be just a bad dream. But it wasn't. I was awake, and this was a nightmare."

One Saturday, as the campaign wound down, Dick was scheduled to make several personal appearances. That afternoon he had been drinking and was involved in a serious car accident. His car went off the road and hit a guard rail. Dick went through the windshield and suffered numerous head and facial injuries. The hospital called Liz and told her to come get Dick. She brought him home and nursed him through his injuries, wondering how much more she could take.

The day before the election, Liz and her children went out early in the day to start campaigning. Dick stayed home in bed, immobilized. When Liz finally came home, she was exhausted. Dick had finally gotten out of bed and had gone out.

When Liz walked into the house, she had a strange feeling. Even though Dick claimed he had given up his apartment months ago, Liz had a feeling this was just one more thing Dick lied to her about.

She called the apartment complex and calmly inquired if Dick Brzeczek had an apartment there. They confirmed that he had.

Liz's decision to divorce Dick was reaffirmed. She immediately phoned her attorney and told him to serve the divorce papers the day after the election. The fate of her marriage was sealed.

Liz knew before the election that Dick would lose. The Republican leaders who had wooed him so vigorously to run had pulled back their support of Dick earlier in the campaign. Rarely will a political party pin its hopes on a candidate who looks like he is about to self-destruct. And Dick Brzeczek was clearly about to self-destruct. His physical and mental condition were obviously on the decline, and there was the cloud of the ongoing state's attorney's investigation, plus Dick's own lackluster campaign appearances and commercials. Dick no longer looked like the winner he had been all his life; he now looked like a loser—to everyone.

Even the newspapers, which at one time had hailed Dick's entry into the political arena, were now blasting him in daily editorials.

Election day dawned bright, clear, and bitterly cold. Dick stayed in bed most of the day, too depressed even to dress himself. Around four that afternoon, he dragged himself out of bed, and the whole family went over to Dick's election headquarters to await the results. Liz was still playing the doting wife, but she knew it would be the very last time. So did Dick.

"I felt like such a fraud. I quietly began telling our friends that I was filing for divorce the next morning. I didn't want it to come as a shock. There were still some people who didn't realize we were even having problems, although they knew something was wrong with Dick. Our families were heartbroken, but they knew I had no choice."

Dick lost the election to Richie Daley. After Dick gave his concession speech, Liz kissed her husband one last time. After all the couple had endured, after all the struggles and hardships, Liz knew she was kissing her husband goodbye.

That night, after Liz had gone to bed, the Brzeczek children called Diane. She wasn't home, but her answering machine was on. The children left a message for her: "Thank you for ruining my parents' life."

The next morning, knowing that Dick would be served with the divorce papers, Liz went to Mass. It was the first time in her life she had questioned her faith in God. Liz had now reached the lowest point in her life. She had lost her husband and her marriage, but, more important, she had lost her faith.

"I deeply resented Dick for taking that away from me. My faith had always been the strong driving force that kept me going no matter what, but that morning, when I told Father Clark there was no God, I truly believed it."

The priest was stunned by Liz's words. He invited Liz back to the rectory to talk. In tears, she sat for hours, telling him all that had happened to her once happy life.

Father Clark prayed with Liz, assuring her that she was doing the right thing for herself and her family. He didn't believe in divorce, but he did understand why Liz had to file. He was convinced that Dick Brzeczek was a very sick man and beyond Liz's help.

When Liz left the rectory that morning, for the first time in almost three years she felt an inner strength and peace. Perhaps, she thought, because she was questioning God's very existence, He gave her the strength to go on. As she left the church that cold morning in November, Liz knew in her heart that she was doing the right thing. Her long nightmare was over.

That morning Dick was served with divorce papers. That afternoon, despite Levy and Erens's assurances that they would keep him on regardless of the outcome of the election, Dick was fired.

Within twenty-four hours, Dick Brzeczek had lost an election, his wife, and his job. It proved too much for his fragile emotional state. That evening, Dick was admitted to a psychiatric hospital. The man who had spent most of his life putting other people behind bars now found himself locked up. The man who had valued control for most of his life had finally lost control.

Chapter Five

Letting Go

Dick's breakdown had been imminent for almost a year. It wasn't just one incident but a series of emotional traumas that finally pushed him over the edge and into a psychiatric hospital.

Liz too had been pushed past her endurance. During the past few years she had tried to tolerate an intolerable situation the best way she knew how: she had put up with her husband's drinking, his lies, and his affairs in an effort to protect him and keep her marriage together. But Liz was sick of pretending, and she was sick of protecting Dick.

Secrecy had not been Liz's friend but her enemy. By protecting Dick, Liz had enabled him to continue his unacceptable behavior. Because she "covered" for him, he was never forced to face the consequences of his actions.

Liz wasn't protecting just her husband but herself as well. Dick's betrayal brought out deep feelings of shame and embarrassment. Liz feared that if her husband's adulterous behavior was publicly revealed, somehow *she* would be blamed. Perhaps people would think Dick had strayed because of some inadequacy on her part; perhaps she had not been a good enough wife, lover, or partner.

Dick's emotional demoralization and psychological abuse fed Liz's lifelong insecurities and renewed her childhood feelings of worthlessness.

"By the time the campaign was over, I was in so much pain I actually thought of suicide," Liz confessed. "I literally wanted to cut my heart out just to stop the unbearable anguish."

Dick was the only man Liz had ever loved. She had built her whole life around him. At one time, Liz had believed that the worst thing in the world that could ever happen to her would be to lose Dick. But by the end of the campaign, Liz realized that divorcing Dick would probably be the best thing that could happen to her.

Finding the courage to make a decision like divorce was extremely difficult, particularly in view of Liz's deep religious beliefs. But it was her first step toward taking control of her life.

For almost twenty years Liz had been totally dependent on her husband. In some ways, she was as addicted to Dick as Dick was to Diane. Liz needed Dick's love and acceptance in order to validate her self-worth. When Dick's love and emotional support were withdrawn, Liz didn't know who she was. She had no inner confidence or resources to draw upon. She had always drawn strength from Dick.

Liz had gone from the security of her parents' home to the security of her husband's. She never had the opportunity or the *need* to develop her own confidence or persona. Liz felt she didn't need confidence; Dick had enough for both of them. Nothing could go wrong with Dick by her side. He had been Liz's tower of strength and her security.

Until now.

Liz's fear of losing her husband and, in effect, losing her identity overshadowed her horrendous pain. Because of her fears, Liz never confronted Dick or forced him to deal with the consequences of his actions. Liz had sacrificed her own needs and self-respect in order to protect her husband and keep her marriage going. She was to learn, however, that her actions and reactions were quite typical for a woman in her situation.

When a husband is unfaithful, fear and insecurity are the dominating factors, particularly when a woman has not developed her own strong identity. Loneliness, fear of single parenthood, financial deprivation, and loss of social status all play a part in a woman's decisions when faced with this kind of crisis. It's difficult to think or act clearly when you're paralyzed by your insecurities.

It takes a great deal of inner strength and courage to end a long-standing marriage and face an uncertain future. Some women *never* find the strength or the courage to take such action. They feel it is better to stay in a bad relationship than to have no relationship at all.

In Liz's case, her pain finally overshadowed her fears, thus giving her the courage to say: "I've had enough. I want out."

Once Liz had made the decision to go through with the divorce, she knew that what lay ahead would be almost as difficult as what lay behind her. She would have no one to depend on but herself. She would go from

being the much pampered wife of a political celebrity to a single
charged with the sole responsibility of raising and supporting herself and
her four children.

Liz hadn't worked outside the home in years. Although she had once
been a registered nurse, she hadn't used her skills since the beginning of
her marriage.

The years Liz would have spent building her career had been spent
building her husband's career. Financially, the couple was already on
precarious ground. Their savings had been almost depleted by the
enormous medical bills they had incurred, so there would be little left for
Liz to live on.

Financial hardships were not the only problems facing Liz. Her
children had become innocent victims of their father's emotional illness.
The security of their lives had been destroyed and they were in deep
emotional pain. Liz would be the one left to cope with the aftershocks of
Dick's behavior.

With all these problems, Liz's future was uncertain at best. But,
despite the hardships, she had no other choice. She was no longer willing
to put up with Dick's unacceptable behavior.

The day after Dick lost the election was his final day of reckoning. A
few hours after Liz returned from Mass, Dick was served with divorce
papers.

"Dick called me from the office," Liz recalled. "He was in shock. I
don't think he actually believed I'd go through with it. "He pleaded with
me to give him another chance. He promised this time he'd change. I
wouldn't even consider giving Dick another chance. I had made the
toughest decision of my life and I wasn't about to change my mind. I told
him I intended to go through with the divorce."

The afternoon didn't get any better for Dick. A few hours after Liz
served him with divorce papers, Dick's partners fired him. It was another
crushing blow for a man who had always prided himself on being a
winner, a blow Dick didn't handle well.

"Dick called me back later that afternoon," Liz remembered. "By
then he was literally out of control. Once again he begged me to give him
another chance. I felt sorry for him, but I wasn't going to give in. I was
no longer going to protect Dick. The time had come for him to face up to
the consequences of his own actions. I had to let him go."

Dick's emotional health rapidly deteriorated. Dick's secretary telephoned his psychiatrist, and subsequently Dick's campaign manager drove Dick to see his doctor.

It was evident that Dick needed immediate hospitalization. Dick's emotional distress was so severe, he couldn't even make a decision about which hospital to enter. The man who just a short time ago had commanded the second largest police force in the country could no longer make even a simple decision.

Dick's psychiatrist finally called Liz and asked her to choose a hospital, then to meet them there and bring along any toiletries or personal items Dick might need for the duration of his stay.

"I called Dick's sister Rita and quickly told her what had happened," Liz said. "Rita and Joe offered to drive me to the hospital so I wouldn't have to go alone."

Liz was shocked when she arrived at the hospital. She hadn't seen her husband since the night before, when they returned home after his crushing electoral defeat. The change in Dick was dramatic. He was slumped in a chair, staring off into space. Listless, silent, Dick seemed oblivious to his surroundings.

Liz never imagined that her once healthy, vibrant husband could dissolve into a lifeless shell. The man who sat before her bore little resemblance to the arrogant young man with the high hopes and dreams Liz had married so many years before.

Liz spoke to Dick's psychiatrist at length. He had been treating Dick and Liz on a regular basis since their marital problems began. The doctor was fully aware of Dick's relationship with Diane, as well as his drinking and his depression.

It was the doctor's opinion that Dick was suffering from acute emotional depression brought on by the stress of his dual relationships. Dick was also suffering a tremendous amount of guilt because of his double life, which only added to his distressed mental state. The doctor said that Dick was much too ill to be helped by one-hour weekly visits. He needed intensive therapy that only a hospital could provide. Liz agreed.

The doctor took Liz aside and told her quite bluntly that Dick would never get well with both his wife and his mistress in his life. One of the women had to give up her relationship with Dick. The doctor went on to inform Liz that Diane had already telephoned twice—from Hawaii.

"In less than twenty-four hours Dick had lost everything that had ever mattered to him," Liz recalled. "As a result of his relationship with Diane, he had lost his wife, his job, and the election. He had also suffered a breakdown, but still he chose to continue his other relationship. That was *his* decision. I had already made *my* decision, and I intended to stick by it."

The doctor wanted Liz to withdraw fully from Dick's life. Walking out on her husband in the condition he was in was abhorrent to Liz. She felt she was deserting Dick at a time he needed her desperately. But the doctor stressed that if Liz didn't walk away, Dick might never recover. Liz did not want that on her conscience. Even though their marriage was over, Liz wanted only what was best for Dick.

"In spite of everything that had happened between us, I still felt tremendously guilty," Liz admitted. "I'm not a quitter. My heart told me to stand by my husband, to support him until he was well, but my mind told me I had to get out for all of our sakes. If Dick was ever going to get well, I *had* to walk away."

Despite her misgivings, Liz promised the doctor she would have no further communication with Dick. When she walked out of the hospital that night, for the first time in her adult life she was on her own. She had no one to depend on but herself.

For over two years Dick and Liz had successfully hidden their marital problems from the public, but Liz's divorce action and Dick's subsequent breakdown were impossible to hide.

The morning after Dick was hospitalized, a Chicago gossip columnist broke the story of Liz's divorce action and Dick's subsequent hospitalization. Liz was portrayed as a power-mad political wife who had abandoned her poor, defenseless husband in his hour of need. The columnist went on to suggest that Liz receive the "Cristina Ferrare Award" for sticking by her husband during the campaign, then dumping him when he was down and out. The story was devastating for Liz.

"For so long I had played the role of the dutiful, supporting wife. I had protected Dick because of his career, and I must have done a good job, because the blame for Dick's breakdown, the divorce, and the loss of the election was placed squarely on my shoulders. I was portrayed as the heartless wife who was interested only in the power and the glory. It would have been funny if I weren't so sad."

Political scandals were nothing new in Chicago. The story of Dick's hospitalization spread quickly, as well as rumors that Dick's hospitalization was for drug abuse. Inquisitive reporters rang Liz's phone constantly, but she refused to talk to any of them. Except one.

Irv Kupcinet, a well-known and well-respected Chicago columnist, had been a friend of the Brzeczeks through the years. After the initial inaccurate story broke about Dick and Liz, Kup called Liz at home.

"Kup was genuinely concerned about Dick's health. He also inquired about me and the children. I was very touched by his call. Kup promised to run a small item in his column stating the true reason for Dick's emotional breakdown and my divorce action."

The next day Kup's syndicated column carried a brief but factual account of the events leading up to Dick's hospitalization, revealing that Liz's divorce petition had more to do with Dick's "lady love" than anything else.

Even though Liz refused to talk to the press, items began appearing in the newspapers almost on a daily basis revealing information about Dick and his mistress, as well as the enormous problems in the Brzeczeks' marriage. Liz had no idea how the media was getting its information, but she later learned that a former member of Dick's campaign staff— someone who professed to be a friend—was leaking the details.

The Brzeczek children accepted their father's hospitalization as just another confusing twist in their young lives. Natalie recalled:

"When my father went into the hospital, I went to see him. I must admit I was scared. I'd never been in a psychiatric ward before. I never expected my father to be a *patient* in such a place. This was *my father*! To see him in this place was sad and just a little bit frightening.

"All the other patients were just milling around looking at us. It was very spooky. I was glad my dad was finally going to get some help. I knew my mom and dad were getting divorced and I was really upset about that, but I still wanted my dad to get better, even if I was mad at him for all the things he had done to us."

The boys, too, went to see their father. For Kevin it was particularly painful:

"I didn't go to see my father because I wanted to—the only reason I went was because I felt I *had* to. He was my father, and I felt I had to go out of respect. But if I had my choice, I never wanted to see him again. I hated my father for what he had done to us.

"When the stories started appearing in the papers about my dad and his girlfriend, it was very embarrassing. Everyone at school knew who my father was. Kids would look at me and whisper; I couldn't help but wonder what they were saying about me and my father behind my back. I had all these feelings inside that I didn't know how to handle. At school

I would sit at my desk with my head in my hands so no one could see me cry."

In addition to the children, several of Dick and Liz's close friends also visited Dick. There were just a handful of people who stood by Dick and Liz, offering their love and support.

Even though both families were angry at Dick because of his behavior, they continued to support him. But Dick's hospitalization was especially hard on his sister Rita. In some ways, Rita had always thought her brother invincible. Dick's breakdown brought home his very human vulnerability.

"I was very sad about what happened to my brother," Rita remembered. "He was the last person I ever expected to end up in a psychiatric ward. But I didn't believe that man was my brother. It was as if someone else had taken over my brother's body. I couldn't imagine my brother doing half the things he did."

Rita was also trying to deal with the enormous anger she had built up. "I wasn't angry at Dick but at his so-called friends. When my brother was on top, when he was superintendent, people crowded around him, wanting to be his friend. But now that he had hit bottom, all these so-called friends abandoned him. My brother was no longer important; he wasn't in a position to help anyone. Not even himself. These so-called friends vanished. I'll never forget that when my brother needed them, they weren't there. I deeply resented that."

Rita's husband, Joe, viewed Dick's hospitalization with a more pragmatic eye. "I knew Dick had some problems, but I never doubted he would get his life together again. I viewed this as a temporary setback. I think what happened to Dick could happen to anyone. Dick had suddenly been thrust into the spotlight with people pulling at him every which way. He was under incredible pressure all the time. I think it just got to him. As for his marital situation, I wasn't about to start telling him what to do with his life. It was *his* life. I didn't understand or agree with what he was doing, but it wasn't any of my business. I just planned to stick around and support him, Liz, and the kids any way I could."

Although Dick's family continued to visit him, Liz did not. She honored her commitment to the doctor. Every day Liz drove the kids to the hospital, then sat in the parking lot and waited for them. After every visit the kids came down with a frantic message from Dick begging Liz to call him. She refused.

Liz tried to keep herself busy and her mind occupied during Dick's hospitalization. She tried to focus on something other than her crumbling life.

Despite her attempts at normalcy, Liz too was suffering from depression. Her life was shattered, her future uncertain. The trauma of the past few years had taken its toll on her both physically and emotionally. Liz became compulsive about cleaning and exercising; it was her release, a way of trying to cope with what had happened to her. At one point, she dropped over thirty pounds from her five-foot-seven-inch frame, leaving her looking gaunt and emaciated.

Withdrawing from Dick after so many years was extremely painful for Liz. Although she had no direct communication with her husband, she kept track of Dick's progress through his doctor, to whom she spoke frequently on the phone. Diane was still calling Dick on a regular basis, so Liz knew that relationship was still going on. It just confirmed that she had indeed made the right decision in filing for divorce.

One week after Dick was admitted to the hospital, his psychiatrist phoned Liz with a startling announcement: Dick was being released.

"I couldn't understand how he could release Dick. It was inconceivable to me that Dick had recovered in just one week. It had taken him several years to fall into the depths of despair, so how could he have this miraculous recovery in just one week?

"The doctor told me Dick had finally made a decision," Liz remembered. "Dick had decided to stay with his mistress. He planned to go to Minneapolis to be with Diane as soon as he was released from the hospital."

Although Liz had been expecting Dick to choose his mistress over his family, it still came as a shock. It still hurt.

"You can say you're ready; you can say he can't hurt me anymore. *But he can and he does.* It's like when a loved one is dying. You know the end is near and you think you're prepared for it, but when death finally comes, it's still a shock, and it still hurts deeply. I don't think you can ever adequately prepare yourself for something like this. I knew then my decision to divorce Dick had been the right thing to do. After all the misery and grief we had all been through, Dick had finally made his choice. At last it was over. Hopefully the kids and I would be able to put our lives back together and find some peace."

Liz had no choice but to tell the children of their father's decision. She knew the kids still held out some hope that once Dick was released from the hospital their family would be reunited. But Liz knew it wasn't to be. To keep the children's hopes alive would be cruel.

"It was the hardest thing I've ever had to do. How do you tell your children that their father has chosen another woman over them? It was the final straw. The kids felt as if their father didn't love them. In their minds, if he did, he never would have done this. I tried to explain that this had nothing to do with Dick's love for *them*. But they didn't understand. How could they? *I* didn't understand it. Dick's decision ripped the children's security out from under them, leaving them on very shaky ground.

"I wanted them to know that just because their father wasn't going to be with us any longer didn't mean *we* couldn't be a family. We still had each other. I wanted the kids to know that no matter what, I was still going to be here; we were still going to be a family.

"I hoped this meant we could go forward and make a new life for ourselves, that we could put this all behind us. The kids deserved to have some peace and stability after all they had been through. We all needed it. In some strange way, I think Dick's decision was a relief. After all the horrendous years of lies and deceptions, it was finally, blessedly over."

Liz tried to be strong, not just for herself but for the children as well. She was determined to do whatever was necessary to repair some of the emotional damage Dick had done to all of them.

When Dick chose his mistress over her, Liz realized it really was the end. After nearly twenty years, Liz had no choice but to slam the door shut on her marriage, and the only man she had ever loved.

Liz Brzeczek had lost her husband; but perhaps, just perhaps, she might be able to find herself.

Chapter Six

Dick's Story: Part 2

Dick Brzeczek's fall from grace had been as meteoric as his rise to the top. For a man like Dick—overconfident, successful, and extremely intelligent—the last place he ever expected to find himself was locked up in a psychiatric ward.

As Dick described it:

I had two great fears in my life. Fear of rejection, and fear of mental patients. I certainly never expected that one day I'd *be* a mental patient.

The last year of my life had been a nightmare. But I sure as hell knew I wasn't crazy. I just had a few personal problems I needed to get straightened out. Maybe I drank a little too much and maybe I was involved with another woman, but it wasn't anything I couldn't handle. I just needed a little bit more time to get things under control.

The campaign just complicated my life. I was so absorbed in my own problems I couldn't really concentrate on anything, least of all a campaign. The race for state's attorney seemed to be the longest year in my life.

Nationally, Illinois was a pivotal state for the Republicans. And *I* was going to be the new Republican Golden Boy; the man with the credentials and the name recognition to finally beat a Daley and the Democrats in Chicago. Knowing that the national leaders thought *I* was the one who would finally be able to oust the Democrats from their stronghold in Cook County really fed my ego. It would have been a real coup. I honestly thought I could pull it off.

During the campaign, I was still drinking a lot, although I thought I covered it pretty well. Drinking seemed to help me forget all my personal problems. Not a hint of my drinking ever appeared in the press, although

76

there had been a great deal of speculation as to what *was* actually wrong with me.

I was so obsessed with my own problems that I had a hard time concentrating on what I was supposed to be doing—campaigning. It was hard to stir up any enthusiasm when my heart really wasn't in the race. How could it be? I was trying to handle a severe personal crisis.

There were rumors Liz and I were having marital problems. It really was just speculation; nothing concrete had ever been proven. Even though I had moved out of the house several times during the campaign, Liz worked very hard to keep up the image of the happy, loving, political couple. Every time a rumor about our marriage hit the papers I'd move back home to try to repair some of the damage done to my campaign. For a while I felt like a yo-yo, moving in and out of the house. I knew if word got out about the problems in my personal life I could kiss the election goodbye.

When the story leaked that my opponent, Richie Daley, was investigating my handling of the police contingency fund during my tenure as superintendent, it certainly didn't help my campaign.

Daley's office had subpoenaed all of my personal banking records for the years 1980 through 1984. They had also subpoenaed my parents' financial records. Daley's office claimed the investigation wasn't political. Daley also claimed he had personally recused (excused to avoid conflict of interest) himself from the investigation, letting other prosecutors on his staff handle the matter. But if it wasn't personal, then what the hell was it? I was running against the guy, the polls had me ahead, and then all of a sudden his office was investigating me. I wasn't the only one who was being investigated, though; the whole police department's financial dealings were under investigation. It just seemed like *I* was the one who got all the headlines. The timing of the news about the investigation was incredibly bad. I really felt it was just a fishing expedition leaked deliberately to discredit me. I was certain nothing would come of it. It was just politics as usual in Chicago.

I have to admit that my relationship with Diane had been deteriorating long before I announced my candidacy. She hadn't wanted me to run for state's attorney in the first place. Diane felt I had been stalling her long enough. First, I had told her I'd never leave Liz while I was superintendent, then four months later I announced I was running for state's attorney. I *was* stalling her.

Diane knew I would never leave Liz during the campaign because of the political repercussions. I used the campaign as an excuse to avoid making a decision I just couldn't make.

Diane was very upset because I hadn't been able to make a decision between her and Liz. We quarreled a lot. And at times she could be very vindictive, like when she told Liz about Laura. The only reason she did that was because she was angry at *me*.

Ever since Liz had confronted us at my apartment, I felt as if Diane was intimidated by Liz. I know she was extremely jealous of her. Liz was my wife, and the mother of my children. That day at the apartment, all Diane did after Liz left was talk about her: how she was dressed, how she behaved. I guess she was surprised that Liz didn't create a scene. But Liz didn't—she acted like a lady, much to Diane's surprise.

It was obvious I was having a hard time leaving Liz, because I really didn't want to leave her. I didn't want to have to give up either woman. I loved Liz, but I needed Diane.

Our relationship had been going on for almost three years. This wasn't just a casual fling, but something much more serious. Although we still continued to be intimate, it wasn't just a physical relationship. If it had been, I think it would have been easier to break off. But it wasn't. After all this time, our lives were very much entwined and our relationship was emotional as well. I have to say I was emotionally hooked on her. I couldn't break it off.

I tried to explain to Diane that I was just having a rough time with the campaign and all my personal problems. I assured her that once the election was over, things would ease, and I would be able to see things much more clearly. But she wasn't interested in any more excuses.

Diane had absolutely no compassion or sympathy for my situation or what I was going through. I received no support from her at all. She just kept accusing me of wallowing in my problems. I couldn't understand why Diane couldn't see what I was going through. This wasn't a picnic for me, either. I was getting pressure from her, pressure from Liz, and pressure from the campaign. Even though Diane could be cruel and vindictive at times, it didn't lessen my physical or emotional desire for her. At this point, I was so confused, I don't even know what I was getting out of the relationship—except pressure and a whole lot of grief. But I was hooked on her; I was sure I needed her—desperately. In a way, I think my wife and my mistress each filled a different need.

My relationship with Liz wasn't any better. But to Liz's credit, she *did* do her best to help and support me during the campaign. I knew I could always count on Liz. I knew she would always be there for me. We were still going for counseling, although I don't know why we bothered. It wasn't doing any good.

As the campaign drew to a close, everything fell apart. I didn't think things could get worse, but they did. Day by day things just seemed to be slipping away from me. I couldn't stop it. I didn't know *how* to stop it. It was the first time in my life I couldn't get things under control.

When Liz told me she was going to file for divorce I went nuts. How could she do this to me? I didn't want a divorce. What I wanted was Liz *and* Diane. I couldn't let go of either of them. I *needed* both of them. Why couldn't they understand that?

I never thought Liz would actually go through with the divorce. I was certain I could talk her out of it. She told the kids she was going to file the day after the election. I guess she also told them the real reason. I don't think they could believe their father was having an affair. My kids have always looked up to me. Words can't describe the disappointment in my children's eyes when they learned about Diane. It hurt like hell to know how much pain I had inflicted on my children, but not enough for me to break off my relationship with Diane.

Everyone was disappointed in me. My folks, Liz's folks, Rita, Joe, everyone; you could just see the bewilderment and confusion in their faces. They all thought I was nuts. At one point during the campaign, I guess I was acting so strangely that Liz began to fear for her safety. She had my father disconnect the electric garage-door opener and barricade the doors so I couldn't get into my own house. My own father! I couldn't believe it. I began to feel as if everyone was against me.

Then, as if I didn't have enough on my mind, the night before the election, while Liz and the kids were out campaigning for me, I went to the airport to pick up Diane. She had flown to Chicago for a twenty-four-hour layover before going on to Hawaii. As I drove Diane to the hotel, she dropped a bombshell. Nine months earlier Diane had put in for, and had now accepted, a transfer to the West Coast! My God, how was I going to see her? Her news sent me into a tailspin. I didn't need this the night before the election.

I begged Diane not to take the transfer. But she turned a deaf ear. I told Diane that Liz was filing for divorce the day after the election, but it didn't seem to make any difference.

Diane just didn't care; she was fed up with me and my lies. I didn't know what to do, but I knew I didn't want her to take that transfer. Somehow I had to talk her out of it. I begged and I pleaded with her to reconsider. I was totally beside myself.

I wanted to stay with Diane and try to talk her out of taking the transfer, but I couldn't. The CBS affiliate, WBBM TV in Chicago, was hosting a live pre-election news special with the candidates. I was scheduled to appear and I had to go. It was the last thing in the world I wanted to do. But it was the final push for the candidates prior to election day. One last chance to show your stuff. I went and did the show, but in the emotional state I was in I didn't do very well.

The day of the election I *still* thought I could pull it off. I still thought I could beat Daley. Hell, I'd always been a winner. I had accomplished everything I had ever set out to do and succeeded at everything I tried. It really never occurred to me that I could lose.

But I did.

On election day I was so consumed by my problems that I could barely drag myself out of bed. Liz was filing for divorce; Diane was transferring to Seattle. I didn't know what to do. Finally around six in the evening Liz, the kids, and I headed down to my campaign headquarters. The place was pitiful. I had disillusioned a lot of my supporters, good people who had worked hard and believed in me.

At one time the polls had me way ahead of Daley. But by the end of election day I had garnered less than twenty-four percent of the vote. I had the distinction of being the most soundly beaten candidate for state's attorney of Cook County, Illinois, since 1964.

Liz and the kids stood on the podium with me as I made a few off-the-cuff remarks to the last of my supporters. Afterward, Liz reached up and kissed me. She had tears in her eyes. At that moment, I think it finally sunk in: the election wasn't the only thing I had lost. I had lost my wife and family as well.

That night I had to face the fact that I had lost everything in the world that mattered to me; I was no longer a winner but a loser. It wasn't a role I was accustomed to, nor one I was very comfortable with.

Losing the election was a hard blow to deal with, but it was nothing compared to what was to come.

The day after the election, Liz left the house before I even woke up. I went down to the office and a few hours later a messenger arrived. Liz had served me with divorce papers. I was stunned. I never believed Liz would go through with it. *Never.* When the papers arrived it was like a slap in the face. I really lost control.

I called Liz. I was hysterical. Couldn't she see that this wasn't what I wanted, that this wasn't going to solve things? I knew I could get my life together. I just needed some more time. Divorce wasn't the answer. But Liz obviously thought it was.

I didn't want to lose Liz; she'd always been there for me. We had been a team for almost twenty years; everything I had attained had been with her help. I couldn't have accomplished all that I had without her. I had always felt that no matter what happened I could always count on Liz's love and support. But not any longer.

Liz turned a deaf ear to my pleas. She refused to believe me. She just wouldn't relent. Liz kept insisting she was going to go through with the divorce no matter what happened.

I was an emotional wreck. I couldn't accept the fact that I had really lost Liz. I *never* thought it could happen. But it did.

I had lost the election and my wife all in less than twenty-four hours, but it wasn't over yet. Despite my bosses' assurances that my job would be waiting for me no matter what the outcome of the election, that afternoon I was fired from Levy and Erens. It was the final blow. I started crying; I couldn't even think clearly. It was as if my emotions overloaded. I couldn't find my way out of the haze of my despair.

In less than twenty-four hours I had lost everything that had ever mattered to me: my wife, my family, my job, and the election. I also had to come to terms with the fact that Diane was moving to Seattle. I still didn't understand how it had all happened. I'd thought I had everything under control.

Walking into that psychiatric hospital was a shock. When those doors slammed shut behind me it was the eeriest feeling in the world. To this day, the sound still haunts me.

I was stripped, searched, and placed in a locked ward. The staff confiscated all of my personal belongings: my shoelaces, belt, pens, lighter—anything that I could hurt myself or someone else with.

It was kind of ironic in a way. I had spent most of my life locking other people up, but now *I* was locked up. As miserable as I felt, I couldn't help thinking about the similarities between being arrested and being admitted to a psychiatric ward. Both places strip you of your personal possessions, your identity, and your dignity. It was a humbling and humiliating experience.

All of my life I had always been in control of my thoughts, my actions, and my deeds. Now someone else was dictating what I had to think and do.

Shortly after I was admitted, Liz, my sister Rita, and her husband, Joe, arrived. In spite of what was happening between us, Liz still came to the hospital and brought the things she thought I might need. She brought my razor, shaving cream, and other personal items, but all of these were searched and then confiscated.

Liz talked to my psychiatrist for quite a while. I just sat there not really doing much of anything. I think I was still in a state of shock over the events of the past day.

After a brief visit, Rita, Joe, and Liz left. I was totally alone. There really wasn't much I could do. I was locked in my room. It was the loneliest feeling in the world. I couldn't even smoke. The staff had confiscated my lighter. I was told that patients were allowed to smoke only at certain specified times, and then only under the supervision of one of the staff.

There is a lot about that night that I don't remember. But there's a lot that I'll never forget. For the first twenty-four hours of my confinement I was not allowed any privileges. I couldn't leave the floor—not even go to the cafeteria for meals. I had to eat in a small room right off the nurses' station so that I could be monitored by the staff.

I was no longer Dick Brzeczek, former police superintendent and political celebrity. I was suddenly Dick Brzeczek, mental patient. It was shocking to me when I realized how far and how fast I had fallen.

The next day I was required to join in the regimented schedule of the ward. I was forced to mix with the other patients, which I found particularly uncomfortable because, as I said, mental patients have always made me nervous. To add to my discomfort, some of the other patients recognized me.

"Hey, haven't I seen you on television? Aren't you that cop, the one who was running for something? What the hell are you doing in here?"

If I heard that once, I heard it a hundred times. One day I was on television, and the next day I was in a mental ward.

It didn't take me long to realize that I would receive no special treatment in the ward. I was just another defenseless mental patient. A lot of good all my degrees did me in there.

I wasn't exactly the most popular patient in the ward. There was a lot of resentment toward me. Some of the other patients began hounding and tormenting me. One patient in particular used to follow me around all the time. He really made me nervous. It got to the point where I began to fear for my safety. The nurses finally stopped him from bothering me.

I began sleeping with one eye open just to be sure someone didn't come after me. I knew everyone had been searched and personal items confiscated. None of the patients were supposed to have anything they could harm themselves or anyone else with, but I'd been a cop much too long not to know about contraband items. I may have been sick, but I sure as hell wasn't stupid.

It wasn't enough that I had to worry about my personal problems. Now I had to worry about my personal safety as well. God, it was a nightmare. What the hell was I doing in that place?

I had always thought I was pretty tough. Nothing scared me. But I was scared in there. You want to talk about fear? Try being locked up in a mental institution. I've never felt so helpless or alone in my life. It was one of the most terrifying experiences I've ever had.

All my life, from grammar school through college, graduate, and law school, I had always followed the rules. I had always been a good soldier looking for approval and acceptance. I had always been the one in control.

As you get closer to the top you're freer intellectually and emotionally. Your thoughts and ideas are your own. You don't have to worry about someone looking over your shoulder, questioning your decisions or approving what you do. It had been a long, long time since I'd had anyone looking over my shoulder. But in the hospital someone was constantly looking over my shoulder, watching and evaluating me. You can't help but feel a little paranoid after a while. I was not accustomed to having someone tell me how to think, what to do, when to do it, and how to do it.

The hospital was more than just a prison of the body; it was a prison of the mind and spirit as well.

At one time I had commanded the second largest police force in the country. I had been recognized as one of the foremost law enforcement officials in the United States. I had socialized with presidents, dignitaries, and international VIPs. Now I found myself asking permission to do something as elementary as shave or smoke a cigarette. It was a thoroughly degrading experience.

My doctor saw me every day. I finally persuaded him to give me some privileges. I was going nuts just being stuck on the ward. I was finally allowed to shave with an electric razor provided by the staff but only under their strict supervision.

I was also allowed to smoke, but only at designated times in designated places. I was given cafeteria privileges, too. I thought it had to be better than eating in that tiny room all by myself with the nurses hovering over me. I didn't realize that patients with cafeteria privileges were lined up and taken to the cafeteria in small groups like schoolchildren so that no one could escape.

As a patient I was required to participate in group therapy. For me this was particularly difficult. I was not used to opening up and discussing my personal problems with anyone, let alone perfect strangers I probably wouldn't even talk to under normal circumstances.

I found group therapy to be one of the most stressful parts of my hospitalization. In group the patients sat around discussing their problems— real or imagined. It wasn't uncommon for someone to totally "freak out" during these sessions. I'd always had a deathly fear of mental patients. After a few sessions in group therapy, I knew why.

I quickly learned all the rules and regulations of the ward. I worked very hard to become a "model patient." I was the Great Impostor, trying hard to use all my mental abilities, reduced as they were, to toe the line and adhere to all the rules. I made sure I did *everything* that was expected of me. I lived in morbid fear of breaking any of the ward's strict rules.

Any infraction, no matter how minor, would result in a loss of all privileges. Any serious infraction earned you a trip to solitary confinement, or what was known as "house arrest." When placed under house arrest, a patient would be strapped into a straitjacket and locked in a padded room—alone.

As emotionally distraught as I was, I wasn't too sick to know I never wanted to be strapped into a straitjacket. I managed to use all of my abilities—as minimal as they were—to beat the system. I strictly followed the rules so that I didn't end up in solitary confinement. I was determined that they would *never* get me into that room.

I spent most of my time trying to outfox the staff. I learned one thing in the hospital: if you weren't emotionally ill when you went into a psychiatric ward, after a few days you sure as hell would be. And they expected me to get well while I was there? I didn't have *time* to get well. I was too worn out from trying to watch my every movement, follow the rules, and keep an eye on the other patients. It was totally demoralizing and exhausting.

While I was in the hospital, Rita, Joe, and a few of my close friends and the kids came to visit me. I was really glad to see the kids. I knew I had hurt and disappointed them. When they came to see me I felt as if they still cared about me.

The kids were scared by the hospital environment. Hell, it was a scary place. But they still came—all except Holly. She's the youngest, and I don't know if she just didn't understand what was going on, or if she was too frightened to come.

My parents also came to see me. Once. They sat across from me and cried the whole time. I felt so ashamed. What could I say to them? I had been their pride and joy. They had been so proud of me, and now . . .

It was difficult to face my parents' anguish. I finally told Rita and Joe not to bring them to the hospital anymore. To see my mom and dad suffering like that only added to my feelings of guilt.

Rita and Joe came faithfully every day. Their love and support meant a great deal to me. Everyone came to see me but Liz. I knew she was filing for divorce. I really couldn't blame her after what I'd put her through, but I still couldn't understand why she wouldn't come to see me.

Whenever I called the house to try to talk to her, one of the kids answered and told me she wouldn't talk to me. Every day when Liz drove the kids over she would sit outside in the car. I would beg them to tell her to come up, but she refused. When the kids left, I'd stand by the window hoping for a glimpse of Liz as she drove off the grounds. It was the first time in all the years we'd been together that I needed her and she wasn't there.

Diane and I kept in touch by phone. She had come back from Hawaii the day after I was admitted to the hospital. On her way home she had a twenty-four-hour layover in Chicago. I begged her, pleaded with her, to come see me in the hospital. But Diane refused. My hospitalization and Liz's divorce action had made front page news in Chicago. The press was having a field day digging up all the dirt not only about the divorce, but my breakdown, the investigation, and my "other woman." Diane didn't want to get dragged into the middle of the media circus, particularly since she was the "other woman." When she refused to come see me, it really hurt.

I think the real reason she didn't come was because she was furious at me. When she had arrived home after her trip to Hawaii, she listened to her answering machine and heard the message the kids had left for her on election night. She called me at the hospital and was absolutely livid. Diane read me the riot act about giving the kids her phone number. Hell, I don't know what the big deal was, she'd already talked to Mark once before. Besides, I hadn't given them her phone number, Liz had. On election night, after I had lost, Liz had allowed the kids to call Diane in an effort to calm them down. I don't know what they said on her machine, but Diane was furious. She just kept screaming at me that I had invaded her privacy by allowing my children access to her home telephone number.

I thought it was kind of sad. As a result of our affair I had lost everything in the world that mattered to me. But all Diane seemed to care about was her privacy being invaded by my scared, helpless children.

It didn't seem to matter to her that I had hit rock bottom or that our relationship might have been the cause. I tried to explain that right then I needed her support more than ever. I was still convinced that I needed her, still convinced that my very life depended on her.

Every time I thought about her transferring to the West Coast I went into a panic. I thought it would mean the end of our relationship. I couldn't bear to face that. Especially now.

I needed Diane. Couldn't she see that? The more I thought about losing her, the more I realized how much I needed her. The more I realized how much I needed her, and might lose her, the more frantic I became. It was a vicious circle.

In spite of how I felt about Diane, I wanted and needed Liz, too. I needed and wanted them both. I didn't want to make a choice between them. And I couldn't.

By the time the weekend rolled around, I was going nuts—literally. Between fighting with Diane, begging everyone to have Liz call me or come to see me, trying to follow all the rules and regulations of the ward and yet stay out of the way of the other patients, I was physically and mentally exhausted.

I wasn't getting better in there, but worse. I realized that if my doctor knew my condition was deteriorating rather than improving, he'd never let me out of that place. And I knew I *had* to get out.

A psychiatric hospital is certainly no place for someone who has any kind of personal or emotional problems. I found my spirits sinking lower and lower. The ward just seemed to magnify my problems. I knew that somehow, some way, I had to get out of the hospital. If I didn't, I feared I really would go nuts.

Before I went into the hospital I had never given any thought to the rights of mental patients; it wasn't my area of legal expertise. But did I learn fast—from the other patients. I was the attorney, yet the patients knew more about their legal rights than I did. I learned more about patients' rights in just a few days in that place than I had learned in all my years practicing law.

I learned that since I had voluntarily signed myself in, rather than having been committed against my will, I could not be held in the hospital for more than five business days without my consent. I had been admitted on Wednesday, the day after the election, so I couldn't legally be released until the following Wednesday. But they also couldn't hold me beyond Wednesday without my consent, which I had no intention of giving.

All weekend I was locked in my room again. I couldn't talk to my doctor because he didn't see patients on weekends. I spent the entire time trying to figure out how I was going to convince him that I was well enough to be released. I wanted out and I didn't care what I had to do to accomplish my objective.

On Monday, when the doctor arrived, I spent most of the day convincing him that I had finally made some decisions regarding my life. I said all the things he wanted to hear, fed him all the answers I knew he expected. I would have said or done *anything* to get out of that hospital. Even before I spoke to the doctor, I had been so confident that I could persuade him to release me that I had called Diane and told her to expect me.

The doctor and I agreed that my dual relationships couldn't go on. I finally admitted that the stress of the double relationships had led to my downfall. It was what he wanted to hear. I also convinced him that I had made a decision regarding my wife and my mistress. I told him I had done a lot of thinking and had decided to stay with Diane. I told him as soon as I was released I was going to Minneapolis to be with Diane and start my life anew. I assured the doctor that I felt much better now that the decision had actually been made. I had my priorities in order once again and was certain I could get my life under control.

The doctor believed me. He agreed to release me the next day so that I could leave for Minneapolis. It was one of the happiest days of my life, knowing I was finally going to get out of that hellhole.

I really *hadn't* come to any decision. In fact, I was probably more confused after I had been in the hospital than I had been before I went in. But I just couldn't think clearly in that place; I really didn't have the energy or the time.

I had no doubt that once I was released my life would improve. I was certain I would be able to get a handle on things. The pressure of the campaign was finally over and I was sure that not having that pressure hanging over my head would help. I could now concentrate on getting my personal life together.

I hadn't seen Diane since the night before the election. The only truthful thing I had told the doctor was that I planned to go to Minneapolis after my release.

I *was* going to Minneapolis, but there was something I had to do first. I had to see Liz.

Chapter Seven

Down and Out

As far as Liz was concerned, her relationship and her marriage were over. She didn't anticipate ever seeing her husband again. She was shocked when he walked in the door a few hours after his release from the hospital.

"I couldn't understand what he was doing here," Liz insisted. "Dick had made it very clear he didn't want us; he wanted *her*. So why did he come home? Hadn't the kids and I been through enough? Why was Dick trying to prolong our agony?

"I had been trying very hard to pick up the pieces of our life. When Dick walked in as if there were nothing wrong, it certainly didn't help matters. It only confused the kids more."

Dick couldn't break the ties that bound him to his wife any more than he could break his ties to his mistress. If he thought he would receive a hearty welcome when he returned home, he was wrong. Liz didn't want him there and neither did his children.

"When Dick came home he told me he'd be leaving for Minneapolis the next day," Liz recalled. "I didn't understand why he didn't just go to a hotel for a night. I didn't want to talk to him, let alone see him. But apparently Dick still hadn't gotten the message. He kept telling me how much he loved me and the kids. I was just sick to death of hearing it.

"Somewhere along the line, my feelings for Dick began to die. I think it was self-preservation. I had been through so much grief and pain, I think my mind simply shut off all my feelings. It had taken Dick nearly three years but he had finally succeeded in killing all the love and tenderness I had ever felt for him. I just wanted him out of my life.

"The week he was in the hospital was the first peace the kids and I had had in a long, long time. We were learning to cope without him. I didn't want the craziness to start all over again. I knew if I allowed Dick to stay, the whole mess would just get worse. I couldn't take it and neither could the children. Their feelings were evident the day he came home."

"I had no idea why my father came home," Natalie revealed. "He was supposed to be going to Minnesota to be with his girlfriend. So what did he expect from us, a welcome-home party? All we wanted was for him to go to *her*, if that's what he wanted, and to leave us alone."

Dick kept insisting that he still loved Liz and his children. He attempted to be warm and affectionate but Liz refused his amorous advances.

She had been slowly coming to terms with the fact that her marriage was over. It was time for Dick to accept it. He could stay the night in order to pack his belongings, but Liz would not let him return to their home or their life. Dick had made his choice.

That evening Liz slept on the couch. It was the only night in their married life she had ever refused to sleep with him. The next morning Liz rose early, dressed, and left the house before Dick awoke. She knew he would be leaving for Minneapolis sometime that day. In order to avoid another scene, Liz made plans to be out of the house until she was certain Dick had left.

When she returned home that afternoon, Dick was indeed gone, but he had left her a note:

"Liz, I love you. When I return from Minneapolis we'll go see your attorney together to arrange for an amicable divorce."

Relieved that Dick was finally gone for good, Liz threw herself into getting her life back on track. The day Dick left for Minneapolis, one of his former campaign workers stopped by to see how the couple was doing. Liz told the woman that Dick had gone to Minneapolis to be with Diane and they were indeed getting divorced.

The next day the item was duly reported in the newspaper. Liz tried to shield the children from the adverse publicity about their father. She canceled the newspapers in an effort to protect them, but it did little good. At school, the children's classmates informed them about items that appeared in the press about their father.

"The children were deeply ashamed of Dick," Liz revealed. "It was difficult enough for the children to handle this privately, but having to deal with it publicly was even more horrendous for them."

The trauma soon began affecting the children in other ways. Mark and

Kevin developed behavior problems at school; they had difficulty getting along with other kids, and their schoolwork began to suffer.

Liz knew she had to get the kids some professional help. She made an appointment for the children to see a family counselor. The counselors, a married couple, made arrangements to come to the house so they could speak to all four of the children together.

The day before the counselors were scheduled to arrive, Liz was driving her daughter Holly to a basketball game. A woman ran a red light and sheared off the front end of Liz's car. No one was seriously hurt, but Liz was badly shaken. She pulled herself together and arranged to have her damaged car towed, then borrowed a car from Joe and Rita for the interim. It was the first time Liz had ever handled a major crisis without Dick's help. She felt understandably proud of herself. Perhaps she *was* going to make it on her own.

That night, after being gone only five days, Dick arrived back home unexpectedly. Liz insisted that he leave. The counselors were coming over the next evening, and she wanted the children to feel free to speak to them without their father present.

How were they ever going to put their lives back together if Dick kept coming back and embroiling them in the same old mess? Liz was not about to start letting Dick drift between her house and Diane's. If he couldn't make a decision, that was his problem. She'd made hers and she planned to abide by it, whether Dick liked it or not. Liz felt she had already given Dick every opportunity to choose what he wanted.

Dick claimed that once he had actually arrived in Minneapolis he had realized it wasn't Diane he wanted, but Liz. He kept insisting he had seen Diane for the last time and the relationship was over. Liz had heard so many lies from Dick for so many years that she no longer was able to believe him, particularly where Diane was concerned. Once again Liz asked Dick to leave.

Dick refused; he claimed he was home for good. Dick tried to convince Liz and the children that this was going to be a new beginning for them all.

Although Liz was extremely upset about Dick's sudden reappearance, as always, she was intimidated by her husband. He adamantly refused to leave the house. He was sad and repentant, almost hysterical again. Liz finally relented and let him stay. For the children's sake, she didn't want another scene.

The next evening, when the counselors arrived, Liz slowly revealed all that had happened in the past three years. The counselors tried to talk to the children, to draw them into the conversation and get them to talk about their feelings, but the kids refused to talk in front of their father.

They were openly antagonistic toward Dick. The counselors finally suggested that Dick and Liz leave the room so that they could speak to the children alone.

Once Dick and Liz were alone, Dick tried again to convince Liz that his relationship with Diane was over. He begged her to let him come home. He wanted another chance to try to repair their marriage.

Liz refused to listen. She told him again that their marriage was over and he'd better get used to it. He was no longer part of her life.

After speaking to the children at length, the counselors called Dick and Liz back into the room. The counselors carefully explained that in spite of everything that had happened, what the children *really* wanted was for Liz to give their father another chance. Despite their anger at him, the children felt sorry for Dick and truly wanted to believe him when he said he was ready to give up Diane, change his ways, and come home.

During the day and a half that Dick had been home he had convinced the kids of his sincerity in wanting to come home and rejoin the family. The children desperately wanted to believe that he meant what he said. For the children, Dick's desire to come home was an affirmation of his love for them.

When Dick had chosen Diane over them, it was a rejection the children simply could not cope with or accept. If their father wanted to give up Diane, come home, and once again rejoin the family, then he *must* love them. In the kids' minds, Dick's love for them was tied to his relationship with Diane.

Psychologists and marriage counselors explain that when parents divorce, no matter what the reason, children tend to blame themselves. They feel responsible. If the children can bring their parents back together, it allows them to absolve themselves of some of their misplaced guilt.

The Brzeczek children had been innocent victims caught up in an emotional crisis that they were unable to handle. They believed that if their father came home and the family was reunited, their problems and emotional turmoil would be resolved, and their lives would return to normal.

The Brzeczek children desperately wanted to believe their father. They wanted to believe that *this* time he was telling the truth.

If the children *didn't* believe Dick, it meant they would finally have to face and accept the reality of the situation. In the children's minds, reality was black and white: either their father loved them or he didn't.

When the counselors told Liz how the children felt, she was stunned. After all that had happened, Liz couldn't believe her children expected her to give Dick another chance. The children might have believed their father, but Liz did not. She was furious with Dick for coming home and once again raising the children's hopes.

"I had fallen for his lies too many times to be fooled," Liz said. "But for the kids' sakes, I had to seriously consider giving Dick another chance. I could tell it was what the kids really wanted.

"I never wanted the children to feel I hadn't given Dick a fair chance. I wanted them to look back on this and realize that I had done everything in my power not only to keep the marriage together but the family, too. They were so hopeful, I really didn't have the heart to disappoint them."

Against Liz's better judgment, she agreed to give Dick another chance. She would let him come home—on one condition: if he saw Diane, or even talked to her on the phone, she would kick him out for good and go through with the divorce. Dick agreed. Once again, he assured his wife and children that his affair was over. Dick promised that this would be a new beginning for all of them. He seemed so sincere, so happy; he even called their families to announce that he had come home for good. Dick apologized profusely, then asked for, and received, forgiveness from everyone after assuring them that his affair with Diane was definitely over.

The children were overjoyed at Dick's return to the family. Kevin recalled: "When my mom agreed to let my dad come home I was really happy. I didn't want my parents to get divorced. I just wanted things to go back to normal. When my dad came home from Minneapolis, he seemed so sad, we truly believed he wanted to come home and stay with the family."

Natalie remembered how she felt that evening: "I don't think my mom really wanted to give my dad another chance. I don't think she believed one word my father said, but for our sakes, she agreed to let him come home. Finally our lives were going to settle down and go back to normal."

The day after Dick's solemn promise to his children, he went down to Levy and Erens. (Although Dick had been fired, he was scheduled to work through the end of the year.) Dick took Natalie with him down to the office.

"We'd been at the office only a few minutes," Natalie recalled, "when I caught my father on the phone with Diane. I couldn't believe it! Just the night before he had promised us it was over. He had *sworn* to us he was through with that woman. We *believed* him. We had even convinced our mother to give him another chance. My father had deliberately lied to us. He *used* us.

"My father didn't care about us or our mother. All he cared about was his girlfriend. I started crying and I couldn't stop. I was so upset I had to talk to someone. I used one of the other phones to call my mom. I didn't know what else to do. I thought if I talked to her maybe I'd feel better."

When Liz received Natalie's heartbroken call she knew it was the last straw. It was one thing for Dick to lie to her and betray her, but to deliberately lie to his children, to raise their hopes, only to crush them once again, was unforgivable. Dick had finally succeeded in breaking not just Liz's heart but his children's hearts as well.

Liz called Dick on his other telephone line and confronted him about his phone call. At first Dick lied and denied he had been on the phone with his mistress. But then he finally admitted it. He said he couldn't help himself; he *had* to talk to her. It was the final straw for Liz.

When Dick and a visibly upset Natalie returned home, Liz gathered the children together. She told them what had happened. Liz told the children that she had no choice but to go through with the divorce. This time the kids offered no protest. In fact, they encouraged her. They were so disgusted and disappointed, they wanted no part of their father.

Liz told Dick to get out. He became enraged. He began screaming and threatening Liz, only frightening and infuriating Liz and the children more. Liz was terrified and nearly hysterical; she had no idea what to do with Dick, but she knew that somehow, for the children's sake as well as her own, she had to get Dick to leave. The couple had a horrible argument that pushed Kevin past his endurance.

He went wild. Kevin began screaming and ran into the basement. Grabbing his prized hockey sticks, he began smashing them against the basement wall. When he finished, Kevin ran hysterically through the house, finally locking himself in his bedroom.

"I hurt so bad inside, I just wanted to stop the pain," Kevin recalled. "But I didn't know how. I was so angry I just wanted to punch something—*anything*. I finally smashed my fist into my bedroom door, knocking a hole through it. My brother, Mark, ran in and tried to hold me to calm me down, but I broke free. Everyone was crying and screaming. I just wanted them all to stop.

"My father finally stopped yelling at my mother and came to my bedroom to try to calm me down. I was crying and yelling, and my dad put his arms around me, but I broke free of him. I didn't even want him to touch me. *I hated him.* I just wanted him to leave us alone."

Liz was at her wits' end. She had no idea how to get Dick out of the house.

"Dick was just out of his mind—crazy. He threatened us, yelled at us. He said he'd never leave. I just didn't know what to do. I knew the kids were scared, terrified, in fact. So was I. The scene just went on and on for hours. I don't think I've ever gone through a worse night."

Things didn't get better in the following days or weeks. Liz was helpless to do anything. She had absolutely no legal recourse to remove Dick from the premises. No judge would issue a restraining order or force a man to leave his own home simply because he was having an affair. In spite of all of Liz's resources and contacts, she felt as if she still had to protect Dick's reputation, protect his image. Besides, she had worked so hard and for so long at keeping up the facade of the happy, loving couple that she wasn't sure anyone would believe her now if she told them what was going on.

She thought about taking the children and leaving, but Dick had begun talking about suicide. Liz realized she couldn't just leave him alone. This was a man she had spent most of her adult life with; he was the father of her children. If Dick did take his own life, Liz knew she would never be able to forgive herself, nor would she ever be able to explain to the children that she had left their father and then he had killed himself.

"Dick was totally out of it," Liz recalled. "He was either on the phone with Diane right in front of me and the kids, crying hysterically and begging her to come to Chicago. Or he was lying on the couch in a paralyzed, depressed stupor. Dick was supposed to continue working at the law firm until the end of the year, but he couldn't even drag himself out of bed to go to work. He'd just lie around and drink and cry. Dick had once prided himself on his impeccable appearance. Now, he lay around in grubby clothing, not bothering to shave or shower."

Dick's irrational behavior only further alienated the children. They were openly hostile toward him. As the days and weeks wore on, the kids began to grow increasingly angry with Liz for not getting Dick out of the house.

"I couldn't force Dick to leave," Liz confessed. "I felt sorry for him.

He was quite clearly so emotionally ill that he didn't know what he was doing. He was so depressed that he was totally incapacitated. I really don't think he even realized what he was doing.

"At times, he would get so hysterical that he threatened to take his service revolver and go into the basement and commit suicide. Then I would get hysterical. We'd both be screaming. I'd grab Dick and hang on to him in an effort to try to keep him from going into the basement because I feared he'd do something crazy. I was convinced that he really would take his own life. I knew it was only further deepening the kids' emotional scars but I didn't know what to do. I was at my wits' end. In the condition Dick was in I knew I would never be able to divorce him. How could I kick him out? He was like a sick, helpless child. I couldn't just walk out on him. I just couldn't."

Liz pleaded with Dick to go back into the hospital, or at least to go to his doctor. He refused, and continued to deny that he was ill. Dick kept insisting Liz had the problem; she was the one who was crazy, not he.

Liz became so distraught over the situation that she finally made an appointment to see Dick's psychiatrist. She needed someone to help her with Dick. The doctor's advice was to try to get Dick back into the hospital.

"How could I get Dick back into the hospital? The only way you can have someone committed is with a certificate from two physicians, a court order, or if a patient voluntarily commits himself. I knew Dick wasn't about to commit himself. *He didn't think he was sick.* I couldn't even get him to go see the doctor, let alone have two of them certify that he needed hospitalization."

Almost daily Liz begged Dick to see a doctor. Months earlier Lee Philip had given Liz the name of Dr. Jan Fawcett, a psychiatrist who specialized in depression. Liz tried desperately to get Dick to see Dr. Fawcett or at least talk to him. But Dick refused.

"One night, Dick was particularly distraught. He had been drinking excessively and was sinking deeper and deeper into depression. He was almost totally paralyzed and in such a state I literally feared for all of us. I had no idea what he would do next.

"That evening Dick finally called Dr. Fawcett at home. I don't know why he chose that particular night. Perhaps he was just feeling so bad he finally realized he had to talk to someone.

"Dr. Fawcett strongly encouraged Dick to come in the next morning and see him. But Dick told him he couldn't; there were some things he had to take care of first."

There was nothing Liz could do unless Dick went willingly to the doctor. The couple's families continued to be supportive of Liz, but from a distance. They called daily, but Dick was so totally out of control, his behavior so unstable and unpredictable, that no one wanted to be around him because they had no idea what he would do next.

"Dick's mother called every day," Liz recalled. "She'd tell me to just hang in there; she'd do the praying for both of us. By this time I couldn't even pray anymore. I didn't have the energy. I was totally drained, physically and emotionally. I think the kids finally realized just how emotionally ill their father was. Dick was totally dysfunctional."

The atmosphere was extremely troubling for the children, but Liz didn't realize just how desperate the situation had become until she received a telephone call from the boys' counselors at Loyola Academy. They wanted to see her immediately to discuss her sons' behavior. Liz went in to talk to the counselors about Mark and Kevin. A meeting was called with all of the boys' teachers so that Liz could explain exactly what had caused such a drastic change in her once happy, stable sons.

Mark's grades had fallen and he had become extremely aggressive. He was having difficulty getting along with the other kids and had started fighting. Mark was rebelling in the only way he knew how—he was simply acting out his anger.

Kevin too was having a very difficult time. Once the counselors were aware of the problem, they were very understanding. They assured Liz that they would do whatever they could to help the boys.

Kevin no longer felt that he had to keep everything inside. When he was having a difficult time, he went to one of the counselors to talk things out. It helped Kevin immensely just to know there was someone he could talk to about what was happening at home. He no longer felt so isolated and alone.

The counselors tried to assure Liz that as long as there was one healthy parent in the household, the boys probably wouldn't be permanently scarred.

"That was part of the problem," Liz recalled. "I didn't think there *was* a healthy parent in the household. I no longer considered myself healthy. I was suffering from depression and severe emotional distress. I felt helpless. Our lives had become totally unmanageable. I couldn't do anything *with* Dick or *for* him. Unless you've actually lived with a person who's truly emotionally unstable, it's very difficult to understand how painful it is. It was hard for me to believe this was the same man I had married twenty years ago."

The counselors, like Dick's psychiatrist, also suggested that Liz immediately get Dick into a hospital. Liz explained that she had no way to do it; she'd already tried everything she could.

The counselors went on to suggest that Liz call one of Dick's close friends, someone Dick trusted. If Liz explained the severity of the situation, perhaps this trusted friend could convince Dick that he needed to seek help and hospitalization.

Although a few of Dick and Liz's close friends had stuck by them, there were a great many more who did not. Many people simply could not accept the fact that Dick was emotionally ill. Dick had been a very respected and admired member of the community, a man who was looked up to and revered. Once again, because Liz had kept their problems a secret, Liz had a difficult time convincing people Dick was seriously emotionally ill and totally out of control.

Bill Hanhardt had been a close personal friend of both Dick and Liz for many years. A career police officer, Bill Hanhardt had been Dick's chief of detectives. Hanhardt had been one of the most admired police officers in the city of Chicago. Dick respected Hanhardt and his opinions.

Hanhardt had always been there when Dick or Liz needed him. Desperate now, Liz called Hanhardt. She told him what had been going on since Dick's release from the hospital. Liz pleaded with Hanhardt to come by and try to talk Dick into going back into the hospital. Hanhardt agreed. If anyone could get through to Dick it would be Hanhardt. He was Liz's last hope.

"It was December," Liz remembered. "Dick decided he wanted to barbecue. I was taking a shower, and the next thing I knew Dick came into the house and said Hanhardt had dropped by. I asked where he was because I wanted a chance to talk to him. Dick told me that he had left. Dick said he had talked to Hanhardt and assured him that there was absolutely nothing wrong with him or our marriage. He'd convinced Hanhardt that he was perfectly fine and didn't need hospitalization. He told Hanhardt I had been exaggerating."

Liz had reached the end of her rope. She had nowhere else to turn. During the weeks following Dick's release from the hospital Liz and her children were virtually prisoners of his madness.

One afternoon a package arrived for Liz. Tessie Johnson was a neighbor who had lived downstairs from the Brzeczeks when their children were little. Tessie had read about the couple's marital troubles in the newspaper. Although Tessie hadn't seen the Brzeczeks in almost eighteen years, she wanted to offer Liz some solace and help. The package contained the book *Love Must Be Tough*, by Dr. James C. Dobson.[1]

Desperate and willing to grasp at anything that might help, Liz sat down and read *Love Must Be Tough* from cover to cover. The book had a profound effect on her. The material reaffirmed all the things she had learned in Al-Anon so long ago. The book made Liz realize that the situation she found herself in was not going to change unless *she* changed it.

Liz decided to take drastic action. Due to her own emotional stress, she feared she would not be able to confront Dick face to face without breaking down. Instead, as suggested in the book, Liz wrote Dick a letter, guided by the one in Dobson's book, but changing it somewhat to fit her own circumstances.

Liz's letter to her husband is reprinted below.

Dear Richard:

It's a curious thing, Richard, how a person loses all perspective when he's so close to a problem. It's become difficult to see the issues clearly, and that has definitely happened to me in the past few months. But in the past few weeks I've been able to pull back from our difficulties and I now see everything in an entirely new light. It is incredible just how foolish I have been since you told me of your decision to leave us. I tolerated your unfaithfulness for over three years now. I can't believe that I really did that. My self-esteem and self-confidence were torn to shreds. I was willing to do anything to keep you from leaving me.

I'll tell you, Richard, those days are over! If you want to go, you can certainly do so. In fact, that may be for the best. I doubt if I can ever trust you again, or feel for you as I once did. I wasn't a perfect wife, to be sure, but you violated my trust not once, but repeatedly for over the past three and a half years. I'm no longer special to you, I'm just one of a crowd. I can't live with that. I'd rather face life alone than as a member of your harem. If Diane is the one you want, I hope the two of you will be happy together. I'm still not sure how something so wonderful became so dirty and distorted, but that's between you and the Lord. We both have to answer to Him in our own way, and my conscience is clear.

So where do we go from here, Richard? I've been doing some intensive thinking, and believe you should pack up and leave. It won't work for you to hopscotch between Diane and me, sleeping with us both and trying to make it seem so normal. You say you aren't sure which one you want? Well, that isn't very inspiring in you. You pledged eternal love and commitment to me on our wedding day, and we shared in the births of four beautiful children, but now, all that could be gone with the toss of a coin. What we both need is some time apart. I think you should find another place to stay, perhaps with Diane if you wish. If in the future, you decide you want to be my husband, then we'll talk about it. I make no promises, however. I'm doing everything possible to remove you from my heart, to spare myself any more pain. It's not going to be easy. You were my one and only love, and the only one I ever wanted. But that was then, and this is now. God bless you, Richard. The kids and I will miss you.

Elizabeth.

After writing the letter, Liz called Dick's sister Rita. Liz explained about the letter and what she wanted to do. She had to get Dick out of the house. She asked Rita and Joe if Dick could stay with them for a while. They agreed.

Liz didn't know how Dick would take the letter. In his emotional state she wasn't even certain he would be able to understand what she was trying to say. But to Liz's surprise, Dick agreed to leave.

"I guess he was just too sick to fight anymore. His spirit seemed crushed. Dick called his sister and told her he was coming over."

Rita had no idea what to expect when Dick arrived. She hadn't seen him since he had been in the hospital and really wasn't prepared.

"My brother was in worse shape than I had ever seen him. He looked awful. My heart just ached for him. Joe and I were afraid to leave him alone. We had to go to work, but knowing Dick would be alone all day was frightening. I was terrified he would do something foolish.

"I love my brother and I'd never turn my back on him. But I don't think anyone realizes how sick a person in a severe depression really is. You look at him and physically he looks fine. But how do you heal a mind?

"Depression is not like a heart attack or cancer, where you can actually see the ravages of the disease. But depression can be just as ravaging on a person and his family as any physical illness. Depression is hard to recognize and understand, particularly if you've never had to experience it on a personal level with someone you know and love.

"No one could imagine what we went through with my brother, or how it affected our whole family. It was pure agony. It's a very helpless feeling to watch someone you love slip further and further away, knowing you can't do anything to help him."

Joe was equally distressed at Dick's declining mental health. "I was terrified Dick was going to do something to harm himself. When Rita and I went to work we called Dick every couple of hours just to make sure he was all right. He talked all the time about taking his life.

"Dick was drinking so much I could smell the liquor as I came through the door. He wouldn't eat anything except chocolates, and he wouldn't listen to anyone, either. He was like a zombie, lying around in a stupor, or on the phone with his girlfriend. Dick was constantly talking to her. I felt his conversations with her only agitated him more."

A few days after Dick moved in with Rita and Joe, something happened that seemed to be the final breaking point. He had called Diane, and they'd had a horrendous fight that further demoralized Dick.

Rita and Joe had no idea what was going on; they only knew that after Dick's phone call to Diane he became hysterical. He just sat on the couch and cried. It seemed that Dick had finally gone over the edge.

Joe and Rita tried to calm Dick, but to no avail. Nothing helped. They, too, were at a loss as to what to do for him or with him. Dick hadn't eaten in days. The only thing he had consumed was liquor. Rita and Joe decided to go out for Chinese food, hoping that if Dick ate something perhaps he might feel better.

While they were gone, Dick called Liz. It was the first time she had heard from him since she'd forced him out of the house.

"Dick was hysterical," Liz remembered. "He was sobbing and talking crazy. He kept saying there was no way out of this mess except to kill himself. Dick begged me to come over and help him. I had no doubt he was absolutely serious about committing suicide, but I refused to go over there. It may sound cruel, but you have to remember what I'd been through. I meant what I had said in the letter. I had finally reached the end of *my* rope. He chose to remain in the relationship with Diane. It was my choice not to put up with him, or the situation, any longer. I felt sorry for him, but my feelings for Dick were totally dead.

"Dick kept begging me to come over to Joe and Rita's. He pleaded with me to do something to help him. I refused to go over there, but I did offer to call a doctor for him. I made it very clear that that was *all* I would do.

"I guess that night Dick realized something I had known for a long time: what he needed was professional help. This thing had gone on much too long. It was the hospital or nothing. Dick had finally hit bottom."

Liz hung up and immediately called Dr. Fawcett. She told him about Dick's phone call and his threats to commit suicide. Dr. Fawcett advised her to get Dick to Rush Presbyterian—St. Luke's Stress Unit as soon as possible. Dr. Fawcett promised to meet them there.

Liz called Dick back to tell him he was going back into the hospital. She knew Dick's opinion of hospitals, particularly after his last stay. But she felt he was sick enough now to accept the idea.

Liz couldn't get through to Dick; the line was busy. He was back on the phone with Diane. Liz kept calling and calling, getting more upset as time passed. Finally, she got through. When she told Dick that he was going back into the hospital, he offered no resistance. In fact, he almost seemed relieved.

When Rita and Joe returned they got Dick into the car, then swung by to pick up Liz. Together they drove to the hospital. Dr. Fawcett met them there and immediately admitted Dick under an assumed name to avoid any further publicity for the family. This time, however, Dick was not placed in a locked ward, but in an open ward with a more hospital-like atmosphere.

"Dr. Fawcett kept asking Dick if he felt suicidal," Liz recalled. "But Dick denied it. I knew he was lying. After all those years I think lying had become a habit with him.

"I had to tell Dr. Fawcett the whole story from the beginning because it was the first time he had seen us or treated Dick as his patient. Dr. Fawcett stayed with us for several hours. He had a very calm demeanor and I liked him very much. Because of Dick's condition, I did most of the talking. Dr. Fawcett didn't seem the least bit shocked by anything I told him.

"When I was finally finished, Dr. Fawcett looked at me and said something to the effect that, I had taken so much crap, I must have some feelings for Dick if I was still sitting by his side. The only feeling I can remember having at that point was relief that Dick was finally going to be back in the hospital, where he belonged."

Dr. Fawcett ordered a complete series of blood tests for Dick, and after he had Dick settled in a room, Liz left.

The next morning Liz received a call from Doris Wineman, the hospital's psychiatric social worker. Earlier in the morning Doris had spoken to Dick at great length and now wanted to speak to Liz, to hear her side of the story. Liz agreed to go to the hospital to talk with the social worker.

"Doris and I had a long talk. She explained to me that Dick was very sick. I was very surprised when she told me she didn't think Dick would get well _without_ me. Previously, I had been told Dick wouldn't get well _with_ me. Doris went on to explain that Dick was not in love with Diane; he was 'addicted' to her. I had never heard of such a thing. I never realized someone could be addicted to a _person_. Doris explained that an addiction to a person or a relationship can be as serious as any other addiction, and just as difficult to break.

"Doris had already talked to Dick earlier that morning and he had expressed a sincere desire to save our marriage. Doris felt our marriage was worth saving, but she needed to know if _I_ felt our marriage was worth saving. Doris wanted to know if I would be willing to give Dick and our marriage another chance."

Another chance? Liz couldn't believe it. Did Doris know what she was asking?

"Whatever Dick and I had, it had died a long time ago. I honestly didn't know if the children or I could ever get over all the hurt and pain Dick had inflicted on us. What had taken us years to build, Dick had destroyed because of his relationship with this other woman.

"I had spent nearly twenty years with Dick. I thought I knew him, but I didn't know him at all. I thought I could trust him with my life and my love.

"Dick had totally demoralized and humiliated me both publicly and privately. He'd made me feel worthless and ashamed. I had absolutely no feelings for Dick by this time, except perhaps anger and hatred for what he had done. I seriously doubted if my love or respect for him could ever be rekindled.

"A marriage has to have some foundation: love, respect, trust, mutual admiration. I had none of those feelings. As far as I was concerned, Dick and I had nothing left. How did they expect us to repair something we no longer had?"

Liz had worked hard to put Dick out of her heart and out of her life. Now, the doctors wanted her to let him back in.

Liz was torn. She wasn't certain she could make a rational decision in her battered emotional state. Knowing that the doctors felt Dick would never recover without her help and support weighed heavily on her.

Liz had a major decision to make and not a great deal of time in which to make it. The doctors wanted an answer from her as soon as possible. Once again, Liz felt she had nowhere to turn.

Liz's deep religious faith had carried her through every crisis in her life. Once again, she turned to God for help and guidance. She was certain He would help her make the right decision.

"Dick and I had twenty years invested in our marriage; twenty good years before all this craziness started. We had brought four beautiful children into the world; children who didn't ask for, or deserve, all the pain and misery we had inflicted on them.

"I just didn't know what to do. I prayed a lot. I just kept thinking to myself: 'God, what do You expect of me? What do *You* want me to do?' "

Chapter Eight

Giving the Marriage a Second Chance

Dr. Jan Fawcett is professor of psychiatry and the chairman of the Department of Psychiatry at Rush Presbyterian—St. Lukes Medical Center in Chicago. Dr. Fawcett is also the national adviser to the Depressive and Manic Depressive Association.[1] The DMDA treats patients and their families who have suffered, or who are suffering from, various forms of depression.

The first time Dr. Fawcett actually met Dick Brzeczek was the night he admitted him to Presbyterian—St. Luke's Stress Unit. However, it wasn't the first time Dr. Fawcett was aware that Dick Brzeczek had been having emotional problems.

"One evening during the campaign for Cook County State's Attorney, I was home watching television when one of Dick Brzeczek's campaign commercials aired. I sat in stunned silence. Dick's outward physical symptoms of depression were so obvious I could have used him as a classic case study for my students. Dick was ashen; his movements were stiff, lifeless, and wooden, and his voice was a flat monotone. Just from Dick's speech patterns, lack of mobility, and outward physical condition I could tell the man was clearly in the throes of a debilitating depression.

"My first thought was: 'Why isn't someone getting him some help?' I couldn't believe that the people around him—his advisers, campaign staff, or whoever else was working with him—couldn't see how desperately ill he was. I turned to my family and said: 'That man needs help.'

"In all my years as a doctor I have never made a diagnosis of a patient from watching television. But from a visual standpoint it was so apparent

105

that Dick was acutely ill, I couldn't believe no one else could see it. In my opinion, to allow Dick to endure the rigors of a campaign put his life, and his emotional well-being, at great risk."

Dr. Fawcett had received several telephone calls from Liz prior to meeting or speaking directly to Dick. But there was little Dr. Fawcett could do until Dick contacted him personally. One evening he finally called.

"After talking to Dick on the phone I knew the man was in serious trouble. Our conversation just confirmed my original opinion when I saw him on television. I tried to persuade Dick to come to the office the next day, but he kept saying he had some things to straighten out first. I think Dick still felt he would be able to untangle the threads of his life on his own. He was not yet ready to admit he needed help. There really wasn't anything I could do for him until he was ready."

It wasn't until several weeks later that Dr. Fawcett received the frantic phone call from Liz.

"The night Liz called me she was very upset. She said Dick was so despondent that he was talking about suicide. From our conversation I had no doubt that Liz truly believed Dick was capable of taking his own life. In my opinion Dick was not making idle threats. I believe he was in a state of such paralyzing, disabling depression that suicide seemed the only way out. I instructed Liz to bring Dick to the hospital immediately."

When Dr. Fawcett arrived at the hospital, there was no question that he was going to admit Dick. Dick was in poor physical condition and emotionally demoralized. His self-esteem was badly damaged and his perspective extremely distorted.

Dr. Fawcett's diagnosis: major depression complicated by probable alcohol abuse.

"One of the first things I did was sit down and talk to Dick and Liz at length," Dr. Fawcett recalled. "From our conversation I knew Dick's depression had escalated to the point where he was definitely at risk for suicide. Hospitalization was the only answer. Dick needed to be in a controlled environment until he was well enough to sustain himself on his own. I had every indication Dick would indeed take his own life if he did not receive the proper medical treatment immediately.

"It was quite clear from our conversation that Dick's relationship with this other woman was obsessive and addictive. He felt as if this woman was his lifeline. He could not break off with her, although he had tried many times. Dick had uncontrollable urges to call her and to remain in constant contact with her.

"I found Dick to be a very intelligent man who knew there was no intellectual justification for these urges, yet he still had an uncontrollable compulsion for this woman and this relationship. Dick *actually believed* his life depended on her.

"By the time I began treating Dick, his depression had distorted his personality. This is quite common. Dick did show compulsive/addictive tendencies, but I didn't know if these symptoms were a result of the depression or part of his original personality."

Depression is an acute emotional illness that strikes one out of five women, and one out of ten men. At any given time almost six percent of the population suffers from some form of depression. It is estimated that over two million people have unsuccessfully attempted suicide while in a depressed state.

When a person is in the throes of a debilitating depression such as Dick's, there are actual chemical changes in the tissue of the brain which can alter or change a person's personality, perspective, and thought patterns.

When depression reaches a crisis stage, the patient needs more than just emotional support and therapy in order to control and correct the illness. Medication is generally recommended, depending on the individual patient.

Upon the results of Dick's blood tests, Dr. Fawcett immediately changed his medication.

"I felt Dick had not received adequate pharmacology treatment. It was important that we find just the right medication in the correct dosage in order to relieve Dick's agitated state."

Dr. Fawcett believed there were three reasons why Dick had not gotten well during his first hospitalization. The first and foremost was Dick's refusal to cooperate with his doctors; the second was inadequate drug treatment; the third was the demoralizing atmosphere of the hospital.

The first hospital Dick was in was a locked unit. The atmosphere was more like that of a prison than of a health-care facility. Being confined in a place where Dick felt all of his personal liberties had been stripped away served only to demoralize him further.

For a man like Dick, who valued control above all else, the loss of control over himself, his actions, and his emotions was frightening and further added to his emotional distress.

Dick had worked harder to get out of the hospital than he had at trying to resolve the conflicts in his life. He had fought the system and pushed to be released before he was ready to come to terms with the conflicts in his life.

The Stress Unit at Presbyterian—St. Luke's had more of a hospital atmosphere. There were no bars or locks on the doors or windows. Dick was allowed to keep all of his personal possessions; nothing was confiscated. He had a private two-bed room with his own shower. Dick could eat his meals in the cafeteria if he chose, or he could go out for dinner. He was allowed to smoke, shave, and attend to any of his personal needs without constant monitoring by the staff. There was no threat of punishment for any infraction of the rules. No padded rooms. No fear of straitjackets. Dick no longer had to fear for his personal safety.

The atmosphere at St. Luke's was much more relaxed and less regimented. There, Dick did not have to fight his own private battles as well as the staff and the system.

It was difficult for Dr. Fawcett to pinpoint exactly when Dick's depression began, or the cause of it, because by the time he began treating him, Dick's depression was already at a crisis point.

"From what Dick and Liz had told me, I believe Dick's situational depression began with his affair. However, it is my opinion that his depression did not gain momentum or escalate to crisis proportions until he left the police department.

"Dick was a nationally recognized law enforcement officer. He had reached the pinnacle of success at an age when most men are still struggling to make their mark in society and business. When Dick resigned as police superintendent, he went from being a nationally recognized 'whiz kid' who was constantly on the front pages of the newspapers, to being just another attorney. It was a very difficult adjustment. Had Dick been emotionally healthy at the time of his resignation, perhaps he might have suffered a *temporary* bout of depression. But since Dick's emotional health was already declining, leaving the police force only increased his anxiety. Leaving the department, particularly under the circumstances he did, only added to Dick's depression and, I believe, began the downward spiral of his emotional health."

When Dick resigned as police superintendent, he had been set adrift from all that was familiar, all that he had known. For almost nineteen years Dick had been a cop; the police department had been his life's work.

Leaving was a drastic life-altering situation that only increased Dick's depression.

Dick essentially had three problems to overcome before he could even begin to consider repairing his marriage: his addiction to Diane, his addiction to alcohol, and his severe depression. The day after Dick was admitted, Dr. Fawcett went to see Dick to give him his initial diagnosis.

"I felt the first thing we had to do was break Dick of his compulsion/addiction for this other woman. I had no idea why he had begun this affair or why this particular woman had been capable of ensnaring Dick in a relationship that not only put him at great risk but also marred his potential and damaged his marriage.

"Why a man or a woman has an affair is a complex question that doesn't always have a simple answer. Dick is the kind of man who has an obvious need for approval. In his highly visible position as police superintendent, Dick certainly had many other opportunities to become involved in an affair. Why *this particular woman* was able to hook him in, and why he took the chances he did, is difficult to say. I could never ascertain what it was this woman did for him that was different from what any other woman would do. There was no obvious reason for this relationship.

"From our discussions, it was clear that the Brzeczeks had had a very sound, close marriage at one time. I could tell that the early years of their marriage were quite successful. Liz had not only been Dick's wife but his best friend as well. There had been a strong bond between them as they worked toward a common goal.

"Dick had met this other woman at the height of his career. I think in some ways he associated this woman with his extreme success. In his mind, the two were somehow interrelated. In Dick's distressed emotional state I believed he felt that if he hung on to this relationship, no matter how detrimental to his health or his life, he would be able to hang on to the enormous success he had enjoyed.

"In addition to Dick's obvious need for approval, he also exhibited some compulsive traits, including perfectionism. Dick also had a clear need to succeed. He was driven. Dick is the type of man who will keep at something until he succeeds. I felt this trait might eventually help in his recovery.

"As for whether the Brzeczeks' marriage was to continue—that decision was left entirely up to them. But by the time they came to see me their marriage was hanging by a thread. I was clearly amazed at what Liz had gone through with her husband. I felt there had to be something left of the marriage if Liz had gone through all that and was still by Dick's side. She was hurt, bewildered, and demoralized, but her reactions were quite common under the circumstances. Liz was also suffering from depression, but her depression was situational, rather than clinical. I was certain that, with some therapy and support, Liz's symptoms would ease. Even though it was my opinion that Liz still cared for Dick, I wasn't certain we could save the marriage, or if Liz even wanted to at this point. I did feel, however, that Liz's participation in Dick's life was paramount to his recovery.

"I told Dick quite bluntly that unless he did something immediately, his marriage was over. Dick expressed a sincere desire to continue the marriage and get his life under control once again.

"We needed to know if Liz was willing to try to recommit to the marriage. If she chose to end the marriage, my staff and I were prepared to help Dick deal with that, if that was what was necessary.

"But if Liz chose to give Dick another chance and continue the marriage, we were also prepared to help them begin the process of reparation. That decision wasn't mine. It was Liz's."

Chapter Nine

Dick's Story: Part 3

When Dick agreed to go into the hospital the second time, he had hit rock bottom. For the first time in three years he was finally ready to admit he had a problem and needed help:

Meeting Dr. Fawcett probably saved my life. By the time I met him, I felt as if I had nowhere to turn and nowhere to go. I had gotten myself into a situation I didn't know how to get out of; for the first time in my life I had to admit I was no longer in control. My life was so totally out of control that suicide seemed the only solution.

The night I was admitted to the hospital, I settled in my room and tried to call Diane to let her know I was back in the hospital. We had already had a big fight earlier in the evening. I had been at Joe and Rita's, and after Diane and I hung up, I really became distraught. Diane had told me on the phone that the state's attorney's office had subpoenaed all her personal records in the course of their investigation of me. They had also been leaving messages for her on her answering machine. They wanted to talk to her.

Diane was furious that she had been dragged into the investigation. That's what we were fighting about.

I wanted to call her back that night, but I couldn't make a long-distance call from my room, so I had to go out in the hall to use the pay phone. When I told Diane I was back in the hospital she didn't seem too concerned. She told me she would have to call me back because she wanted to see the sports segment of the news. Diane is a big football fan and the Minnesota Vikings had just announced they were bringing back retired coach Bud Grant to handle the Vikings' next season. Diane was so excited that she wanted to listen to Grant's plans. She promised to call me back after she listened to the sportscast.

After we hung up I guess it finally hit home just how Diane really felt about me. I had lost everything in the world because of my relationship with her. I was ready to commit suicide, back in a psychiatric hospital for the second time, and all Diane cared about was next year's football season. Reality reached up and slapped me in the face, sobering me. I can't tell you how empty and defeated I felt.

The next morning Dr. Fawcett came back to see me. We had another long talk. He told me point-blank that unless I did something immediately I would lose Liz and my marriage would be over. Liz actually intended to go through with the divorce.

Dr. Fawcett's words were neither didactic nor dogmatic. I had heard all this a million times over the past three years, but it had never really hit home before. Liz had threatened divorce, but I'd always been sure I could talk her out of it. Every time I had moved out, I'd been able to convince her to take me back.

But as I talked to Dr. Fawcett that morning, I realized that Liz was really going to leave me. I knew I couldn't let that happen. I had to do something. I couldn't lose Liz. *I just couldn't.*

After Dr. Fawcett left, I sat in my room thinking about my life. I was forty-two years old, and I sure as hell had never expected to find myself in a psychiatric hospital—not once, but twice. What the hell had I done to my life?

Liz and I had such plans, such dreams, but everything we had worked for lay in ruins around us. A marriage that had endured almost two decades, through tremendous hardships and sacrifice, was annihilated.

Everything Liz and I had worked for was gone: not just our past, but our future as well. I had managed to destroy not only the faith my wife had in me, but also her love—something I thought could never happen.

That day in the hospital I was forced to face all the consequences of my actions. I finally had to look at what my relationship with Diane had cost me: *everything*.

My mind, which had always been my most precious asset, was as mixed up as my life. I had always prided myself on my intelligence. Now I was in such bad shape that I couldn't even put a coherent thought together.

Honesty, respect, and integrity were words I had lived by. Now those words were just a mockery. I had always taken pride in the fact that I had been an honorable man. But no longer. I had disappointed and disgusted everyone who had ever loved or believed in me. I had told so many lies to so many people that I no longer knew *what* the truth was.

At one point I had been one of the most respected and admired men in the city of Chicago. What was I now? As I sat in my room dressed in grubby clothes and with a three-day growth of beard, I was forced to take a long, hard look at myself, and I was deeply ashamed of what I saw: I had become a liar, a cheat, and an alcoholic.

My God, what had I done? What had I done?

I was the one person in the world Liz was supposed to be able to count on, to trust. We were partners. She should have been able to turn to me no matter what, but she couldn't because I had *turned* on her, betraying her for another woman. The shame of my actions rose up like bile, nearly choking me.

Until that day, I never realized how deeply I had hurt all the people I loved. No one deserves the kind of misery I had put Liz through. Yet, when I hit bottom and looked up, she was still there, holding out her hand to me. After all I had done to her, she was still there for me. That says a lot about her.

I was finally ready to admit that there were some things even *I* couldn't control. This was hard for me to accept at first, because I had always prided myself on being in control. But I was no longer in control of anything: not my thoughts, not my actions, not my life. I had to acknowledge the fact that I couldn't help myself. I had tried for three long years.

All my life I had thought I was invincible. Hell, I was Dick Brzeczek. I had always thought I was brighter, smarter, more intelligent than everyone else. I didn't need anything or anyone. I was a winner and I'd always been a winner.

But that day in the hospital I knew I was no longer a winner. I was a pathetic, selfish, self-serving asshole. I had been so arrogant. But what the hell did I have to be arrogant about now? You sure don't need two advanced degrees to screw up your life the way I did.

I knew then that I couldn't get through this life on my own. Dying would have been easy; it's living that's the bitch, especially after all the things I had done—things I certainly wasn't proud of.

But I didn't want to die. *I wanted to live.* I wanted a chance to get my life together and my family back. But I knew I couldn't do it on my own.

I didn't even know how or where to start. I was so desperate, and in such despair, I had nowhere to turn but to God.

At one time He had been an important part of my life. I knew that day that I needed Him in my life again, like I had never needed Him before. This problem was too much for a mere mortal like myself. I needed the kind of help and support that only God could give me.

I had stopped going to church when I began my affair with Diane. Religion, like everything else, had taken a backseat to her. But that day, when I was finally forced to come face to face with my actions, I knew I needed the help and support that only God could give me.

I could never before admit I needed help. That day, I humbly got down on my knees and prayed—no, *prayed* isn't really the right word—*begged* God to hear me and help me. I prayed that somehow, some way, He could forgive me and help me find my way back to the man I had once been: a man of honor and integrity; a man who had the love and respect of his family.

I knew the first thing I had to do in order to get my life together was to give up Diane. I hadn't been able to do it on my own; I'd tried many times. But maybe with God's help and Dr. Fawcett's I might be able to break free of her.

I knew it wasn't going to be easy. I begged God to walk with me every step of the way because I knew I could never make it alone.

I humbly admitted my sins and my failures and asked for forgiveness. I wasn't even sure He'd hear me, let alone help. I had broken so many sacred vows that I didn't even know if I deserved His help, but I knew I wanted it and needed it now, more than ever.

That day I begged God to give me another chance. Just one. A chance to turn my life around.

More important, I prayed with all my heart that it wasn't too late to get back the most important thing in my life—my wife.

Chapter Ten

Beginning Anew

In spite of Liz's deep religious convictions, she was emotionally torn over the decision the staff at Presbyterian—St. Luke's wanted her to make.

"I was so battered at this point that I really couldn't think clearly. I prayed for guidance because I knew I wasn't in any condition to make this decision on my own.

"Twenty years ago I had vowed before God to stay with Dick 'for richer, for poorer, in sickness and in health, until death do us part.' How could I break that vow?"

After a great deal of prayer, Liz had her answer. She knew she couldn't break the promise she had made. Liz knew she had to give Dick and their marriage another chance.

"Maybe it wasn't what *I* wanted to do at the time," Liz said, "but I felt very strongly that it was what God wanted me to do."

After all that she had endured, why would Liz choose to remain with Dick? Dr. Fawcett explained:

"It's my opinion that Liz's religious beliefs and faith had a great deal to do with her decision to remain in the marriage. Liz preserved her marriage on religious grounds rooted in her belief of family integrity and the value of the family in the Church.

"Liz is a woman of uncommon strength. For her to go through what she did, and yet still make the decision to continue with the marriage, exhibits the depth of her strength. Clearly from her point of view it would have been easier just to walk away. But she chose not to.

"Although Liz has never viewed herself as a strong person, I believe she *is* strong, perhaps in some ways even stronger than Dick. Her deep faith sustained her throughout this ordeal. Liz is quiet and soft-spoken; it's not always necessary to be loud or pushy to be strong.

"I also think the strength of the couple's very early relationship, the bonding between Dick and Liz, and the closeness they had once shared helped them both to survive and enabled them to take a chance on continuing their marriage.

"I was convinced that without Liz, Dick would never get well. Despite all Dick had done to Liz, I never doubted that he loved her. Liz was, and is, a very important, integral part of Dick's life. Dick did not *love* this other woman; he was *addicted* to her and the relationship.

"I believe Liz is the backbone of that marriage," Dr. Fawcett continued. "And of the family. Liz kept *everyone* together during the worst crisis in her life. Despite her own horrendous pain, she was strong for her children and her family.

"I felt Liz's participation in Dick's life was paramount to his recuperation. He *needed* her. But before we could even begin to counsel the couple on the reparation of their marriage, before they could begin the long road back toward each other, we first had to break Dick's obsessive addiction to the other woman."

Liz had made a commitment to take Dick back, but it was based on the fact that he would give up his relationship with Diane.

Liz wasn't certain that Dick would be able to break off with his mistress. For nearly three and a half years Dick's life and his thoughts had revolved around Diane. Liz realized that Dick's relationship with his mistress went far deeper than just a physical bond, there was an emotional bond as well. He had to be able to break the ties that bound him to her. But that decision had to be Dick's. Liz would not and could not force Dick to make the decision. She had tried many times in the past. If he truly wanted their marriage to continue, he would have to break off the relationship on his own. It was his choice.

Liz knew that if Dick chose not to break off the relationship, their marriage had no chance. She would no longer be a willing participant in a triangle. Liz was fully prepared to deal with the end of her marriage if necessary. She now had the confidence in herself to know she could go on.

Liz was no longer the same woman Dick had married twenty years ago. In a little more than three years, Liz Brzeczek had come into her own. She was no longer a shy, insecure woman intimidated by life, her husband, or the world around her. Liz had handled a life-shattering problem with more strength than she had ever dreamed possible.

If the couple's marriage was to continue, their relationship would be quite different from what it had once been, because *Liz* was different. Liz had finally realized *she could survive*, even if her marriage didn't.

The day after Dick was admitted to the hospital, Diane called him to announce that her mother would be arriving for a visit just before the holidays. She ordered him not to call her during this time. (Diane's mother had been greatly distressed about her daughter's affair with a married man. She had encouraged Diane to break off with Dick, and almost a year earlier Diane had convinced her mother that the relationship was indeed over.)

Diane didn't know it, but her ultimatum was just the psychological boost Dick needed in order to break his addiction to her.

For the first time in over three years Dick was not in daily communication with Diane. Because of therapy, correct medication, and Diane's absence from his life, some of the guilt and pressure Dick had experienced began to ease; his constant state of melancholy and hopelessness lifted.

"Dick's self-esteem was badly damaged," Dr. Fawcett said. "His perspective was dramatically impaired by this affair and his subsequent depression. I believe Dick's insecurities *increased* with his dependence on this other woman. This dependence only led to further depressed thoughts."

In the controlled environment of the hospital, Dick's absorption with Diane began to wane. She was no longer the sole focus of his life. As communication between them was interrupted, Dick's attitude and behavior slowly improved.

He was finally able to use his intellectual abilities to see just how destructive their relationship had been. It had taken a long time for Dick to be able to step back and look at Diane and their relationship from a fresh perspective. Once Dick's mind cleared, he began to recognize the destructive path his life had taken since his relationship with Diane began.

Dick hadn't talked to Diane in days, and, to his surprise, his heart hadn't stopped and his life hadn't ended. All the irrational fears Dick had lived with for so many years had failed to be realized.

Dick finally was able to acknowledge that his life did *not* depend on Diane. It was a startling revelation. To Dick's surprise, he began to feel much better. In some ways, the knowledge freed him.

Working daily with the hospital staff, Dick learned that he had harbored a great deal of resentment since his childhood. Controlling and hiding his emotions had taken their toll. Over the years he had kept things bottled up inside him and finally those resentments had erupted. During therapy, Dick exorcised a lot of old demons.

As Dick's emotional health gradually improved, he began to see the impact of his actions over the past few years and was finally able to recognize just what he had done to Liz and his children.

For three long years, Dick had refused to admit that his actions were causing pain to those he loved. Because of his deep depression, he felt only his *own* pain, not the pain he inflicted on others.

"I never realized how much I loved Liz, or how much courage she had," Dick said. "When I finally realized just what I had done to her, and what she had put up with, I found my respect for her growing, not just as a woman and as my wife, but as a person.

"You want to talk about courage? Talk about Liz. What I did to her and to our life takes no courage. There are a million guys in the world just like me, screwing around, hurting the people they love, and not giving a damn about the consequences of their actions.

"For Liz to have put up with what I did to her—the pain, the humiliation, the public disgrace—yet still hold her head up high, and go on with her life, now that's what I call courage. For the first time in my marriage, I realized my wife was a pretty remarkable woman. She was someone to admire. *And to love*.

"As I began to get better, I began to see Liz differently. It was almost as if she *were* a different woman. A woman who was strong, independent, and had her own mind. Liz was no longer intimidated by me. I realized just how much Liz had changed and grown during this crisis in our life.

"I also realized she didn't *need* me anymore. I think that frightened me at first, but as my emotional health began to improve, I realized maybe it wasn't such a bad thing. Liz didn't need me anymore. *But she still wanted me*. Considering all I had done to her, to us, and to our family, I thought that was pretty remarkable."

During therapy, Dick finally was able to admit not only that he had problems but that he needed help. It was a huge emotional hurdle for him to overcome. But the first step to recovery was admitting he had a problem.

"I guess I was always afraid to say, 'I'm an alcoholic,'" Dick confessed. "I always thought alcoholics were people who had some character flaw, people who weren't strong. My reasoning came from all the propaganda associated with alcoholics. I thought that because I went to work every day, and managed to carry on in a somewhat normal state, I *couldn't* be an alcoholic. I was wrong. I am an alcoholic.

"Now, I'm not ashamed to admit it. I'll bet if you looked around, you would see lots of alcoholics, people you'd never believe were drunks. There are bankers, lawyers, priests, and teachers. Alcohol is not prejudiced toward any gender or any racial or professional group. It crosses all socioeconomic backgrounds, too. Alcoholism touches all of us.

"I just hated to admit I had a weakness. I was convinced that I was infallible. I thought I was too strong to be an alcoholic. But I'm not. *Strength has nothing to do with being an alcoholic.*

"For the first time in my life I was forced to take a good hard look at myself. I thought I was better, smarter, more sophisticated than everyone else. I had always tried harder, done better, and succeeded at everything. I thought nothing could touch me. I was wrong. I'm just a human being. I have all the human frailties that everyone else has. I can't handle alcohol. It's as simple as that. There's no shame in admitting you can't handle liquor; the shame is in *not* admitting it.

"I was also afraid to admit that my relationship with Diane was out of control. In fact, my whole life was out of control. I was in so deep, and had done so much damage, I didn't know how to get myself out of the mess. That's why suicide seemed the only answer. In therapy, I was finally able to admit that there were a lot of things I couldn't control. But once I admitted it and accepted it, it helped me get well."

Although Dick was gradually making progress and his emotional health was improving day by day, Diane remained an unresolved problem. Her presence still hovered over the couple.

As Christmas approached, Diane called and said that her mother had left and Dick was now free to call her. But he didn't call her. Drawing strength from within, Dick resolved to try to break off the relationship permanently.

"In just a few weeks, without Diane in my life, I felt a dramatic improvement. I was beginning to feel like my old self again, and I could finally see my relationship with Diane for what it was—destructive. I no longer wanted to continue the relationship. I knew I didn't *need* to, as I had previously believed. I finally realized that my life did not depend on Diane.

"Liz and I had come very far in our relationship. I had made a commitment to her and to the doctors to try to repair our marriage and get my life back together again, and I didn't want to risk all that we had achieved by reestablishing daily contact with Diane. I felt strong enough finally to break the powerful bond between us."

Dick's emotional condition improved so much that Dr. Fawcett allowed him to go home for Christmas. It was to be the first true test for Dick.

Under the controlled and structured atmosphere of the hospital Dick had been able to cope with his life without Diane and alcohol. How would he cope with life outside the hospital?

Even though Dick's pass was only for twenty-four hours, Liz was extremely nervous about his coming home. She had no idea what to expect. Would Dick race to the phone or sneak around to contact Diane? Would he begin drinking again?

Surrounded by their families, Dick and Liz enjoyed a very pleasant holiday, something they hadn't done in years, not since Dick's affair and illness began.

"I will always remember that Christmas as one of the happiest," Liz recalled. "It was just like the old days before all this craziness started. There was no fighting, no screaming, no running to the phone to call Diane, or sneaking around trying to contact her. Dick was perfectly content with me and the children. He was so calm, so relaxed, I finally began to hope that he was eventually going to get well. Dick was almost like his old self. He was warm and attentive, and very loving toward me. And he didn't have one drink the entire day. It was the first time he'd been out of the hospital, so I expected him to start drinking as soon as he walked in the door, but he didn't."

Joe and Rita were also surprised at the change in Dick. "When my brother came home for Christmas we were all pretty nervous," Rita recalled. "We had gone through so much together—so many lies, so many broken promises—we really didn't want to get our hopes up again. But as the day wore on, we began to feel cautiously optimistic. For the first time in a long time, I began to see traces of my brother again. Or at least the brother I had remembered. Dick wasn't completely well, but he had made such progress, we couldn't help but feel overjoyed. It was such a wonderful experience for all us. It was as if my brother had gone on a long journey and had finally come home to us."

Once home with his family, Dick realized just how lucky he was to still have so much support and love.

"I knew I had to return to the hospital that night. But I also knew I *needed* to go back. I wasn't completely well. I still had a lot of things left to work out. Liz and I had a lot of things left to work out, but at least I was finally beginning to feel like my old self. I remember laughing that Christmas. It was the first time in a long time I felt like laughing."

After spending Christmas Day with his family, Dick returned to the hospital and to therapy feeling better than he'd felt in years. He finally had some hope that one day soon he would be healthy enough to cope with life outside the hospital.

Although Dick's emotional health had been improving, he did suffer a temporary setback. Shortly after Christmas Dick suddenly realized he had not spoken to Diane in quite a while. The knowledge brought on an acute flash of panic.

"I tried calling Diane, but her answering machine was on," Dick revealed. "It was an old trick of hers that had been going on almost as long as our relationship. She did it whenever she was angry with me because she knew when I wanted to reach her and couldn't, it drove me crazy. I guess that was Diane's way of controlling me, and our relationship. I guess the only thing I can equate it to is when you can't have something, it makes you want it even more."

The old compulsive/addictive cycle seemed to be resurging. When denied the object of his obsession, Dick began to suffer severe withdrawal symptoms once again. His panic seemed to increase as the day wore on.

"I finally reached Diane and she admitted she had deliberately refused to answer my calls because she was mad at me for not calling her once her mother had left. She was also furious because I had gone home for Christmas with Liz. For the first time in our relationship, I realized I was totally disgusted and appalled by her behavior. I never really saw any of Diane's flaws before, I guess I had been too blind. But I wasn't blind any more. I knew I had to put an end to our relationship once and for all. If I didn't, I knew I would never be able to recover completely, nor could I ever hope to save my marriage. I suddenly realized then that my wife and my health meant far more to me than Diane.

"That day on the phone, I told Diane it would be the last time she ever heard from me. Our relationship was over."

It was January 14, 1985, almost three and a half years after his affair began and his life and his marriage unraveled.

Dick Brzeczek was finally free.

PART
TWO

Chapter Eleven

Dick's Story: Part 4

I have to admit I was a little shaky about breaking up with Diane at first. But I was well enough on my way to recovery to know that I couldn't fully recover until Diane was out of my life—permanently. The relationship had been totally destructive, but up until that point I don't think I could have broken off with her and made it stick. I had been too sick to see the relationship for what it really was.

Do you know what it's like to want to kill yourself because living has become too painful? Or how frightening it is to know you are truly emotionally ill? It is the most terrifying, helpless feeling in the world.

I'd rather have a terminal illness than ever have to go through such a debilitating depression again. Depression isn't like a cold or the flu; you don't get well in a week or ten days. It can take years to recover from severe depression and some people *never* recover. I was lucky.

Dr. Fawcett claims no one is ever cured of depression; it just goes into remission. Well, I'm in remission now and I've never felt better in my life.

I had been so emotionally ill that I truly believed my life depended on Diane. *I believed it.* I was as addicted to her and the relationship just as strongly as someone can be addicted to heroin or cocaine.

The worst part of all of this was that I never realized how sick I was until I went into the hospital the second time.

In defense of the other doctors and therapists, I hadn't really given them a chance to help me. First of all, I lied to them—all of them. Second, I deliberately intimidated them. I didn't like anyone poking around in my

125

business. And finally, I had no desire to cooperate because I was absolutely certain there was nothing wrong with me: I had my life under control. But, in reality, I'd never been so out of control in my life. I *had* to be sick. Because of my affair, my own mother had a heart attack and I still couldn't break off the relationship.

I truly believe that without Liz and Dr. Fawcett I might never have recovered; I might never have been able to break free of Diane. But I knew with their help I could make it the rest of the way without Diane. I didn't need her; what I wanted and needed was my wife and my life back.

All those years Liz and I were married I had always thought of her as my other half. Liz had always been there. She was someone I could count on no matter what; whatever I dished out, she took without complaint. I was a real bastard to Liz. Even before my affair with Diane I took Liz for granted. During the counseling sessions I began to see a different Liz; she was not the woman I had married twenty years ago, but I loved the new Liz. I knew I would never again take her for granted. I finally began to appreciate what a lucky man I was.

I wanted to regain my self-respect and the respect of my family and friends. I never realized how much damage I had done. Repairing relationships wasn't going to be easy, but I sure as hell was going to try. I finally realized just how much I had lost; I wanted it back—all of it. I was determined to do whatever I could to make things right for Liz and for our kids. They didn't deserve what I did to them.

I wasn't so different from a lot of other men who get caught up in affairs. Marriage is a reality; affairs are a fantasy. Men get so caught up in the emotional and physical high, it's difficult to see things clearly. By the time a guy is into an affair, he's not thinking with his mind, but with another part of his anatomy. It doesn't take long before his head and every other part of him are caught up in the craziness. I know. I've been there.

I believed the rules applied to everyone but me. I was Dick Brzeczek. I was above it all. It happens to a lot of men who get too full of themselves. They get so caught up in their own importance that they actually begin believing they are infallible.

Because of this affair I destroyed my life, hurt my wife, and ruined all the things we had worked a lifetime toward. I became a drunk and ended up in a mental hospital. Not once, but *twice*. I threw away a career I had worked twenty years for, a career that most men would have given their eyeteeth just for a crack at. I threw it all away. I blew it. I had no one to blame but myself.

Everything in this life has a price. I learned that the hard way. You play, you pay. There are no free rides. Not for me. Not for anyone. I finally accepted that I was no different or better than anyone else.

When Liz agreed to give our marriage another chance, I knew it was the chance I had begged God for, a chance to make things right in my life again. I sure as hell didn't intend to blow it. I *needed* that chance to make things right, not just in my life but with my wife.

Whatever it took, no matter how long, no matter how painful, I intended to prove to Liz how much I loved and valued her. I almost had to lose her to appreciate just how much she meant to me. I didn't ever intend to let her go again.

I had a lot to make up for, but with God's help, I prayed that someday I would be able to convince Liz how sorry I was, and how much I loved her and wanted our marriage to work.

Chapter Twelve

Picking Up the Pieces

With Diane permanently out of his life, the correct pharmacology treatment, and intensive therapy, Dick's emotional health finally stabilized.

But there were other consequences he still had to face. The destruction of his marriage and his family weren't the only casualties of his three-year affair. His career, his reputation, and his credibility lay in ruins.

Dick had been a powerful, influential man with a brilliant future. Now, he faced the stigma of alcoholism, a mental breakdown, an adulterous affair, and the possibility of criminal charges due to the ongoing investigation by the state's attorney's office. What had started out as an investigation of the whole police department had turned into an investigation of Dick and his handling of the police contingency fund during his tenure as superintendent. The couple was also facing financial ruin. The years of medical treatment had nearly depleted their savings, and Dick was no longer bringing in an income.

As he slowly began to recover, the couple's precarious financial position began to weigh heavily on Dick. Although Liz had been working part-time since she filed for divorce, the money she made wasn't nearly enough to support the family. Dick had no prospects for employment.

While he was still in the hospital he began phoning some old friends in law enforcement circles looking for a position. To Dick's surprise, he found that although some of his old friends were warm and cordial, no one was interested in hiring him. In fact, some of his calls were not even returned. For the first time in his professional life, Dick had to face rejection. There weren't many law firms willing to consider an applicant who was inquiring about a job from a psychiatric hospital.

The professional reputation Dick Brzeczek had spent nearly twenty years building had been systematically destroyed by his own behavior. But Dick was confident that once he was released from the hospital he would be able to find employment.

After three more weeks of hospitalization, Dr. Fawcett felt Dick was ready to be released. Although Dick was not totally recovered, he was *recovering*. His depression was, in Dr. Fawcett's opinion, in remission. No one ever fully recovers from depression because it is an illness that can recur at any time. However, when a patient like Dick is well enough to maintain himself outside the hospital environment, and when his thought patterns and perspective are no longer distorted, he is considered "recovering," and his depression is termed *in remission*.

Dick had made such dramatic improvement that Dr. Fawcett was confident that as long as he continued his medication and his weekly counseling sessions, Dick could manage life outside the hospital.

Dick looked forward to his release; he was eager to get his life and his marriage back together. But the day of Dick's release from the hospital was marred when the Chicago newspapers broke the story that twenty-one grand jury subpoenas had been issued by the state's attorney's office in connection with Dick's handling of the police contingency fund during his tenure as superintendent. One of the twenty-one subpoenas issued was for Diane.

Dick finally had to take the investigation seriously. Certain he had done nothing wrong, Dick never really thought anything would come of the investigation, even when the focus of the investigation had been shifted from the entire police department onto him.

When the story hit the papers, a well-respected and nationally renowned Chicago attorney called Dick and offered his legal services. Dick decided he'd better accept the attorney's offer.

From the moment Dick was released from the hospital he and Liz were hounded by reporters demanding a reaction to the grand jury subpoenas. Dick adamantly refused to speak to the press or issue any type of statement. He had developed a deep resentment toward the press because of their treatment of Liz.

The first few days Dick was home were extremely tense, not only because of the press but because of the tension that existed between Dick and Liz. They had to learn to live together as man and wife again.

For Liz, those first few days were particularly difficult. She had promised to give Dick and their marriage another chance, yet for her own sake she remained cautious. Liz took things one day at a time; it was the only way she could handle the situation.

"It was rough," Liz remembered. "We walked on eggshells around each other. I wasn't really sure how I felt about Dick. Part of me hated him for what he had done, yet another part of me must have still cared for him.

"As much as I wanted to make things easier for Dick, I couldn't just say: 'I love you. I forgive and I trust you, so let's just forget what happened and go back to the way things were.' I couldn't say those things because I didn't love or trust Dick, and I didn't know if I'd *ever* be able to forgive him. I wasn't certain our life could ever go back to the way it had been. As for forgetting about what happened, I knew it was going to take me a long, long time.

"All the positive emotions I had felt for Dick were dead. The only emotion I had was anger. And I had a right to be angry. Neither the children nor I deserved to be treated that way. We had loved and trusted Dick, and he had betrayed our trust.

"Before Dick went into Presbyterian—St. Luke's he had been too sick to realize how he had hurt us. But now he was well enough to know. How could I ever forgive him if he didn't even realize what he had done, or what he was being forgiven for?

"I knew if our marriage was going to survive I was going to *have* to forgive him. I couldn't carry all this anger and resentment around for the rest of my life. I also knew that if we were ever going to repair our marriage I had to get rid of all these miserable, resentful feelings I was harboring."

During Dick's affair, Liz had buried her pain in order to deal with the situation. She had allowed Dick to heap guilt and blame on her because she felt responsible for his betrayal. She believed Dick had strayed because of some inadequacy on *her* part.

The wife of a man involved in an affair suffers humiliation and pain. She *allows* her spouse to heap guilt and blame on her because she somehow feels responsible for her spouse's betrayal. It is common for a wife in this situation to feel as if there is something lacking in her that has persuaded her man to stray; perhaps her husband has insinuated that some deficiency on her part has encouraged his betrayal.

If a wife accepts these beliefs, both parties are hurt. The *offended* party (in this case Liz) is made to feel guilt, shame, and humiliation, which result in the shattering of her self-esteem and confidence.

Dick had always been Liz's ideal man, a larger-than-life person she had never expected to live up to. Liz felt lucky to have such a man and his love. She accepted all the punishment and blame Dick doled out because she thought she deserved it. Liz truly believed that if she had been a better wife or a better person, perhaps her husband would not have had an affair.

Because of the way Liz felt about herself, she continually forgave Dick, no matter what he did, no matter how many times he lied to her or betrayed her. By continually forgiving him, Liz *enabled* Dick to continue his affair, thus, in effect, *accepting his unacceptable behavior.*

Spouses should never accept an adulterous situation. *Never.* But in most cases they do, because of their own fears and insecurities, which are naturally heightened during this type of crisis. The offended spouse may feel it's better to stay in a relationship that is no longer viable than face life alone.

If the offended spouse does not make it clear that this type of behavior is unacceptable, it is a form of acceptance.

In Liz's case, it took her nearly three years to find the courage to say: "I've had enough. I want out." She had finally reached the point where her pain outweighed her fears. Regardless of the personal consequences, Liz could no longer accept Dick's unacceptable behavior.

During Dick's affair, Liz also denied her own feelings. She would have done *anything* to keep her husband and save her marriage. She tried to improve and mold herself into the type of woman she thought Dick wanted. But no matter what she did or how hard she tried to change in order to please Dick and gain his acceptance, his affair continued because it had nothing to do with any inadequacy of Liz's. The responsibility for Dick's affair rested squarely on Dick's shoulders.

Because Liz had never developed an identity or persona outside of her husband's, in her mind she had no self-worth, except what she received through Dick's love and acceptance. If Dick thought she was worthy, then he would love her. If he didn't love her, then it seemed obvious to her that she must not be worth his love.

Throughout Dick's affair Liz continually buried her painful feelings and emotions in an effort to please her husband and hang on to the marriage. Pleasing Dick and gaining his approval became of the utmost importance to her. Liz found herself constantly trying to live up to Dick's expectations of excellence in order to keep the marriage going.

If Dick came home and yelled at her because she had neglected to do some household chore, instead of standing up to Dick and his anger, Liz would cry and promise to be a better wife and a better person. At the time, Liz felt Dick had a *right* to criticize and belittle her because she wasn't living up to his expectations.

Her self-esteem had been so low that she felt Dick was justified in his behavior. Her husband was like a god who could do no wrong. She felt she needed Dick in order to go on living.

But after Dick's affair, Liz could not and *would not* bury her feelings and emotions in order to gain Dick's approval or acceptance. Liz had grown and changed through her pain. She no longer *needed* Dick—his approval *or* his acceptance. Liz finally realized that her strength, her security, and her confidence had to come from within herself, and not from her husband. It had been a very painful lesson.

Liz Brzeczek emerged from this personal tragedy with a great deal of confidence in herself and her abilities. She finally knew who she was; Liz finally realized she was worth something.

Liz knew she had changed, but what she didn't know was if Dick would accept the person she had become. During the years of Dick's betrayal, Liz had learned to care *about* herself and *for* herself. If Dick could not or would not accept the "new" Liz, their marriage had no chance. Liz Brzeczek knew she would never go back to the person she had been.

"I knew I would never be a victim again," Liz stated firmly. "I would never allow Dick or anyone else to use me as a whipping post. Never again would I allow anyone to trample my self-esteem. I would not accept or tolerate that kind of behavior again. Ever.

"Dick strayed because he wanted to, not because I did something to force him to. *I* had been giving one hundred percent to him and our marriage, while Dick had been giving all of his time and energy to his other relationship. I knew that if our marriage was going to be saved, we were both going to have to give one hundred percent."

In order to find their way back to each other after an affair, both spouses have to learn to grow and change; they have to learn to accept the person the other has *become*.

Before they can begin repairing a marriage, though, the offended spouse and the offender must first repair themselves by ridding themselves of all the negative emotions they have buried inside. Anger, resentment, bitterness, guilt, and shame must be expelled. *You must know who you are in order to know what your relationship will be.*

When a spouse has an affair, not only is the marriage jeopardized, but both partners suffer severe emotional damage. In Dick and Liz's case, both experienced acute pain and anguish. Liz had buried her pain in order to cope with her situation and keep her marriage going. Dick had buried his pain in order to justify and continue his actions. Drinking was a false outlet for his pain, because it only further increased his anxiety and guilt, and led to other emotional problems and dependency.

During the throes of a marriage-ending crisis it's difficult for either partner to see the other's pain.

During Dick's affair, Liz had allowed him to draw her into his madness. She found her life revolving around Dick's relationship with his mistress: her thoughts, actions, and her very life were obsessed by Dick's affair. She too suffered from depression and its accompanying symptoms: sleeplessness, fatigue, and disturbed thought patterns. Liz found her own life had become unmanageable. Normal day-to-day life was impossible because of her obsession with Dick's behavior. Liz became almost as emotionally ill as her husband because of the situation she found herself in, a situation she could not control.

Liz had tried to make Dick break off his affair, but she couldn't. Only Dick could make that decision. *You cannot control your spouse, nor can you control his behavior.* The only person you can control is yourself.

Dick suffered tremendous emotional pain because of the lifestyle he had to lead in order to keep two relationships going. He felt guilt about the situation and his behavior. Once his affair was over and he was forced to face the consequences of his destructive behavior, he suffered even more guilt, shame, and embarrassment because of what he had done to his loved ones.

To save a marriage damaged by adultery, both parties need to work through their negative feelings, in order to find their way back to each other and reestablish a healthy relationship. They must heal themselves *before* they can heal their marriage.

Love, respect, honesty, and trust are the emotions that bind a couple together; these emotions grow and strengthen with the passing of time. When an affair destroys the basic foundation of a marriage, these emotions wither and in some cases die.

Honesty is one of the keys to rebuilding a marriage. During an affair there are so many lies between a couple that basic trust is lost. In order to start over and rekindle the flow of positive emotions, the couple must begin by being honest with themselves and with each other. Once they work through their own negative emotions, they can go on to repair their marriage.

Liz had many negative emotions to deal with. It wasn't easy for her, because for so long Liz had hidden behind a sweet, loving nature, burying her feelings in order to please her husband.

Before Dick's affair, Liz would have tried to shield her husband from the knowledge of her pain. But Liz was no longer willing to deny her feelings.

"I finally confessed to Dick how I felt," Liz admitted. "I let out all the anger raging inside of me, anger that was directed at him for what he had done."

Anger is probably the most energy-draining emotion. If you continue to harbor anger and resentment, it only increases your pain and bitterness. Liz had to get all of her anger out; by expressing it, she took away its power and thus began healing herself.

Liz finally began to open up to Dick and honestly admit her feelings. To her surprise, Dick didn't get upset or express disapproval. He listened to her and offered emotional support for what she had gone through and was still experiencing.

When Liz confronted Dick about her feelings, and her anger, it was another way of forcing Dick to take responsibility for his actions. His behavior had caused Liz's pain and his own feelings of guilt. Now the couple had to work together to come to terms with all of these emotions.

Together, Dick and Liz talked openly and honestly about what had happened, the consequences, and how each felt. They tried to discuss and work through all the painful feelings Liz had buried inside.

At times it became quite stressful, but it was a process the couple needed to go through in order to begin anew. Liz found that as she expressed her anger, some of it began to fade.

Dick had also changed a great deal. He was no longer controlling, arrogant, or intimidating. Dick was learning to express his emotions rather than control them. He seemed much more compassionate and caring than Liz had ever seen him. Although Dick had always had difficulty opening up to people, now he began opening up to Liz and sharing his inner feelings. He had a sincere desire to save his marriage and to make amends for the tremendous pain he had caused Liz, their family, and their marriage.

"I guess when I realized what Dick did wasn't a deliberate attempt to hurt or destroy me, I began to feel much better about myself and about our relationship," Liz said. "I didn't feel quite so resentful. Dick's affair had nothing to do with me. It had to do with him. I finally began to believe that Dick was truly remorseful. He was constantly reassuring me of his love and concern. I needed to hear that; I needed to know Dick did indeed love me, because I finally knew I was worth loving."

In addition to Liz's anger, she had a number of questions about Dick's affair, questions she would never have dared ask before. There were things she needed to know for her own peace of mind in order to finally put the matter to rest.

When a spouse has an affair, the offended party is often plagued with questions. It's difficult to make sense out of something you don't understand. It's like trying to put a puzzle together with several pieces missing. *Why* anyone has an affair is an enigma; the reasons are as varied as the participants. While sex seems the obvious culprit, generally an affair has less to do with sex and more to do with the offender's emotions.

If offended spouses do not have all of their questions answered, it is difficult for them to put the matter out of their minds, thus making forgetting or forgiving impossible. The questions will remain forever, haunting them and hurting the reparation process.

Dick and Liz discussed his affair and its causes inside and out. There were times when Liz's questions and Dick's answers led to hurt feelings and flaring tempers, but at least they were communicating. More important, they were being totally honest with each other.

"No matter how intimate the question, no matter how probing, Dick held absolutely nothing back. By answering all of my questions, by not being evasive, Dick showed he truly cared about me and our marriage. I could see Dick was genuinely trying. He was finally telling me the truth. I think that alone was a major breakthrough."

Dick had been lying to Liz for so long that when he finally began to tell her the truth, she found it helped dissipate her negative emotions. Dick's honesty and his genuinely caring attitude gave Liz hope.

"If Dick had been evasive or tried to discourage my questions about his affair, it would have perpetuated my distrust and fear and totally killed whatever chance our marriage had. But he didn't. I think his honesty and openness helped us both a great deal. I began to understand a little better why Dick had the affair. Dick's always had such a tremendous need for approval, and I think he viewed his relationship with Diane as a chance for some sort of new approval. When he accomplished his life's goal at such an early age, it made him feel as if there was nothing left for him; no more mountains to climb. The affair was a new challenge that came at just the right time in his life. Dick viewed Diane's attraction to him as another chance to win approval."

Liz began to see a new consistency and stability in Dick's behavior. She also began to see shades of the man she had married so many years ago, a man she had once thought was lost to her forever.

"I realized at some point that if our marriage was ever going to have a chance, I would have to begin to trust Dick. Without trust, I don't think you can go anywhere in life. I'm not saying I gave my trust to him blindly. It was too soon, and the memories were still too painful. But at least I was beginning to believe our marriage was going to work out."

Liz gave her trust very slowly. It wasn't until she felt Dick was truly committed to her and their marriage, and content with their relationship, that she was able to give Dick the benefit of her trust. It was another major step.

As a result of the couple's evolving relationship, Liz decided to withdraw her divorce petition. There was no point in letting it hang over Dick's head. If she was truly willing to give their marriage another chance, she, too, had to give one hundred percent to the relationship. But Liz received opposition from an unexpected source: her children.

"The kids became very angry with me when I withdrew the divorce petition. I know they thought I was being foolish and perhaps a bit naïve, but I felt it was an act of faith and something I had to do."

Although Liz and Dick were making real progress in rebuilding their relationship, the children's relationship with their father was far from idyllic. The kids were openly wary and very antagonistic toward Dick. They found it hard to believe that their father had really given up Diane. They began to spy on Dick, watching him carefully for any signs of betrayal. Every time he picked up the phone to make a call, they would sneak around and try to listen in, all the time wondering if he was calling Diane. They also refused to acknowledge or accept Dick's parental authority.

"When my father finally came home from the hospital the second time, we really didn't believe that he had broken off his affair," Natalie recalled. "Why should we? He'd said that so many times that we no longer believed *anything* my father said. He told us he was sorry, and that he and my mother were going to put their marriage back together, and we were going to be a family again, but it wasn't the first time he'd said those things, and we had no reason to believe he meant them. We totally distrusted him.

"At times I really felt sorry for my father because he did seem to be trying so hard. Maybe we were unfair to him, but it was almost too late for us. I didn't know if we'd *ever* be able to forgive him for what he had done, or if we could ever be a family again. When my mother withdrew the divorce action we thought she was a fool. How could she even think about trusting him after all he had done? We were not only angry at our father, but at our mother as well. We were truly a family divided."

Mark was particularly upset with both his parents. Knowing how much his father wanted all of the children to get a good education, Mark, in a seemingly defiant act, failed all his courses in school and refused to fulfill his academic responsibilities. He flunked out of Loyola Academy and had to repeat his entire junior year at another school.

Dick was clearly upset with Mark and tried to counsel and advise him on the value of his education, but Mark wasn't ready or willing to accept his father's new involvement in his life.

"My father hadn't exactly been a sterling example, so I don't know why he expected me to start taking advice from him," Mark explained. "If he truly cared about us, how could he have done what he did? I wasn't about to just welcome him back with open arms. I loved my father, but I hated him, too. When my mother decided not to go through with the divorce, I couldn't believe it. I thought she was being incredibly naïve. How could she believe my father after all the lies he had told?

"My dad tried to exercise his parental authority with me, but I refused to accept his advice or control. Why should I? It was hard for me to respect him, or even listen to him. Who was he to be giving advice?

"Looking back on it now, I probably hurt him a lot because of the way I treated him, but I just wasn't as forgiving as my mother. At the time, I just figured she had to love him one hell of a lot, or be incredibly stupid."

If Liz was disturbed by her children's anger, she didn't show it. She knew her children weren't the only ones who thought she was a fool for taking Dick back.

There was also a great deal of public speculation about the couple. But Dick and Liz refused to talk to the press, which only caused more speculation and added fuel to the fire. Liz knew that some believed she had "stuck *by* Dick," and now she was "stuck *with* Dick." But Liz continued to hold her head high and go on with her life. She had enough self-confidence at this point to feel that she had a right to choose what she wanted to do with her life. She had stayed with Dick because she wanted to: not because she needed to or had to. The choice was hers and hers alone. Liz Brzeczek was happy with her choice; she no longer felt she had to please anyone but herself.

In spite of the children's animosity, Dick and Liz had the full support of the rest of their families.

Dick's sister Rita recalled: "When Liz took my brother back I must admit my admiration for her grew. After all she had been through, no one could blame her if she just turned her back on him. It would have been easy; he was down and out, with no friends, no job, nothing. It would have been easy for Liz to walk away and start a new life. But she didn't.

"Liz always said that God had a reason for putting her through what He did; she just didn't know what that reason was. Maybe she'd never know. But even if she wasn't sure of her feelings for my brother, *I was*. I knew in spite of everything she loved him. I knew he loved her, too. I've always believed Dick and Liz were destined to be together. Watching them work toward putting their marriage back on track only confirmed my feelings. I was happy for them, and happy for the whole family. My brother, the man I had looked up to, loved, and respected for most of my life, had finally come home. I couldn't have been happier."

Dick and Liz's parents were equally overjoyed with the couple's reconciliation. "I always told Liz to keep the faith and keep saying her prayers," said Liz's mother. "I always knew that one day Dick would come back to the family. Through it all, I never once told my daughter to leave Dick. Never. Dick's mother and I went to Mass every morning to pray for the children. I always believed our prayers would work miracles, and they did."

Regardless of their families' reactions to the reconciliation, Dick and Liz still had other, more practical problems confronting them, especially their financial crisis.

The day after Dick was released from the hospital, Liz began a second job as a nurse. They needed the income. Dick and Liz Brzeczek were broke. Their savings had been depleted, their medical bills were staggering, and they had no money coming in. In addition to everything else, they now had the increased worry of Dick's legal bills.

Dick continued to try to get hired by a law firm, but to no avail. No one would even talk to him. While Liz worked, Dick took over the household chores and the full-time care of the children.

"At one point the kids were calling their father Mr. Mom," Liz recalled. "It was so out of character for Dick. This once high-powered man was now spending his days scheduling Scout meetings and car pools."

The couple's finances continued to be a source of constant worry. When the boys needed new school clothes, Liz bought them two shirts each and the boys alternated wearing them.

"The kids went to school in gym shoes because we couldn't afford to buy them anything else," Liz recalled.

Dick was becoming increasingly depressed about his professional status. Liz ended up taking a third part-time job just to put food on the table and pay their living expenses. Dick knew he couldn't remain unemployed much longer. Even with three jobs, Liz wouldn't make nearly enough money to support the family, nor could she make a fraction of what Dick could earn as an attorney.

Dick *had* to get a job.

He continued calling old friends in the hope that someone would give him a lead on something, but nothing worked out. No one wanted to give Dick a chance or take a chance on him. Sometimes his calls weren't even returned. Finally, in desperation, Dick called an old friend and former client.

In the early 1970s Dick met Art Smith, a black businessman who had wanted to start a school-bus company. Art had only two thousand dollars, which he had borrowed, to invest in his new company. Dick had served as Art's attorney and helped him to form a firm called Art's Transportation. Knowing Art needed every penny he had borrowed to put into his new business, Dick accepted his three-hundred-dollar legal fee in installment payments.

Through 1979 Dick had continued to represent Art on numerous legal and business matters. By early 1985 Art had built his bus company into a successful minority-owned business with over five hundred buses in his fleet. Liz was already working part-time for Art at home doing public relations work by phone.

"Art knew all about my personal troubles," Dick recalled. "I don't think there was a person in the city who didn't know about my problems, thanks to the press. With my past history, personal and emotional problems, and the ongoing state's attorney's investigations still hanging over my head, I didn't think I was ever going to be able to get a job. I decided to call Art and see if he had anything for me. It was a long shot, but I was desperate."

When Art got on the phone, Dick said, "Art, I'm in trouble. I need a job." Dick fully expected to be turned down, but instead, to his surprise, Art simply said, "No problem, Dick. I'll take care of it, don't worry about a thing."

Dick immediately started working for Art as an in-house consultant at a salary of one thousand dollars a week.

"When I was on top of the mountain, I helped a lot of people," Dick said. "I gave more people jobs than even I can recall. But when I was desperate, when *I* needed a job, no one knew me. Hell, I couldn't even get anybody on the phone. It's like the old saying, 'Nobody knows you when you're down and out.' I finally realized how true that statement was. But I had no one to blame but myself.

"I don't know what I would have done if Art hadn't given me a job. I was at my wits' end. Liz was worried that I'd slide back into a depression. But I knew that I would do everything in my power never to let that happen to me again. I never wanted to go back to feeling so ill or so desperate again.

"We continued to see Dr. Fawcett on a weekly basis. It really helped me air some of my frustrations and keep a handle on my emotional state. I also continued to take my medication. After what I went through, I never, ever wanted to sink that low again. Once in a lifetime is enough."

As Dick settled in at his new job, he began to hear rumors that Art Smith was receiving pressure from Mayor Harold Washington's administration for giving Dick a job. The animosity between Dick and the mayor ran deep. Art was a minority business owner who did business with the city of Chicago. Dick knew he wasn't going to be able to stay with Art for long, at least not without possibly hurting Art's business, which Dick would never do.

Whether the rumors about the pressure from the Washington administration were true or not (and nothing was ever proven), the last thing Dick wanted to do was cause problems for his old friend.

"I'll never forget that Art Smith was the only person who would even talk to me, let alone hire me with no questions asked, at a time when I was truly desperate. He is not only a wonderful friend but a good and kind man, and the last thing I'd ever want to do is hurt him."

Knowing his position with Art was not going to be permanent, Dick came to the conclusion that if he was ever going to be able to support his family and get his financial house in order he would have to practice law. But since no firm would hire him, Dick decided the only way he was going to make a decent living was to open his own law firm.

"I talked it over with Liz, and she supported the idea all the way. It was a very exhilarating experience for me," Dick recalled. "Although I had been in law enforcement my whole life, I'd only spent a short time actually practicing law. I knew my emotional health was getting better because I began to feel some of the old drive and ambition that had always been so much a part of my life. Feelings and emotions I had thought dead were beginning to resurface. It was the first time in a long time I felt excited about something. Life was really beginning to look up."

Liz was openly optimistic about Dick's decision to go into practice for himself. It was the first time in years that she had seen shades of the old Dick. When he hadn't been able to get a job, his confidence had seemed to collapse. Liz had feared he would have a relapse.

"Dick was excited about his new venture. His spirits lifted immediately. It reminded me of the old days when we were working our way toward Dick's becoming superintendent. Dick now had a purpose in his life, a goal that he could work toward, a goal *we* could work toward. I knew he was going to need my help. We were as broke as we'd been at the beginning of our marriage. We were starting all over again from the bottom. We'd gone from the bottom, to the top, to the bottom again. But this was something we could do together, build together. I was certain that it couldn't help but draw us closer, and perhaps further heal some of our wounds."

While Liz and Dick were excited and optimistic about the idea of opening their own law firm, Dr. Fawcett was appalled.

"When Dick and Liz came in for one of their weekly sessions and announced that Dick was going to set up his own law firm, I couldn't believe it. I was stunned. Dick had been out of the hospital for a short time. While I knew he had been concerned about his career and the family's finances, I certainly didn't feel he was in any condition to tackle such a monumental project so early in his recovery. Although Dick's depression had eased enough for him to control it with medication and weekly therapy, it was not yet in total remission. I advised him against tackling this project so soon.

"Dick was in what I call the 'demoralization period of recovery,' " Dr. Fawcett continued. "During this time a patient is usually totally demoralized. His self-esteem is low and he has little confidence in himself or his abilities. It's generally not a good time for a patient to begin a taxing and exhaustive physical or emotional endeavor. Clearly, starting up his own practice was going to be taxing physically and emotionally for Dick. I expressed my concerns and reservations quite bluntly to both Dick and Liz."

Dick took Dr. Fawcett's concerns into consideration but felt he *was* strong enough to tackle this project. Dr. Fawcett wasn't really surprised.

"Despite his emotional problems, Dick Brzeczek is not only a supremely intelligent man but a very strong one. Had Dick not been as strong as he was, considering the circumstances and the stress he was under both personally and professionally, I think his collapse probably would have come a lot sooner. I think his depression had matured him in a lot of ways.

"There are not many people who would even attempt to tackle such a monumental project so soon after such a severe, debilitating depression, but again, Dick is not like many people. I felt as long as he continued his weekly therapy and his medication, he just might be able to pull this off. But I made it very clear that at the first sign of any emotional discord or problems, he was to contact me immediately. I still wanted to keep a very close eye on Dick."

Dick continued working for Art Smith during the day, and Liz kept her jobs, but in the evenings the couple would drive around their Chicago neighborhood, looking for a vacant office to rent.

"It was the first time in years Dick and I had done anything constructive together," Liz recalled. "It really was a lot of fun. I was beginning to feel much more secure with Dick, partially due to the consistency in his behavior and his attitude toward me. His criticism and complaints had turned to compliments. I found myself feeling much more comfortable and at ease with our relationship.

"Dick really was very excited about the prospect of setting up his own practice and getting our lives back on track. I could see he was trying very hard, and it made all the difference in the world to me."

Dick is one of the few attorneys in the city of Chicago who is fluent in both English and Polish. He wanted to find a location in a predominantly Polish area of the city. After driving around night after night, Dick and Liz believed they had found the ideal location.

"It was a small storefront office right on Central Avenue," Dick said. "It was accessible by all modes of public transportation and in a Polish neighborhood. It seemed perfect."

But the office itself was a disaster. The ceiling was falling down, the walls were crumbling, and the floors had been damaged by water. The linoleum was old and peeling, and there wasn't even adequate lighting. The night they found the office, Dick and Liz had to view the premises with a flashlight because there was no electricity. Despite the condition of the office, Dick and Liz signed a lease. Dick was ecstatic. It was February 1, 1985, and Dick Brzeczek was in business—almost.

Their savings were nearly depleted and Dick needed money not only to repair and improve his office but to buy all the necessary office equipment as well as law books that he would need to set up his practice.

A member of the couple's family (who wishes to remain anonymous) gave the Brzeczeks a nonrepayable loan of six thousand dollars to help them get started on the office repairs.

"We put every penny into fixing up the office," Liz recalled. "Dick, his brother-in-law Joe, and our families helped with all the repair work to keep the costs down. The rest of the office equipment—desks, copiers, file cabinets, typewriters, law books—we purchased on credit. It was the only way we could afford to do it. We certainly didn't have the funds to pay cash for everything. We hadn't realized—or at least I hadn't realized—just how enormously expensive it was going to be for Dick to set up his own practice."

Dick couldn't afford to hire a secretary, so he had his office phone connected to his house. When calls came in during the day, someone would be at home to answer the telephone. But the calls rarely came, from February until August of that year. For almost seven months Dick continued working for Art, Liz held on to her jobs, and the couple tried vainly to get Dick's practice off the ground.

"It wasn't easy," Dick said. "At times I felt like just throwing in the towel. But I knew I could make this work. I had to. I wanted to practice law and make enough money to support my family. It killed me to see Liz have to work. After all the struggling we had done in our early years, this should have been a time when Liz could relax and enjoy herself, but she couldn't, because I had systematically destroyed the life we had built."

The couple was still working hard on their marriage. Day by day, despite the other pressures they were under, their relationship began to improve. Liz finally began to believe that her marriage might have a chance.

"I guess one day it hit me that Dick was really going to get well," Liz recalled. "While all of the craziness was going on, I used to pray so hard that he would miraculously wake up one day and be the person he had once been. At the time it didn't seem possible, but now I really began to believe again. With Diane totally out of his life, Dick seemed very much at peace. There wasn't that constant agitation. We worked hard together toward common goals. The practice, the financial difficulties, and even Dick's problems with the children were problems we worked out together. Our communication was better than it had ever been. I found that I could talk to Dick about anything, without any fear. Dick continued to be loving and attentive toward me, constantly reassuring me of his love. It was almost like a second honeymoon. I began to see the man I had originally fallen in love with. I found myself falling in love with Dick all over again."

The children also began to see a gradual improvement in their father. They began to have more faith in him as his behavior confirmed his promises.

"I guess when we started doing things as a family again, when my dad started acting like my dad, we began to realize that maybe this time he really had broken off with Diane, and was now home to stay," Natalie said. "We were still wary, though. It was a very gradual process, but we began to have some hope."

Two things happened in August that turned things around for Dick. His affair with alcohol ended permanently when he joined Alcoholics Anonymous and began attending weekly meetings. He had now been exposed to the Twelve Step program that Liz had found so helpful during the Al-Anon meetings.

The second thing that happened was an act of fate. A salesman for a local Polish newspaper stopped by to see Dick. The salesman offered to run a free ad in the local Polish newspaper for one month, if Dick would agree to sign up to use their after-hours answering service. Deciding he had nothing to lose, Dick agreed. It turned out to be one of the wisest decisions Dick ever made.

"Up until the time the ad appeared in the neighborhood paper, I'd say I was making less than one hundred dollars a month in my practice. Hardly enough to buy groceries, or pay the rent and utilities at the office, let alone our expenses at home. As soon as the ad began appearing, my practice turned around almost overnight. During the month of August, my office was jammed every single day. I continued on with Art until early November, effectively working two jobs. Then in November I quit working for Art to devote myself full-time to my law practice. One of the happiest days of my life was when I told Liz to quit her jobs—all three of them. When she offered to come to work for me, I jumped at the chance to have her help."

"I started out doing a little of everything," Liz said. "From answering phones to making coffee. We were just so busy, I didn't have time to think. Dick and I had never worked together before, and I found it fun. Dick finally had to schedule evening hours, because we just couldn't accommodate everyone during the day."

Financially, things improved immediately. The couple was able to pay off some of the crushing medical bills that had been a source of worry. Working together, *being* together, cemented their new and growing relationship.

"Dick and I were too busy to dwell on the past because the present was so exciting. I wish I could say I woke up one day and realized I loved Dick again. But it didn't happen that way. It probably took almost a year before I could even begin to *admit* that I had some feelings for him. It was a very slow and gradual process. But eventually I did realize that I not only loved him but was *in love* with him, or at least in love with the man he had *become*. Dick was a totally different person. I guess we both were. I very much liked the new man I was married to. He was kind, considerate, loving, and attentive. He was constantly reassuring me of his love and his remorse over what had happened.

"I think it was the beginning of the real healing process for me," Liz revealed. "A healing process that never could have begun until I had rid myself of some of my anger. I guess love is letting go of fear and anger. I found that as our relationship and our communication got better, my fear and my anger dissolved as my love grew.

"I found I could finally think about forgiving Dick. Forgiving is really nothing more than healing yourself of the painful memories of the past. It's definitely not an overnight process.

"Forgetting is more difficult because the memories are so very painful. During the time when we were trying to work things out and get our marriage back on the right track, I would find something would jog my memory. A song, perhaps, or some other incident that would remind me of that horrible time, and the pain would start again. As time went on, it became easier and easier. I think once the anger and the fear are diminished, forgiveness gets easier. Forgiveness takes the power away from the anger. You can't forgive or forget, though, until you heal yourself and learn to build a bond of trust, and that can take a long time. You just have to be patient."

Because Dick had inflicted so much pain on *her,* Liz never realized just how much pain Dick was feeling.

"I think when we finally opened the doors to communication I began to understand that Dick, too, had been in pain. When a man is involved in an affair, he's living a lie. It can't help but take a toll on him emotionally. I think that's why so many men sink into depression and alcoholism. It's the only way they can cope with their own behavior."

Dick's relationship with his children continued to improve. Once the children realized that Dick's affair with Diane was over, and they could see how hard their father was trying, the kids once again opened their hearts to him.

"When we realized my dad was serious about our becoming a family again, serious about his regrets and his sorrows, I guess we, too, were beginning to forgive him," Mark recalled. "But it wasn't easy. It was probably harder for us than for my mother. At least we were all trying. We had a long way to go, but at least we were starting to feel like a family again."

From the time Dick was released from the hospital, he had received numerous requests from the press to do interviews. But Dick continued to refuse. He wanted no part of the media after the way they had treated Liz.

But the press was persistent; reporters were eager to learn how the former superintendent was faring in civilian life after his dramatic fall from grace.

"I had my moment in the spotlight," Dick said. "I was quite happy to live my life in the shadows. Power is an aphrodisiac. I was seduced by power and all the perks that went with it—so much so that I forgot all the things that really mattered to me. I have no one to blame but myself. I became so full of my own arrogance, and all the other bullshit, that I almost destroyed not only my family but myself as well.

"Now, all I wanted was to be left alone to live the rest of my life in peace and quiet with Liz and the kids. Every time a reporter called, I just hung up. I didn't ever want to start that merry-go-round again.

"I was the one who was the bastard, yet Liz was the one who took the brunt of criticism. She suffered abuse from me, and then from the press. It was a two-fisted punch she didn't deserve. I wasn't about to let the media start taking potshots at her again. I already had all the press, the power, and the influence in my life, and once was enough. I sure as hell didn't want to start the whole thing over again. Not for my sake, but for Liz's. No one was ever going to rake her over the coals again—not if I had anything to say about it."

Despite Dick's refusal to talk to members of the press, they continued to call. Tom Lee, the political editor for the Chicago *Daily Herald,* a local suburban paper, wanted to do a follow-up interview of the former superintendent to see how he was doing. Once again, Dick adamantly refused.

But Tom Lee was persistent. He didn't want to do an exploitation article or an article opening old wounds. What he wanted was a chance to interview Dick and Liz to learn how they had repaired their marriage.

"Liz and I discussed the interview for a long time," Dick recalled. "She wasn't nearly as opposed to it as I was. We thought it might be a chance to finally set the record straight about what had happened and end a lot of the public speculation that was still swirling around us. I finally called Tom Lee and told him I'd do the interview on several conditions: Liz had to be present, and he had to come to the house to do the interview. I just didn't want to get involved in that whole media circus again. I wanted people to know Liz and I were a team once again."

Tom Lee set up the interview and arranged to bring a photographer with him. During the interview, Dick and Liz talked very candidly about the problems they had encountered because of Dick's affair: Dick's alcoholism, his depression, and his hospitalization. Most of the article focused on how the couple had managed to pick up the pieces of their life and go on to repair their marriage.

It was the first time a public official and his wife had ever talked so openly about their very private tragedy. Dick discussed his affair and all that it had cost him.

Liz, too, was very open and honest about the anguish she and her children had been through. It was a shocking and revealing article that told the whole truth—the real truth—behind Dick's fall from grace and the couple's subsequent problems.

The article hit the newsstands on Sunday, the largest circulation day, complete with color pictures of the Brzeczeks at home. The response was immediate and overwhelming.

Dick and Liz were inundated with telephone calls, not from other reporters as they had expected, but from other couples who had gone through or were going through similar problems with adultery.

Liz and Dick were receiving calls both at home and at the office, so many that it was difficult for the couple to keep up with all of them.

Everyone wanted to know the same thing: how had Dick and Liz managed to save their marriage after what they had gone through?

"I did the best I could to help these couples," Liz said. "The funny thing was that the stories were all the same; just the players were different. There wasn't anything these couples could tell Dick or me that we hadn't gone through or felt ourselves. We never realized how much pain and suffering there was out there. *I'd* never realized how much adultery there was going on. People think they're the only ones in the world this is happening to; everyone feels all alone. Your spouse's infidelity is not a subject you discuss over afternoon tea. There's a great deal of secrecy on both the offender's and the offended's part. But when Dick and I talked openly about this subject, and our own personal experience with it, it was as if we opened up the floodgates. People now knew that someone else had gone through this experience and *survived;* they weren't alone.

"But the people who called *felt* they were alone. They all felt as if they had no one to talk to, nowhere to turn. There was a great deal of shame and humiliation because of the situation the callers found themselves in. I could relate to everything everyone told me because I had been there; I'd felt the same pain, the same loneliness, the same despair. I never realized how widespread this problem was until then."

One couple who called was desperate. After thirty-eight years of marriage, Louise had discovered that her husband, Jim, had had an affair. (Their names have been changed to protect their privacy.) Although Jim had broken off with his mistress after Louise found out, their marriage was still in deep trouble. They were in therapy, but it was not helping.

"When Louise called, my heart went out to her," Liz said. "I could hear the anguish in her voice. She was going through every single thing I had gone through. She sounded desperate. During Jim's affair, he, too, had emotionally abused Louise. Her self-esteem was gone. By the time they called us, the situation between them had deteriorated to the point where she had consulted an attorney.

"Louise didn't think she could ever forgive Jim or forget what he had done to her and to their once happy marriage. She was having a great deal of difficulty coping with the aftershocks of her husband's infidelity.

"Jim, on the other hand, was having difficulty coping with Louise's feelings and emotions. They were at their wits' end. They didn't really want a divorce, but they didn't know how to go about saving or repairing their marriage. They wanted to know what we had done; how we had managed to save our marriage after what we'd been through."

Dick and Liz both spent a great deal of time with the distressed couple. Using their own personal experience, Dick and Liz explained to Louise and Jim what they had done in order to repair their marriage.

"It was important that Jim and Louise realize that they could save their marriage *if they really wanted to*. But that was the key. *Both partners had to have the desire and the willingness to work on their relationship.* If Dick and I could repair and save our marriage after what we'd been through, I truly believe *any* marriage can survive an adulterous affair as long as both parties have the desire and the commitment to make it work."

Dick and Liz worked with Jim and Louise in order to help them over the initial emotional hurdles, to help them find their way back to each other.

Liz knew what it took for the offended spouse to heal herself in order to heal their marriage. Dick knew what it took for the offender to heal himself, and then go forward to help heal their marriage. The two of them used their own personal pain to help Jim and Louise find each other again.

But Louise and Jim weren't the only couple who appeared in deep trouble. From the numerous calls she received, Liz knew there were a great many couples who had a genuine desire to save their marriages after an affair, but they had no idea how to begin. There were support groups for almost everything—except adultery.

After talking at length with many women, Liz realized that the negative feelings she had experienced during Dick's affair were the same as *all* offended victims feel: guilt, blame, worthlessness, and shame. Dick found that the feelings he experienced after his affair were the same as all offenders felt: guilt, shame, and remorse. There were hundreds, perhaps thousands, of couples who had also been emotionally harmed by adulterous affairs. It was a startling revelation for Liz.

The desperate calls she had received weighed heavily on her mind. Liz began having trouble sleeping. She would wake up in the middle of the night and not know why. At first Liz thought it was the stress of the past few years finally catching up with her. She also began to wonder if the phone calls she had received from other couples were triggering flashbacks of her own painful past.

When Liz finally fell asleep she would have strange dreams. She began dreaming about starting a self-help support group for other couples who had been emotionally harmed by adultery yet wanted to repair themselves and/or their marriages.

"I immediately dismissed the idea," Liz recalled. "Despite my recent personal growth, I've always been a follower, not a leader. I didn't have any idea how to go about forming such a group, let alone understand how it would function."

As much as Liz tried to dismiss her dreams, they continued. Night after night she had the same dream about this self-help group. In her dreams, the group even had a name: WESOM.

Liz had no idea what WESOM would stand for, but each night she'd get a different idea. One night it would be: We Saved Our Marriages. Another night it would be: We Saved Our Minds. Yet another it would be: We Served Our Master (God). (In all cases, the WE would encompass the offended, the offender, and God.)

The idea for this self-help group was continually on Liz's mind. No matter how she tried to ignore the dreams or dismiss them, she couldn't. Liz soon found herself consumed with the notion of creating this self-help program. She finally decided to talk to Dick about her strange dreams and her ideas for the group.

Dick thought her idea was wonderful. Not only was Dick encouraging, but he agreed to be a working and willing participant in the group.

As the idea for WESOM began to take form and shape in Liz's mind, she began contacting some of the people who had originally called her and Dick after Tom Lee's article. Liz found that without exception, everyone thought the idea was wonderful. Perhaps for the first time, the veil of secrecy and shame over adultery and its devastating effects was going to be torn away.

"I decided that WESOM would stand for We Saved Our Marriages," Liz said. "It would be the first self-help group in the country for people who had been emotionally harmed by infidelity; that would be the only requirement for joining WESOM. WESOM would be a place for married individuals and couples to put their lives and their marriages back together. We would offer help, hope, and support to both the offended (the victim), and the offender. There would be no shame or embarrassment, because all of us had been through the same thing; all of us had shared the same experiences. I believed those experiences would be the backbone of WESOM.

"For all those terrible years when I thought my world had come to an end, I could never understand why God had done this to me. Why had I been given this cross to bear? There *had* to be a reason. I truly believe He never does anything without a reason. I just never understood what that reason was. But as WESOM slowly became a reality in my mind, I think

I finally began to understand just why God had chosen me to carry the burden and endure such pain.

"How could I possibly help other people, or even begin to understand what they had gone through, or what they were feeling, if I hadn't experienced it myself?

"Whether you are the offended party or the offender, unless you've actually experienced the acute anguish and devastation brought on by an adulterous relationship, you cannot begin to understand what it does to a marriage or a family. You can *say* you understand, but you really don't unless you or a loved one has actually experienced the pain. And I had experienced it firsthand.

"I was happy *now*, but I always wanted to remember that at one time I hadn't been. I could smile now, but I never wanted to forget that at one time I, too, had cried.

"I just prayed that God would walk with me and guide me every step of the way. I had no experience with starting a group, but maybe experience wasn't necessary. What *was* necessary was an understanding of the problem, an understanding of the suffering that one has to endure, and that was something I definitely had.

"There were a lot of wives (and husbands) going through exactly what I had gone through. Maybe I could use the painful experiences of my past to help others save their future. I finally began to understand why I had been chosen to carry the burden of Dick's adultery. And that reason was WESOM."

Chapter Thirteen

Dick's Story: Part 5

When Liz first came to me with the idea of a self-help group for married individuals and couples who had been emotionally harmed by adultery, I thought it was a wonderful idea. From all the phone calls we had received after Tom Lee's article hit the paper, I knew a group like this was really needed. I never realized how many other people were suffering.

Men don't often think about how their behavior damages and destroys the people and the relationships they love. *I* didn't. If someone had been able to tell me just what my affair was going to cost me, maybe I'd have been able to stop before I got in too deep.

Liz and I had had great success repairing our marriage, but I have to give her a lot of the credit. She was the one who was willing to give me another chance. If it wasn't for her, we would probably be divorced right now.

After I got out of the hospital, with all the problems we had, Liz hung in there and stuck by me. It wasn't easy—for either of us. The knowledge of how much I hurt Liz was difficult for me to deal with; I love Liz and always have. I never meant to hurt her. When Liz told me at one point that she had actually thought about suicide because of what I had done, I guess it really made me realize just how destructive my behavior had been.

Together, we had to learn how to deal with the aftershocks. If we hadn't, our marriage could never have been saved. After an affair, when you finally come to your senses, you have to face the consequences of your actions. It's not easy, but if you really want your marriage to survive, you have to, there's no other way around it. You created the pain, now you have to deal with it, and heal it.

I truly believe that most men who have affairs don't want a divorce; if they did, they'd just leave their wives and families. Like me, most guys who get caught up in an affair just want to have their cake and eat it too. For a while, *some* think they can handle it, but they can't. The consequences aren't worth it.

A new relationship is exhilarating and exciting, but the exhilaration and excitement wear off fast because of what you have to do in order to live a double life. I began drinking, lying, and scheming.

When your affair is over, and you want to return home (that is, if you still have a home to return to), you have to face the consequences of your actions. Guys have a tendency to think: "Okay, my affair is over, let's just forget about it and go on." But it's not that simple. You have to deal with the damage you've done.

When you're involved in an affair your defense is to lie and deny. I learned to lie right up there with the best of them. I was the biggest and best bullshitter of them all.

You don't realize or recognize the pain you're causing other people. At the time, you're so caught up in the emotional and physical high that you forget there are other people involved, *innocent* people.

You figure, "Hell, this is a breeze, I can handle this. So I'm having an affair, big deal, it's the American macho thing to do; something to brag about with the boys." Another notch on your belt. But you don't realize until it's too late the price you have to pay. And there's *always* a price.

A lot of guys are probably thinking, "Sure, *he* couldn't handle the situation. But *I'm* in control. *I* can handle it." You've never seen a more in-control guy than I am—or at least I used to be. If anyone could have handled an affair I was the one. And look what it cost me.

No one can handle an affair, not any man or any woman, without its taking a toll on you, your emotions, your life, and your family. You're always maneuvering, always scheming. The guilt, the lies, and the double life take their toll, whether you realize it or not. Men who have affairs do some incredible things, things that lead to the emotional devastation of a lot of people, including themselves. The mind games—the psychological warfare you have to play in order to appease your own guilt and selfish desires—is incredible.

Guys don't talk about the destructive side of an affair, because it's not macho. But any way you look at it, an affair is destructive. It's hard to believe the devastation that occurs unless you've actually lived through it yourself.

All a man had to do was look at me and my life to see what was in store for him down the road. When Liz talked about starting this group, I told her I'd be more than happy to do whatever I could to help her. I even offered to be a willing participant. I had no problem sharing my experience with other guys. Men involved in affairs all do the same things; we say the same things, behave the same way. There wasn't anything a guy could say or do that I hadn't said or done myself. *Everybody* knew what I had done; it had been plastered bit by juicy bit on the front pages of the newspapers, so it wasn't like I was telling people something they didn't know. It didn't take a lot of courage to talk about my behavior. I wasn't proud of it, but I thought maybe some good could come out of this experience after all.

My affair cost me everything I had ever valued: my wife, my kids, my career, and my integrity. Some things were easier to repair than others. None of it was easy; some of it was just *easier*.

Take my relationship with my kids. They had a real hard time accepting me back into their lives. I couldn't blame them; I had acted like a raving lunatic. My children lost all respect for me because of my behavior. It took a long time for the kids to forgive me and begin to trust me again.

After all I had gone through, if I could prevent one man from ruining his life, his marriage, and his family by telling him what I had done to my life, my marriage, and my family, then maybe something positive could come out of this. I truly believed we could make WESOM work. I was behind Liz all the way.

Chapter Fourteen

WESOM, Inc.

With Dick's full support, Liz swung into action in order to get WESOM off the ground. She decided the group would be a nonprofit corporation that would meet weekly. Dick volunteered the use of his office without charge for the meetings and also handled all the legal requirements in order to get the group incorporated.

The basic premise for WESOM, Inc., would be very simple, its purpose twofold: it would be a support group exclusively for *married individuals* who had been emotionally harmed by adultery and wanted to help heal themselves. But it would also be a support group for *couples* who wanted to heal themselves and their marriages after an adulterous affair. There would be no professional counselors or therapists, only people who had actually experienced and understood the effects of adultery.

During Dick's affair, Liz had drawn a great deal of strength from Al-Anon. It was there that she had first been exposed to the Twelve Step Principle. The Twelve Steps had been extremely helpful in helping Liz deal with Dick's alcoholism, and were used by Alcoholics Anonymous, Al-Anon, and other successful self-help groups. Liz decided that the basic format for WESOM would be founded on A.A.'s original Twelve Step formula, but adapted to WESOM's particular problems.

Liz knew she would be breaking new and perhaps sacred ground. Never before had couples or individuals been encouraged to discuss either their own or their spouse's adultery. WESOM would be the vehicle not only to discuss adultery but to recover from it.

"People in this situation desperately needed a 'home,' " Liz said. "No matter how strong, no matter how independent, when you learn your spouse has been unfaithful it's a gut-wrenching, life-altering problem.

"These people needed somewhere they could feel comfortable discussing an uncomfortable situation. They needed help and guidance to learn how to deal with their pain and all their negative emotions, then to be able to go on and heal themselves, and their marriages, if that was what they wanted.

"If Dick and I could save our marriage after all we had been through, I was convinced that *any* marriage could be saved. I truly believed that out of a pile of garbage, roses could grow."

Dick shared Liz's optimism. He too believed that more marriages could be saved if couples knew exactly how to heal themselves and their marriages.

But Dick and Liz were aware that not every marriage would be saved. In some cases, a spouse, either the offender or the offended, might not have the desire to save the marriage. In order to save a marriage, *both* partners had to have the desire, and the commitment, to make the marriage work.

For those individuals whose marriages were beyond saving, for whatever reason, WESOM would provide the emotional support necessary to pick up their lives, heal themselves, and then go on.

Even before the first meeting was scheduled, Liz adapted the Twelve Step program to WESOM, and also the Twelve Traditions. The Steps would be a program for individuals to apply in their daily lives in order to cope with their spouses' adultery, while the Twelve Traditions would outline the basic ideals of WESOM, Inc.

Next, Liz decided on the format of each meeting, again adapting what she had learned at Al-Anon. They would begin with an Opening Prayer. Although Liz and Dick were Catholic and had deep religious beliefs, Liz knew that not everyone was religious or even associated with any religion. She wanted everyone, regardless of their faith or lack of it, to feel comfortable in the group. Liz chose prayers that were spiritual, rather than religious, so that no one would feel uncomfortable.

"Even if someone didn't believe in God, I was sure *everyone* believed in some Higher Power, whatever it might be."

The Opening Prayer would be followed by a Welcoming Statement. Then people would introduce themselves (first names only, fictitious ones if preferred. As with other support groups, all members would be granted anonymity).

After the introductions, the Twelve Steps of WESOM would be read, followed by the Twelve Traditions of WESOM. After the Traditions were read, the members would discuss one of the Steps and how it applied to their lives and their situations, starting week one with Step One, and then each week working their way through a new step, until all Twelve Steps had been discussed. Then the group would begin again with Step One.

This would be the "meat" of the meeting, when everyone could participate. Each person would be able to discuss individual problems. All would be encouraged to talk about how they felt that week's Step could be applied to help them deal with their lives and particular situations.

This would also be the time the group could offer support in order to help someone who was having difficulty working the Steps or handling a situation.

"I knew firsthand how valuable the Steps could be," Liz said. "They were the only things that helped when I was in such deep despair. While I had originally gone to Al-Anon to get help with Dick's alcoholism, it also helped me deal with his adultery. I knew that if people worked the Steps and lived their lives accordingly, any life or situation could be improved, no matter how desperate."

A sample of a WESOM meeting, with an explanation of the Twelve Steps of WESOM, and the Twelve Traditions of WESOM, follows:

Opening Prayer
The Serenity Prayer
God grant me the Serenity to accept the things I cannot change,
Courage to change the things I can, and the Wisdom to know the
difference.

"I chose the Serenity Prayer because I felt it fit in with WESOM's basic premise," Liz explained. "When there is an adulterous situation in a marriage, the offended party has a hard time accepting that he or she *cannot change* a mate's behavior.

"I knew how hard it was for me to accept. I finally realized I couldn't change Dick's behavior, but I could change my own. When I found the courage to change *my* behavior, to say: 'I'm not going to stand for this anymore,' I filed for divorce. I finally realized I had to *accept* that I couldn't change Dick's behavior; I had to find the *courage* to change the only thing I could—my own behavior. I felt the Serenity Prayer was something a lot of people in the same situation could relate to."

After the Serenity Prayer is read, the Opening Welcome is read:

Opening Welcome

We welcome you to WESOM, Inc., the support group for those married people who have been emotionally harmed by infidelity and yet have decided to save their marriage if at all possible.

We who live or have lived with the problem of infidelity are in need of someone to share our feelings with, someone who understands what emotions we are feeling and who accepts us for what we are.

The WESOM, Inc., program is adapted from the Twelve Steps of Alcoholics Anonymous, which we try, little by little, one day at a time, to apply to our *lives along with the Serenity Prayer. The loving interchange of help among members allows us to place our problem in its true perspective so it loses its power to dominate our thoughts and our lives.*

WESOM, Inc., is an anonymous fellowship. Everything that is said here, in the group meeting and member-to-member, must be held in confidence. *Only in this way can we feel free to say what is in our minds and hearts, for this is how we help one another in WESOM, Inc.*

"The Opening Welcome was very important," Liz said. "I felt people needed to know that WESOM was for them. This was *their* group. Shame and secrecy are a vital part of the adultery experience both for the offender and the offended. At WESOM, adultery would no longer be a secret shame. Here, finally, the veil of secrecy would be stripped away. People could talk openly regardless of whether they were the offended or the offender. There would be no ridicule or criticism, no judging or condemning. We would accept them, listen to them, sympathize, and help them as well as protect their identity. No one had to fear coming and opening their hearts or their spirits.

"All of us at WESOM had gone through the misery of an adulterous situation. We had all felt ashamed, and we had all felt helpless. *But there would be no more shame. We were no longer helpless.* WESOM would be the vehicle to show people how to rid themselves of these negative feelings and find inner strength."

After the Opening Welcome comes the individual introductions. Each person is then asked to throw away a negative thought. Liz explained the negative-thought theory:

"During Dick's affair I was constantly plagued by negative thoughts about myself, Dick, his relationship with Diane, and about what was happening to our lives and family. I was totally obsessed by Dick's affair.

"During the meeting, we believe it helps if each person picks one negative thought and throws it away, in effect saying: 'I won't think about this particular negative thing for one day.'

"Some of the negative things we can throw away are fear, blame, self-pity, anger, and remorse. Now, of course, these negative thoughts aren't going to go away overnight. But by using the Twelve Step program of WESOM, I felt we could teach people how to rid themselves of negative thoughts, if only for one day."

After the introduction and the "throwing away the negative" comes the reading of the Twelve Steps of WESOM, Inc.:

The Twelve Steps of WESOM, Inc.

(The Twelve Steps are reprinted and adapted with permission of Alcoholics Anonymous World Services, Inc.)

1. We admitted we were powerless over our spouses—that our lives had become unmanageable.

During an adulterous affair, normal life is disrupted and we feel as if everything in our lives is unmanageable. We want our spouses to behave in a way *we* consider acceptable. We try to force them to give up the other person or relationship in their lives. We must learn that we cannot force anyone—not even our spouses—to do something they don't want to do. We must realize we are totally powerless over our spouses. We cannot control our spouses or their behavior. All we can do and must strive to do is control ourselves and our own behavior.

This is probably the hardest of all the steps because we have to admit to God or to a Higher Power that we are powerless over our spouses. No one wants to feel that life has become unmanageable. It takes a lot of strength to be able to admit these things. When a relationship goes awry, the natural reaction is to try even harder to control your spouse's behavior.

But once we can *admit* we are powerless over our spouses, we can finally *accept* the fact that we cannot change them or their behavior. We have now shifted the responsibility for our spouses' actions where it belongs—on their shoulders. *We must accept responsibility only for our own actions and behavior.* In this way we can once again gain control over our own lives and thus begin the first step in the healing process.

2. Came to believe that a Power greater than ourselves could restore us to sanity.

By practicing and living Step 1 we can finally admit and accept that we are powerless over our spouses. Now, we need to know that there is *someone or something* that can help us out of the craziness that our lives have become. We need to believe that someone or something will help us restore our sanity. Once we have released ourselves from the terrible burden of responsibility, a belief in a Higher Power reminds us that there is hope for recovery.

In order to find some serenity and sanity in our lives and find some peace, we must believe in a power Higher than ourselves. Only then can we truly find serenity and sanity once again.

3. Made a decision to turn our will and our lives over to the care of God as we understood Him.

By practicing and living Step 1 and Step 2 we now need to begin the healing process within ourselves. This is where "letting go and letting God" comes in. We have to actively work at releasing control, and actively work toward letting God or a Higher Power take care of our will and our lives. We've tried to control things on our own; now it's time to let God take charge.

4. Made a searching and fearless moral inventory of ourselves.

This step is very difficult for the offended spouse. When your mate is involved in an affair, it's very easy to point a finger and say, "He did this, and he did that." It's very difficult to turn that finger inward to see our own flaws. For our own personal growth and happiness we *must* look inward to see our *own* flaws, then work on correcting them. Not even the offended party is perfect. Both the offender and the offended must take moral inventory in order to see themselves as they really are. We must each admit our own flaws and weaknesses, then work on them in order to become the best person *we* can be. If we each bring the best possible person we can be into a relationship, then we can't help but have a better relationship.

By taking inventory of ourselves we are reminded once again that we are only truly responsible for ourselves. We need to rekindle our feelings of self-worth. Only by understanding ourselves can we begin to see what it is that makes *us* special. Now we have a focus for change. We are no longer dealing with a massive world we cannot control; we are dealing with one area we can control—ourselves. When we begin to understand and see ourselves as we really are, then we can work on improving our self-image and our confidence.

5. Admitted to God, to ourselves, and to another human being the exact nature of our wrongs.

During an affair the offender and the offended do all sorts of things they wouldn't do under normal circumstances. We must admit to ourselves, to God, and to *another human being* the exact nature of our wrongs. It's very difficult to admit that we have been wrong, let alone admit it to God and another human being, particularly if you are the offended party. But we must remember that no one is perfect. Only by being honest with ourselves can we hope to change and improve our lives.

The focus here is on honesty and confession. We have to honestly and clearly look inward and try to see our own wrongs so that we can free ourselves from the pattern our lives have taken and find an inner peace and strength.

6. Were entirely ready to have God remove all these defects of character.

It's very difficult to let go of anger and resentment. It's also very difficult to honestly admit our own wrongs. But both the offended and the offender must.

Once we've admitted our wrongs we must learn to say: "I don't want to act like this anymore. I don't want to do these things anymore because they are not healthy. I don't want to live like this anymore. I want some peace and serenity in my life and only God or a Higher Power can help me to accomplish this by removing all the defects of *my own* character."

7. Humbly asked Him to remove our shortcomings.

We can't just say "Okay, God, I'm ready to have you remove all of my defects of character," then sit back and expect to do nothing. We have to honestly and earnestly work on eliminating our own shortcomings in order to try to become the best *we* can be. When you've done all you can do, then you must humbly ask Him to remove your shortcomings.

8. Made a list of all persons we had harmed and became willing to make amends to them all.

Making a list enables us to see the far-reaching effects of our actions. It's also another area of honesty. Once we've made the list we must be willing to make amends to *all* the people we have harmed. This applies to both the offended and the offender.

9. Made direct amends to such people wherever possible, except when to do so would injure them or others.

First, we must make amends to ourselves. The offended parties are generally very hard on themselves; they blame themselves for their spouses' affairs, and they suffer immeasurable guilt and terrible loss of self-esteem. We must make amends to ourselves first because we have harmed ourselves more than anyone else.

The offender must also make direct amends to the people he or she has harmed. It's not enough to make amends in your own mind; you must make amends *directly*. If there are any rips in any relationships, *you* must heal them. You're not doing it for others, but for your own personal growth and serenity.

When an affair disrupts a couple, generally the entire family is involved. We must make amends to any and all of these people who have been harmed. For example, if your husband is involved with another woman, and his parents seem to be taking his side, it's very easy to become bitter and resentful toward your in-laws. If you have been bitter and angry, you must make amends to these people. Maybe what they did was not right, but you need to master this step for your *own* spiritual growth. Both the offended and the offender must each learn to become a better person. This is not easy, but once we accomplish it, it really allows us to grow, both spiritually and emotionally.

10. Continued to take personal inventory, and when we were wrong, promptly admitted it.

This is a continuing process. When you're the offended party, you want to talk about your spouse and what the person did or said. But we have to stop this, and start looking inward. We must look at ourselves and honestly see what we're doing that's wrong. Then we must promptly admit our wrongs, and try again.

The same applies for the offenders. They must continue to take personal inventory of themselves and when wrong, promptly admit it and try again.

11. Sought through prayer and meditation to improve our conscious contact with God, as we understood Him, praying only for knowledge of His will for us and the power to carry that out.

We must reach a level of spirituality in which we pray only for the knowledge of God's will and the power to carry it out. This goes along with letting go with love and letting God do His work. We need to maintain a level of spirituality, to believe that everything that happens is "His will." This Step will bring about peace and serenity in our lives and give us the strength to grow both spiritually and emotionally.

12. Having had a spiritual awakening as the result of these Steps, we tried to carry this message to others, and to practice these principles in all our endeavors.

We must practice the Twelve Steps of WESOM faithfully and honestly. When we do, we will find our own inner peace. Then we can go forward and practice the principles we have learned in all our endeavors, and help other people who may be suffering reach a level of peace and serenity.

We feel it's very important to help other people. We must remember how alone we once felt and how much strength we gained from knowing that there were others who had gone through similar situations. God speaks through other people.

The Twelve Steps of WESOM, Inc., are an individual program. Only the *individual* who works the Steps will learn and grow from them. By practicing the Twelve Steps we show by example how we ourselves are being helped by the program. This is not a temporary fix; this is a program for living that will help us in all areas of our lives.

After the Twelve Steps of WESOM are read aloud, the Twelve Traditions of WESOM, Inc., are read:

The Twelve Traditions of WESOM, Inc.

These guidelines are the means of promoting harmony and growth in WESOM, Inc. Our group experience suggests that our unity depends upon our adherence to these Traditions:

1. **Our common welfare should come first; personal progress for the greatest number depends upon unity.**

2. **For our group purpose there is but one authority—a loving God as He may express Himself in our group conscience. Our leaders are trusted servants; they do not govern.**

3. **The WESOM, Inc., members, when gathered together for mutual aid, may have no other affiliation. The only requirement for membership is that there be a problem of infidelity in a spouse or in themselves.**

4. **Each WESOM, Inc., group should be autonomous.**

5. **Each WESOM, Inc., group has but one purpose: to help those who have been emotionally harmed by infidelity. We do this by practicing the Twelve Steps of WESOM ourselves, by encouraging and understanding our spouses, and by welcoming and giving comfort to those suffering the pain of infidelity.**

6. WESOM, Inc., ought never endorse, finance, or lend our name to any outside enterprise, lest problems of money, property, or prestige divert us from our primary spiritual aim.

7. Every group ought to be fully self-supporting, declining outside contributions.

8. WESOM Twelve Step work should remain forever nonprofessional, but we may employ social workers.

9. Our groups, as such, ought never be organized; but we may create service boards or committees directly responsible to those they serve.

10. WESOM, Inc., has no opinion on outside issues; hence our name ought never be drawn into public controversy.

11. Our public relations policy is based on attraction rather than promotion; we need always maintain personal anonymity at the level of press, radio, TV, and films. We need guard with special care the anonymity of all WESOM, Inc., members.

12. Anonymity is the spiritual foundation of all our Traditions, ever reminding us to place principles above personalities.

"*Remember, you must heal yourself before you can heal your marriage.* Working the Steps is not easy for anyone," Liz said. "Practicing the Steps, and living your life accordingly, will not only help you grow spiritually but will hopefully help heal you and your marriage.

"If the offended use the Steps, it will help them to learn to cope with whatever has brought on the despair in their lives. It will help them to deal with situations they cannot control. What the Steps *won't* do is prevent a spouse from straying. But it will help the offended spouses live their own lives to their optimum potential. *But the Steps will only help those who apply them to their lives.*

"For the offenders, the Twelve Steps of WESOM will help them deal with their own emotional pain and problems in order to grow and find some peace within themselves. They can then use the Steps to repair and heal their marriages through honesty and communication.

"In working the Steps, honesty is the key for the offender and the offended. The Steps will not work if a husband practices them or attends WESOM only to pacify his wife, or to take some of the heat off of him because of his behavior. The offender must have an honest desire to repair his or her marriage, and practice the Steps honestly. It's an individual program for those who choose to use it.

"Once you've found some peace within yourself, and have healed some of your own pain, then you and your spouse can work the Steps in order to heal and repair your marriage.

"If you are having difficulty, sometimes just listening to someone else who has already found peace and serenity in his or her life helps us to know that we, too, can find peace.

"Others can learn and grow from our pain. We are all here to help one another. Any kind of growth or change is painful. But if we really believe in the Twelve Steps of WESOM, then that growth becomes easier and the pain becomes less."

At the conclusion of the WESOM meeting the Closing Statement is read aloud:

Closing Statement

In closing, I would like to say that the opinions expressed here are strictly those of the person who gave them. Take what you like and leave the rest.

The things you heard were spoken in confidence and should be treated as confidential. Keep them within the walls of this room and the confines of your mind.

A few special words to those of you who haven't been with us long: Whatever your problems, there are those among us who have had them, too. If we try to keep an open mind, we will find help. You will come to realize that there is no situation too difficult to be bettered and no unhappiness too great to be lessened.

We aren't perfect. The welcome we give you may not show the warmth we have in our hearts for you. After a while you'll discover that though you may not like all of us, you'll love us in a very special way—the same way we already love you.

Talk to one another, reason things out with someone else, but let there be no gossip or criticism of one another. Instead, let the understanding, love, and peace of the program grow in you one day at a time.

Will all who care to, join me in the closing prayer? [The closing prayer Liz chose was The Lord's Prayer.]

The evening ends with everyone taking away a positive thought. This is very much the same as throwing away a negative thought. Liz explained: "We can take away peace, hope, or forgiveness. Or it could be something as simple as the WESOM meeting. When you're in a situation like adultery, there's very little that's positive in your life. You need to force yourself to look at your life and find something to be positive about, even if it's something you don't feel at the moment. It's something to work toward."

Once the basic format and foundation for WESOM, Inc., were laid, Liz knew it was time to let the group fly. She never had any doubt that WESOM would become a success.

"First of all, I knew I wasn't alone in this. I truly felt God was at my side, guiding me all the way. I also had Dick's total support. We knew how much pain there was out there. We also knew that these people who were going through this pain had no outlet. There were counselors, therapists, psychiatrists, and psychologists, but while these experts could counsel about the problem they generally had no hands-on experience. I felt that was the big difference.

"I truly believe that there are no ideal marriages, or ideal people, only real people with real problems. We wanted to offer hope and help. All marriages have problems. We wanted to try to help these people who had been emotionally harmed by adultery to become the best people they could be in order to have the best marriages they could have."

Liz and Dick did no advertising for WESOM. They called Louise and Jim, the couple who had first called them after the Tom Lee article appeared, as well as a few of the other couples who had called for advice. Several agreed to come to the first meeting.

The week before the first meeting, Dick met a woman in court who told him about her husband's affair. Dick invited her to the meeting.

"I think people felt more comfortable talking to Dick and me about their problems because everyone knew that we had been through it," Liz revealed. "The whole city knew because of the press coverage. Looking back on it, as much as I hated it at the time, perhaps it wasn't so bad. Had people not known about us, they might not have had the courage to come forward and speak to us about their own problems."

That same week, one of the Brzeczek children came home with the news that the father of one of his friends was involved in an affair. Liz invited the couple to the first meeting, although only the wife came. Another woman called and said her husband had molested another woman. Liz invited her, too. The first few meetings were comprised solely of women—except for Dick.

"The first meeting was really quite extraordinary," Liz recalled. "The thing that stands out most in my mind was all the pain."

That first meeting laid the groundwork for all the meetings to come. Dick and Liz explained exactly what the group was about and how they could all help one another.

"I thought it was very important for these women to know this was a self-help group," Liz said. "We were all there to help one another. While Dick and I may have started the group, there were no leaders. We were all just people who had been emotionally harmed by our spouses' infidelity. I wanted the women to know they were not alone. Everyone talked that first night. It was probably the very first time any of these women were able to talk openly about what was happening in their lives; the first time they felt that someone else had gone through the same thing and could understand the pain and shame they were feeling. It was really incredible, and there were a lot of tears. But there was a bond between us, a bond that helped us all learn and grow."

Dick was particularly helpful to the women. Up until then, most of the women hadn't realized that their husbands might be in just as much pain as they were. Dick talked openly and candidly about his affair and the mind games that go on when a man is trying to lead a double life. He also talked about the pain he went through because of his affair.

The women found they could relate to what Dick told them. The lies and deceptions he had carried out were almost identical to what their husbands had been doing. Hearing the man's side of it helped these women understand a little better just what their husbands had been doing, and why.

"When I talked to these women I didn't pull any punches," Dick said. "I wasn't out to win any Prince Charming awards. I did what I did, I admitted it, and now it was time to go forward and put my life back together. Maybe in the process I might be able to help someone else learn from my experience."

"I guess the women were kind of shocked at first to hear Dick discuss his affair so openly," Liz recalled. "You have to remember, when a man is having an affair, secrecy is of the utmost importance. All the lies and conniving that go on are mind-boggling. Dick gave a man's perspective. In a way, it was kind of funny, because Dick would be talking about something he had done, and we could see all the women nodding their heads. They could relate to what he was saying, because their husbands had been doing the exact same thing."

Dick continued: "I explained how I had deliberately found fault with Liz in order to appease my guilty conscience. I simply sat there and told these women the truth. It's amazing, but all men who are having affairs say and do the same damn things.

"Once these women saw that *their* husbands weren't the only ones who had suddenly taken leave of their senses, I think it gave them a feeling of hope. If Liz and I could pull our marriage back together after all I had done, and all that had happened to us, it *had* to give them some hope."

It was very important to Dick and Liz that everyone at the meeting understand that WESOM, Inc., wasn't an instant solution to a devastating problem. Coming to WESOM would not stop their husbands from straying. What it could do was help the women deal with the crisis in a more positive way.

But it was very difficult at first, particularly for some of the wives, because working the Steps meant that *they* had to change not only their attitudes but their behavior.

"Of the women who came, most of their husbands were still actively involved in affairs," Liz reported. "We tried to show them, by using the Steps, how they could help themselves. They couldn't control their husbands—they had all tried and failed. The wives had to learn to accept the fact the only thing they could *control* was their own behavior.

"A wife should never accept an adulterous situation, but we do because of our own fears. Until a wife reaches the point where her pain overshadows her fear and she can say: 'Look, I will not accept or tolerate this behavior,' a husband will continue his affair. A wife must make it clear this behavior is *not acceptable*. It takes a lot of strength and courage to do this. It's difficult to overcome our own fears and tell the man you love you will no longer accept what he's doing. Once you tell him, though, you must be ready, willing, and able to file for divorce and then go through with it if he does not break off his affair.

"At WESOM, we tried to show these women how, by working the Steps, they could grow and find a peace and serenity within themselves in order to reach this point. It's not easy for anyone. It took me almost three years before I finally had the courage to tell Dick: 'No more. I've had enough. I want a divorce.'

"In a great many cases when a wife tells her husband she won't tolerate this behavior and then goes ahead and files for divorce, the husband will break off his affair. When a husband realizes he is going to be forced to face the consequences of his actions, and those consequences are the loss of his home and family, he generally breaks off his affair.

"Most men who are involved with another woman don't really want a divorce, they just want a wife *and* a mistress. But a wife must make it clear that this is an unacceptable situation. When the offenders realize they can't have both relationships because their wives will not tolerate another woman in the picture, most men are forced to put their priorities in order.

"If a man does *not* break off his affair, though, the wife must let her husband go, but let him go with love. By working the Steps a wife learns to let go of her husband and let God take over. You must believe and have faith that whatever happens is His will.

"If a man *wants* to leave we must let him go. *Then, let him be.* Let go with love. You must not call him, beg him, nag him, or do anything like that. No matter what you do or say, you're not going to be able to stop him from doing what he really wants. *You are powerless over him.* Remember Step One. Since you've told him you won't accept this type of behavior any longer, you don't want him to return home until he's resolved his other relationship.

"If a man has left you for his mistress, you cannot allow him to remain a part of your family relationships until his affair is over. Otherwise he will never be forced to face the consequences of his own actions.

"If you *do* allow your spouse to continue as part of your family environment while his other relationship is still going on, you will be drawn back into the craziness of his affair, and your life will once again become unmanageable. You'll begin to think you can control him again. For your own sake and emotional well-being you must remember that you cannot control your spouse.

"With any growth there is pain, but in order to find peace in your own life, and gain control over your life so that it is once again manageable, you must be able to find the inner strength to change your own behavior, and that means no longer accepting an unacceptable situation.

"Some women *never* reach the point where they say, 'No more.' No one wants to be divorced, and no one wants to break up a family. But is it better to live your life in a constant state of panic and crisis? One woman I spoke to had put up with her husband's adultery for almost eleven years. Her life had been a living nightmare. It was clear that she was just as emotionally ill as her husband. Until she finds the strength within herself to say: 'No more,' her husband will continue his behavior. No one can give her the strength; she has to find it within herself.

"I wanted WESOM to be able to show these men and women how to grow to the point where they could say, *'No more,'* if that's what was necessary for them to find peace and serenity and to restore their lives to sanity.

"But I also wanted WESOM to be a place to help heal and restore a marriage once the couple was reunited. When a wife tells her husband she will not tolerate his behavior any longer, and the spouse breaks off the affair and returns to the family, the couple then needs to work through the aftershocks and pain that remain because of the betrayal."

The initial meetings of WESOM were a learning and growing process for everyone, as explained by one early member who wishes to remain anonymous:

"Going to that first meeting was so humiliating. I was certain I was the only woman in the world whose husband was cheating on her. Learning about my husband's affair was hard, but dealing with my emotions after I learned the truth was probably the hardest. Even though I was ashamed to walk into that first WESOM meeting, I went because I had nowhere else to go, no one to turn to.

"No one knew about my husband's affair. I was afraid people would blame me. I was certain everyone would think my husband had strayed because I wasn't a good wife or a good lover. I couldn't tell anyone because I was too ashamed. I kept all of this inside me because I just couldn't talk about it. It hurt so bad.

"I was in such pain and so desperate that I thought the only way to stop this nightmare was to commit suicide. Death would have been merciful. My husband's affair made me feel so worthless I felt I didn't have a right to live. WESOM was my only hope.

"When I walked into that first meeting, I felt like I had come home. I'd finally found a place where I belonged. I *wasn't* the only woman in the world this was happening to; there were a lot of us. I found I could talk about things I'd kept buried deep inside. It was as if all the pain just came pouring out. *Someone finally understood what I was going through.* We had all been going through the same thing.

"My husband's affair was still going on when I first joined the group. At the time all I did was worry about my husband: his anger, his words, his affair, his behavior, his drinking. I was obsessed with my husband and his affair. It was all I could think about.

"I had always been dependent on him. I had always been worried about what he thought of me, and if he approved of me. I never said what I thought or how I felt. I didn't even know how to think, or how to really feel. I was so dependent on him that I did anything and everything I could to please him. I would have stood on my head or walked on my knees for this man and this marriage.

"But it didn't help. He still kept seeing that other woman. I couldn't understand what kind of a relationship he had with her. Was it so celestial, so unworldly, that he was willing to throw away almost forty years of marriage? Was I such a bad wife, such a bad person, that he had to go find another woman? It's hard to understand what we don't know. I kept going over and over our marriage, wondering if I had done this differently or that differently, maybe he wouldn't have cheated on me.

"After that first WESOM meeting I learned that I had nothing to do with my husband's affair. It was *his* choice to have the affair. It wasn't something I had or hadn't done that made him cheat on me. It was his choice, his decision. I couldn't force him to stop his affair any more than I forced him to start it.

"WESOM taught me that no matter what I did, I could not control my husband or his behavior. My own life was totally out of control because I kept trying to control him. I kept trying to force him to break it off with her and I couldn't. Step One of the Twelve Steps really put things in perspective for me. I finally learned that I had to give up trying to control him and his behavior. It's like a psychological wrestling match. When we try to control our husbands it's like we're always trying to anticipate what they're going to do. What kind of way is that to live? It took a lot for me to come to the realization that nothing I ever did would make him stop. I had no control over him. But what I could do was control my own actions. It took me a long time to realize that.

"By working the Steps I finally reached the point where I would no longer allow him to play mind games with me. No more psychological warfare or emotional intimidation. That was my way of gaining control of myself. I finally had the inner strength and confidence to say: 'No more.'

"The group taught me that in spite of everything that was happening around me, I had to learn to respect myself. How could anyone else respect me if I didn't respect myself? When I first went to the meetings I had no self-respect, no self-esteem. My husband had taken it away from me. Emotionally, he battered me into the ground. He totally blamed me for his affair and I accepted the blame. I *allowed* him to take away my self-esteem. I allowed him to shift the blame to me.

"When I first listened to Dick talk about *his* behavior during his affair I was shocked. It was my husband all over again. The lying, the drinking, the emotional abuse. I couldn't help but wonder if there was some kind of secret code book men have that tells them how to behave when they're having an affair.

"Maybe I couldn't control my husband's behavior, but I could control my own. If he chose to continue his affair, that was his choice. I was no longer going to accept his behavior. It was my choice to live my life the best way I could in spite of what was happening around me. I decided to stop worrying about my husband and *start worrying about myself.* I felt such a tremendous relief. For the first time in my life, I respected myself. I was finally in control of my own destiny. No longer would my life and my thoughts center on him, but on *me*.

"My life had become unmanageable because of him and his affair. When I made the decision to turn my will and my life over to God, it brought such peace. I knew then, with each passing meeting, with the support I found, that I would be able to go on and face each day and go forward. I found a sense of peace that had been lacking for a long, long time.

"After nearly forty years of marriage I realized I *could* survive without my husband. I still loved him, but I didn't *need* him. I could make it on my own if I had to. The knowledge was such a release. I found I was able to let go of all the fear I had harbored for so long.

"When I told my husband I would no longer accept his behavior and was filing for divorce, he broke off his affair. I think I shocked him. Now we're both attending the meetings. He wants to repair our marriage. I guess he finally realized I was worth something. I still love him, and I want to make my marriage work, but there's a lot of pain and anguish to get over. We're both working the Steps. WESOM has helped both of us and our marriage. It's not easy, but at least we're both trying."

Dick and Liz also learned a lot from those first few women and those first few meetings. Almost without exception, in nearly every case of infidelity, the offender was involved in alcohol and showed signs of depression.

"It was strange," Liz recalled. "We began to see a pattern after listening to so many stories. We found out from the wives that almost all of the men had started drinking heavily after their affairs began, or their drinking increased once they became involved with another woman.

"A lot of the women talked about their husbands' emotional health. It was clear that there were a lot of men who were also suffering from depression."

It was a premise Dick clearly understood. "Men aren't used to discussing their emotional feelings, particularly when they're in pain. While women will sit and talk about things that are bothering them, men more than likely will hit the bottle. They think that a drink will make their problems go away. Maybe the first one does make you feel better, but pretty soon one isn't enough, and before you know it you're an alcoholic. I knew from my own experience that drinking didn't help, it just made the situation worse. The depression was quite understandable. You can't live your life in an emotional hurricane, lying all the time and trying to cover your tracks, without it taking some toll on you. Between the alcohol and the emotional trauma, depression is a natural progression."

For the women whose husbands were clearly having problems with alcohol, Liz recommended Al-Anon.

From those first few meetings, the word spread. Soon the WESOM meetings were filled to capacity. Initially there were very few men who attended, but soon the husbands began coming too, much to Liz's satisfaction.

"I found that most of the husbands who came to the meetings had a real desire to save their marriages. Once again, they'd never had any place where they could talk openly and honestly about what they had been feeling. Most had never openly discussed their affairs with anyone, especially their wives.

"These men wanted to save their marriages but they had no idea how to begin. At WESOM we tried to help both partners overcome the emotional hurdles they were facing in order to find their way back to each other."

During the initial meetings most of the women were so relieved to finally have someone to talk to and share their anger with, they spent most of the time just pointing a finger at their husbands and saying, "Look what he did." But Liz would not, could not, allow the meetings to become gripe sessions.

"That wouldn't help anyone. What we needed to do was show these women how to dispel their anger at their husbands. How to use their anger constructively in order to go forward, in order to repair the damage that had been done to themselves and their marriages. They had to process all those negative feelings and emotions and get them out in the open. We could not allow these negative emotions to become buried inside or they would never heal."

Once the husbands began attending, Liz found the meetings had to change in order to suit the men's needs and to help them.

"We really had to put the Twelve Step program into action. I felt it was the only way to make any real progress with these marriages. A lot of the women resisted the Twelve Steps at first because it meant they had to take personal stock of themselves, and in some cases it meant *they* had to change. Remember, not even the victims are totally faultless. Even the victims had to learn to take inventory of themselves, their actions and their own behavior. Attacking their husbands certainly didn't allow growth, and I knew from my experience, *my* personal growth was what allowed me to change, and in the end to save my marriage.

"Honesty is a very important part of repairing a marriage. The husband *must* be honest with his wife. He must answer all her questions about the affair honestly. A word of caution, though. Only tell your wife as much as she wants to know. It's not necessary to blurt everything out in one day. That can be very upsetting to someone who is already emotionally harmed. Tell her just what she wants to know at any given time.

"It's not easy for a husband to sit down and tell his wife things he knows will hurt her. But he created the problem; now he has to deal with the consequences if he truly wants to save his marriage. He has to learn to accept responsibility for his actions, and dealing with the pain he has created is part of it. This can be very painful to both parties.

"By practicing the Twelve Steps we can get through all this pain. Truth is imperative in order to come together once again and rebuild the bond of trust that was shattered. But it will not happen overnight. You have to be patient; repairing a marriage and restoring love and trust can take years. But if you truly want to save your marriage, all you need is the desire and the commitment.

"Those first meetings with the husbands weren't easy," Liz recalled. "There was a lot of anger, resentment, and bitterness. More than a few times, there were some very heated words between couples. You have to learn how to deal with all of those negative emotions, because unless you do, it will destroy you. The women had to change how they reacted and responded to their husbands. The husbands had to learn how to respond and react to their wives' pain. Again, that's where practicing the Steps becomes so important.

"A man has a tendency to think, 'Now that my affair is over and done with, let's just forget it and go back to the way things were.' What he doesn't realize is that they can't just go back to the way things were. His wife is no longer the same person and their marriage is no longer the same. The very foundation of the marriage has been destroyed and the couple must slowly rebuild it.

"A lot of men were not comfortable coming face to face with just what their actions had done to their marriages and their wives," Liz said. "But if they truly wanted to return to the fold of the family, they had to learn to deal with the consequences of their actions. They created the problem; now they had to face the consequences and work things through.

"Repairing a marriage that has been shattered by infidelity is a long, slow, painful process. It isn't easy. Anyone who says it is, is lying. Adultery can destroy people's lives, their faith and their trust. Look at Dick and me. Because our case was so dramatic, because of what Dick's affair had cost us, I think it gave the other couples hope that their marriages could be saved.

"Even though there was pain involved, the couples kept coming back, week after week. Each week we could see an improvement. Sometimes it was only something slight, but at least they were trying to work things through. Divorce is easy, but staying together after something like this is truly difficult. But Dick and I proved you could do it. You *can* save your marriage after an affair, and go on to be happy and have a successful, and perhaps even better, marriage. But both partners have to want it and work at it."

Liz knew that despite the progress they were making with some couples, there were going to be some marriages that were beyond saving.

"For those men and women whose marriages were beyond repair, we offered hope and help. We helped the offended cope with the pain. We tried to show them they *could* go on without their spouses. It's not easy, but they can do it. Using the Twelve Step program, we tried to help these people grow as individuals, to become the best people they could be, and learn to stand on their own, alone, despite what had happened to them."

From its shaky beginnings, WESOM became a viable entity in the community. Each week more and more couples came, couples who were eager to learn how to repair their marriages.

Liz became a tower of strength, not just to her family but to other women and to many couples. By her personal example, Liz became an inspiration to other women in their quest to repair and save their marriages, and to grow spiritually and emotionally.

On the following pages you will read about some of the individuals and couples served by WESOM. Their names have been changed to protect their identities, but their stories are factual. In almost all instances each person or couple credits Dick, Liz, and WESOM for saving not just their marriages but in some cases their very lives.

Chapter Fifteen

Stories from WESOM

LARRY AND SUE

Larry and Sue have been married for thirteen years. They have two children, a boy, six, and a girl, ten. This is Sue's first marriage; Larry's second.

Larry's first marriage ended because of his first wife's adultery. When he discovered that his wife had been unfaithful, Larry became a drunk. He lost forty pounds and developed a gambling problem. His wife's infidelity emotionally destroyed Larry to the point where he contemplated suicide.

LARRY'S STORY

No one should ever feel like I felt when I learned my first wife was unfaithful. It was the most destructive, devastating feeling in the world. But I didn't think about it before I began my own affair. Sue and I had a pretty good marriage. She worked nights; I worked days. We kind of saw each other in passing, mostly on weekends. There wasn't anything really wrong with our marriage. Sue and I just seemed to be at a dead end.

Alice moved in next door to us, and she had a daughter the same age as mine. Naturally the kids became friends and started playing together. Sometimes at night Alice would come over to keep me company.

At first, there really wasn't anything to it. Alice's daughter was usually at my house, or mine was at hers. One night Alice's daughter was spending the night with my daughter. Alice came over, and she said some

178

things that led me to believe she was interested in me. Very interested. She was eleven years younger than I am, and I was very flattered by her attention. Before too long, things got a bit more personal and we started having an affair.

When guys are together having a few beers it's kind of a jock thing to talk about all the women you've slept with. Then this woman came along and it was hard to turn down. She was there, and my wife wasn't. It was too easy for me. I couldn't say no. We just kind of fell into this relationship.

While my wife was working we'd go out for a few beers, or we'd go to some sporting events. I didn't think anyone would suspect anything because our kids were always together. But pretty soon the neighbors started talking about us.

As soon as I became involved with this woman I knew it was a mistake. I felt terribly guilty. I was always down in the dumps. I was incredibly angry at myself for what I was doing. I knew what it felt like to be on the other end of something like this, how horrible it made you feel, but I guess I wasn't thinking about that at the time. Maybe if I had, I never would have become involved with Alice. I didn't love her; I loved my wife, Sue. But once the relationship started, I had a hard time breaking it off.

Every time I tried to break up with Alice, she'd threaten to tell my wife. I didn't know what to do. I was getting scared. I couldn't break it off because I was afraid Alice would tell my wife. *I* couldn't find the courage to tell my wife, either. It was just an impossible situation that I just couldn't seem to get myself out of. I felt trapped.

A lot of people in the neighborhood saw us together, and eventually my wife did find out. One of the neighbors told my wife about Alice and me, but I lied when she finally confronted me about it. A week later my daughter was talking to Alice's daughter on the phone. *Her* kid told *my* kid that her mother and I were kissing and stuff. My daughter was very upset. She told my wife all about it. Pretty soon my wife put two and two together and figured it out.

My wife stayed home from work one night. I had been out with Alice, and when I got home, Sue confronted me about my affair. I told her everything. I guess I was relieved it was finally over. It was a very stressful situation. I felt lower than dirt for what I was doing to my wife and family. I wanted to end the affair, but I didn't know how. I was going crazy; I didn't know what to do or where to turn. I knew it was my own fault for getting myself involved with this woman in the first place, but God, I never expected things to turn out like they did. I certainly didn't expect her to start threatening me.

The night Sue found out, she was absolutely livid. She went next door and starting screaming at Alice. Sue was so angry she started throwing beer cans and stuff at Alice's house. Alice called the police and two squads came. My wife and my mistress were screaming and yelling at each other and the whole damn neighborhood knew what was going on, including my own children.

When I finally persuaded Sue to come home, we spent most of the night arguing. She was really hurt. I told her I loved her and wanted to stay with her, not the other woman. Sue didn't believe me. I tried to explain to her how and why this had happened, but it didn't do much good. After my wife found out about my affair she was devastated. Knowing I had caused Sue all that pain made me feel like the lowest thing on earth. All we did was fight and yell. I should have understood how she felt, because I had gone through it myself, but I didn't.

I had read an article about the Brzeczeks, and I called Dick at his law office the next morning. The first thing he asked me was if my affair was over. I told him yes. He said Sue and I should come to the WESOM meeting. Thirty-six hours after Sue found out about my affair, we went to our first WESOM meeting.

It was a two-and-a-half-hour round trip for us, but we went. I would have done *anything* to save this marriage. I didn't want to lose my wife or my family. I made a stupid mistake. I love Sue, but I knew she didn't believe me. In her mind, I'm sure she thought that if I loved her, I wouldn't have done this to her, or to us.

Looking back on it now, I can honestly say that had we not gone to that first WESOM meeting, we probably wouldn't be married today. WESOM saved our marriage.

My affair totally destroyed my wife's confidence and self-esteem. She was so angry, so hurt, so bitter, I didn't think we'd ever be able to get our life back together. But WESOM taught her how to deal with all the pain and anger I had caused. If my wife had not had WESOM, she would never have been able to forgive me. WESOM was really a godsend for her. And for me. It helped me grow and change. I think I'm a better person now than I was before; I hope so.

At that first meeting, my wife talked primarily to Dick, and I talked to Liz. Talking to Liz made me realize exactly what my wife had been feeling and what I had put her through. It made *me* feel incredibly guilty. I knew I wanted this marriage to work, and I would have done anything to save it. I love Sue and never meant to hurt her. But I did. I had to learn how to deal with all the hurt I had caused. WESOM taught me how.

Even after Sue found out about my affair, and even after we started attending WESOM, there were still some things I hadn't told Sue because I was *afraid* to tell her. But at WESOM I learned that Sue and I could never begin anew or hope to repair our marriage until I was absolutely truthful with her. Honesty was the key. She knew I hadn't told her everything; she didn't know why, but the *why* didn't seem to matter. The only thing that mattered was the fact that she thought I was still lying to her. I wasn't lying. I just didn't want to tell her something that would only cause her more pain.

It wasn't easy, but I finally told her everything. Some of the things I revealed did hurt Sue, but at least I was being totally honest with her. It showed her I really did want to save our marriage. We learned how to communicate in a way we never had before. I had been lying to her for so long, it was a relief finally to tell the truth.

Using the Twelve Step program, we were both forced to look at ourselves and our own faults. We had to put our pride away and really take a good, hard look at ourselves. The Twelve Step program forces you to be honest *with* yourself *about* yourself.

Everyone at WESOM had gone through the same problems we had. We weren't the only ones. I didn't feel so guilty or ashamed talking about our problems there. There were guys there who had been in the same situation. Some of them had been going to the meetings for quite a while. It had really helped their marriages, so I was hopeful that it could help ours. Until we actually went to WESOM, I really didn't think our marriage would survive. Once we started going, I began to believe it could, but it was going to take a lot of work on both our parts. Sue and I both wanted our marriage to work, but we just didn't know how to begin.

I try very hard to live my life according to WESOM's Twelve Step program. I wish I could say it's easy, and that I do it all the time, but I can't. That would be lying. But I'm *trying* to live by the Twelve Step program because I know it's the only way to really heal things between us. Sue wanted me to go to A.A. and eventually I did go. I'm just sorry it took me so long to realize what a great wife and a great woman Sue is.

Sue isn't the only one who suffered because of my affair; our kids have suffered, too. Alice still lives next door to us. Her daughter torments my daughter, saying things like, "Your father slept with my mother." It's been very, very hard on my kids. My daughter is now in therapy. She's trying to deal with what's happened but I don't think she really understands. This has definitely hurt my children, far more than I could ever have imagined.

Just a few months ago Alice's daughter had a sleepover party. During the night she and her friends vandalized our home. They took peanut butter, markers, and crayons and wrote vile things all over our house. I called the police, and the kids were forced to clean everything off the house, but still, the damage was done. Sue and the kids were really upset. Again, the whole neighborhood was involved. It's kind of hard to keep something like this a secret.

Alice just won't let up on me, my wife, or my kids. She's constantly tormenting and antagonizing my wife and children. Since my affair ended I have been struggling to overcome the enormity of my financial problems. I recently changed jobs and am now working to clean up a lien on our house, which we have just put up for sale.

Every time something happens with Alice, it's another reminder to my wife of what I did. WESOM has really helped her deal with these feelings, although I think Sue still harbors a lot of anger at Alice.

As for our marriage, we're still working on it. Things have improved dramatically since those first tormented days. Things aren't perfect—yet. We're still working on it. We both want this marriage to work, and as long as we're both trying, I'm hopeful we can succeed.

What hurts me is the knowledge of how much pain I brought my wife and kids. This thing has hurt everyone. If I had it to do over again, you can bet I'd never, ever get involved with someone else. It's just not worth it.

My marriage to Sue right now is so good, so special, I would never even consider looking at another woman. I realize now how much I hurt her when I cheated on her. I don't ever want to make her feel that much pain again.

Our communication is better than it's ever been. I guess all aspects of our marriage are better. Without the group I think we'd probably be divorced right now. There was no way we would have been able to deal with this thing on our own. Knowing that everyone else in the group has been through the same thing helped. We all learned from one another.

I love Sue more than anything else, and despite everything I think she loves me. I don't think she'd be trying so hard to save our marriage if she didn't. But it's not over yet. There are still some aftershocks.

Sue is still afraid to show her full emotions. She's holding back because she's afraid she'll get hurt again. She doesn't trust me. I don't really think she ever will. I've assured her over and over again that it would never happen again. But I guess I can understand why she doesn't trust me. I destroyed that trust when I betrayed her.

As for our sex life, Sue wouldn't let me make love to her until I went for an AIDS test. Alice had not only been involved with quite a few men, but drugs as well. I went for the test and thankfully it was negative. But I have to go in about once a year. I worry about AIDS a lot. It's always in the back of my mind. I could get the disease, give it to Sue, and we could both die. Our kids could be orphans. The ramifications of this thing just never seem to end.

If I had it to do over again, I would never, ever cheat on my wife. It's a high price to pay for a few minutes of pleasure.

If someone asked me for advice, I'd tell them *don't*! There is no way you can ever anticipate the total effect an affair can have on your life, on your marriage, and on your family. It's just not worth it.

As for the future, Sue and I are very optimistic. But we're taking things one day at a time. We're friends now, as well as husband and wife. No matter what, we both know we're in this together. We just have to learn how to cope with all the anger, resentment, and pain. We're learning day by day.

We are so thankful to WESOM, all I can say is God bless WESOM. We don't know what we would have done without it. Dick and Liz have been so wonderful to us. They have helped us so much that Sue and I are starting a WESOM chapter in our area.

If my experience can help just one person, or one couple, maybe then it will all have been worth it.

Sue's Story

I never expected Larry to have an affair. Throughout our marriage Larry has been emotionally and financially immature. He's always been emotionally dependent on me. We've had a lot of financial problems over the years, some left over from his first marriage. I finally went to work to help out. While I was out working twelve hours a day to get our financial situation in order, my husband was having an affair with the woman next door.

I first suspected something because some of our neighbors had seen Larry and Alice together while I was at work. At first I ignored it because our daughters were friends, so I thought it natural that people see Larry and Alice together once in a while. I used to watch Alice's kids when I was home from work. I later found out that while I was watching her kids, she was out with my husband!

Alice's daughter finally said something to my daughter about Larry and her mother. My daughter was very upset. She loves her father very much and she didn't understand what was happening. My daughter came to me and told me what she'd been told, and it didn't take long for me to figure out exactly what was going on. The night I confronted Larry I just went berserk. I wanted to kill Alice. I ran next door and started throwing cans and bottles at her house. I was screaming and yelling at her to open the door or I'd break it down. I fully intended to; if I could have gotten my hands on her I *would* have killed her. I was so furious I couldn't control myself. Alice must have gotten scared because she called the police. They pulled up and asked what the problem was. So I told them. They asked me to please stop screaming and throwing things because I was disturbing the peace. Larry picked me up and carried me into the house but I broke away and ran right back outside again. I started yelling at the top of my lungs and throwing things at Alice's house again. I was so furious, I really lost it. The police finally got me to stop.

I went inside and I was just numb. I started yelling at Larry and hitting him. I couldn't believe he could do this to me. Alice was such a lowlife. The whole neighborhood knew about her. She was always picking up strange men and bringing them home. I don't know how many times she'd been married, and to add insult to injury she was also heavily into cocaine.

I felt terribly betrayed. I learned that Larry had told her a lot of personal information about me and about *us*. That probably hurt more than anything. I couldn't believe my own husband could betray me like that. That first night was horrible. We stayed up all night arguing. The next morning promptly at six, I went out and resumed banging on Alice's door. She called the police again. This time a woman officer came. She talked to me for a long time. I finally calmed down and went back into my house.

During that first WESOM meeting I spent most of my time talking to Dick, and Larry talked to Liz. I think the group devoted that whole meeting to us.

I can't say I was angry at Larry as much as I was hurt. I didn't know if I loved him or hated him. I was numb. I felt so used. I was the one who was always worried about our financial situation. I was the one who always shouldered all of the responsibility. I did it because I loved him and I wanted our marriage to work. I did what I had to do to support our family. Larry should have been helping me. But he wasn't. He was too busy fooling around with another woman.

That night, I talked to Liz for a little while and she told me I had to get rid of all my anger; killing Alice wasn't the answer. At the time, *I* sure thought it was. But Liz was right. I *had* to get rid of all the anger and hostility I had inside. I just didn't know how; WESOM showed me the way.

After the first meeting I knew we had to go back. Larry's affair had ripped apart my self-worth. My pride was badly damaged. At the meetings there were other women and couples who had gone through the same thing. They could relate to how I felt. They helped me to regain some of my self-esteem.

Larry and I kept going to the meetings and our relationship gradually improved. We talked about his affair a great deal, both privately and at the meetings. I learned how to deal with all the negative feelings that were eating at me.

At WESOM you're not alone. You can admit your flaws, your inadequacies, and not have anyone judge you. Going through the Steps is very personal, and sometimes difficult to do because you have to be honest with your spouse and honest about yourself. The Steps helped Larry to open up to me. For the first time in a long time he was honest with me about a lot of things. And I was honest with him. I learned to quit being so strong. I no longer have to carry the burden of all our problems alone. Larry is now much more responsible, financially and emotionally. I now feel like he's there for me when I need him.

We're friends now. We can talk about things and share things. It took me a long time to open up to Larry because he had violated the sacred trust I had given him by telling his mistress private things about me and about us. I'm learning to trust him again.

I stopped working overtime. I'm not going to worry about our financial situation. Larry and I will worry about it together. I don't want all the responsibility anymore. WESOM forced Larry to grow up emotionally. He really is a different person now.

We're working on our marriage. It's not perfect, but it's a lot better. There are still a lot of open wounds. My daughter was terribly hurt by this. She was in counseling for a while. She doesn't understand what happened or why her father was sleeping with Alice. She just knows it was wrong. When it first happened, my daughter would go into her bedroom and just lie on the bed and cry. It was difficult for her to make friends at school. She was a very lonely child. Alice's daughter had been her best friend. Everyone in the neighborhood and at school knows about the situation. Kids talk. It was very hard on her. But she's doing better. She loves her father, but she's very angry at him for hurting me.

I still worry about Larry getting AIDS. When he first told me, we both talked to an AIDS crisis center. I was terrified. Larry went for the test, but it's still on my mind. Something else for me to worry about.

The day I learned my husband had been unfaithful I thought it was the end of the world. I never would have believed we could get through that terrible time and come out of it with our marriage intact, let alone so good. WESOM got me through the worst time in my life. I don't think I would still be married to Larry if it weren't for WESOM.

A lot of people have said: "Oh, I would have divorced him." But then what would you have? Two people who still love each other, and a family torn apart. Larry made a mistake. I had to learn to forgive him because I do love him, and I do want this marriage to work.

At this very moment somewhere in the world some woman has just learned that her husband has been unfaithful. There are a lot of us out there who have thought we would die at that moment.

Before WESOM there was no one to help any of us get through all those horrible feelings. But now there is help. You don't have to go through the pain alone.

Larry and I have started a WESOM chapter in our area. If we help one couple save their marriage the way Dick and Liz helped us, then we'll consider ourselves lucky. WESOM is about bringing couples back together.

R OBERT   AND   F RAN

Robert and Fran are both in their early fifties. They have been married for more than thirty years and have three children.

Robert began drinking at an early age and over a period of years became an alcoholic. He readily admits he could never say no to a drink.

F RAN ' S   S TORY

For almost fifteen years Robert had a severe drinking problem. The whole time he denied he had a problem and resisted any effort of help. I joined Al-Anon to try to learn how to handle it. Al-Anon helped me learn to live with an alcoholic. Because of his drinking problem, Robert missed a lot of the kids' youth.

It took a long, long time, but finally Robert admitted he had a drinking problem. He decided to go into an alcoholic detoxification center. I was glad he was going to finally get help. You have no idea what it's like living with an alcoholic on a day-to-day basis. It's not a great way to live, but I did the best I could.

When Robert came out of the center he was still very distant from the family. He was living at home, but we knew something was wrong. The kids and I started doing things on our own, just trying to live our lives. This went on for almost three years. Robert wasn't drinking, but he was still depressed. I knew something was wrong, but I never suspected another woman.

One day I found a bottle of pills in the car with a woman's name on it. I asked Robert whose they were, and he claimed he didn't know. I didn't ask him if he was having an affair. I didn't think he would ever cheat on me, not after thirty-four years of marriage. I told my daughter about the pills and she said she thought maybe her father was involved with someone else. I never asked Robert about it, though. Almost a year later, someone Robert works with told me that some woman was calling Robert at work, but I still didn't ask him about it. I never thought he'd cheat on me.

We had made plans to take a cruise. One afternoon Robert talked to the travel agent, who is a friend of mine, and he mentioned that he really didn't want to go on this cruise. She couldn't understand why we were spending all this money on something Robert really didn't want to do.

I finally added things up and suspected that the reason he didn't want to go was that he did have another woman. I finally confronted him. I said: "I know why you don't want to go on the cruise. It's because of that other woman, the one whose pills I found in the car." I told him I knew all about it, when in fact I really didn't know anything.

He, of course, denied it. I insisted we go for counseling because something was obviously drastically wrong with our marriage. Robert wasn't drinking, but our marriage wasn't getting better. During the counseling sessions Robert lied to me and to the psychotherapist. He kept denying that he was seeing someone else. I didn't know what to do. We stayed in counseling for quite a while, but it didn't help at all.

Things between us kept getting worse, and Robert finally admitted he was having an affair. It had been going on for almost three years. Although I had suspected it, and in my heart I think I really knew it, the reality of the situation just totally destroyed me. It's very painful to live your life with an alcoholic, but that pain is nothing compared to what you feel when you learn your husband betrayed you with another woman. After so many years, and all we had been through, I couldn't believe he could do this to me. I didn't think he could hurt me any more, but I was wrong. I didn't know how to cope with all the things I was feeling.

It's a difficult feeling to describe and I still have trouble discussing it. It's still very painful. Robert and I have been married thirty-four years. I never, ever expected him to cheat on me. I trusted him implicitly. But he betrayed my trust. Learning about the affair was very hard, but dealing with the aftermath was incredible. I didn't know how to deal with it; I didn't know if I wanted a divorce or if I wanted him to stay. I didn't know what to do. My self-esteem and confidence were totally deflated.

I had read about Liz and WESOM and wrote her a letter. Liz called me and we talked for almost an hour. She invited me to a meeting, and both Robert and I went. I think Robert went only to pacify me. He's never really been very honest about things. I knew in WESOM you had to be honest with yourself, and with your spouse, if you wanted the marriage to work.

At WESOM I found other women who had been through the same

thing and felt the same way. Their experiences taught me how to handle my situation and feel better about myself. I learned how to use the Twelve Steps to make myself happy. I also learned I couldn't control Robert: not his drinking, his lying, or his cheating. Before I went to WESOM, I was so hurt and in so much pain that I didn't think I would survive. But after I started going to WESOM I knew *I would survive* even if my marriage didn't. I don't know what I would have done without WESOM. I stayed with Robert all those years because I loved him. I still love him, but I don't trust him and I don't know if I ever will. I still have a lot of pain to process through, but I'm working on it. Robert has really changed since we started attending WESOM. I think our marriage has a real chance to work now. I *want* the marriage to work. But if my marriage doesn't make it, I know *I will.*

R O B E R T ' S   S T O R Y

I never had just one beer, I had to get plastered. I graduated from beer to Jack Daniels. You know how it is, you go out with the guys for a few drinks after work, and the next thing you know it's too late to go home, at least without getting into a hassle. So you don't bother going home at all.

Fran and I always fought about my drinking. I'd get up in the morning and we'd have words about my not coming home on time the night before. She kept telling me I had an alcohol problem, but I denied it. I even went to a doctor but it didn't really help.

I was also physically abusive to Fran. I was in such a fit of depression for so many years that I didn't know what I was doing. But I finally realized I did have a drinking problem and needed help. I went into a detox program. I didn't understand any of it; they fed me the Twelve Steps of Alcoholics Anonymous, which I thought was just bullshit. I went through all the verbal mockery of the program, but I really didn't understand the Twelve Steps. When I was in the detox center everyone had to go to group therapy. I wasn't about to bare my soul to anyone, particularly strangers. I didn't think my personal problems were anyone's business.

After I was in the center for a while they let me out for a weekend pass. I went home and realized I couldn't wait to get back to the center. I guess it hurt Fran that I would rather be at the center than with her and the kids. I later found out it's quite normal for people who are let out on a pass to feel more comfortable at the center.

When the program was over, I went home to Fran and the kids. I wasn't drinking, but I still had problems with "dry drunks." Even though I wasn't drinking I was still the same ornery son of a bitch I'd always been.

Fran had started going to Al-Anon years before, and she and the kids had learned to kind of fend for themselves and do things on their own. When I came home it was like no one even cared about me. I didn't feel like I was part of the family.

Every morning I met the guys from work at a restaurant for coffee. They used to tease me a lot because I was no longer drinking. Well, this one waitress always used to wait on me. She'd save me a danish and always seemed to give me special attention. We got to talking and she told me she was in A.A., too. She asked me what meeting I went to, and I told her. She said it was the same one she was attending, but I'd never seen her there. That week I did. At first we just started going out for coffee. She had a pretty rough life. She was divorced with two kids and was on welfare.

I lied to her, too. I told her my wife had been killed in a car accident, and pretty soon we became more than just friends. As I became more involved with her, and her kids, I became less and less involved with my own family. I became her sugar daddy. I spent a lot of time at her house and gave her a lot of money. Over the course of our three-year affair I probably spent twenty thousand dollars on her and her kids.

I didn't feel I was part of my own family; they seemed to be doing fine without me. But I was part of *her* family, and I got pretty close to her children.

All this time, I really wasn't thinking about my wife, but about this other woman. I didn't like what I was doing, but I denied a lot of what I was feeling. It was easier than having to face it. Even though I wasn't drinking, I was still very depressed over my life. I suffered a lot of guilt.

When Fran finally confronted me about the other woman, I lied to her and denied it. She insisted we go for counseling, but I lied to the counselor, too. I have been a chronic liar my whole life. I lied to the other woman, and I lied to my wife. My whole life was a lie. The guilt gnaws at you. You're always wondering, When is she going to catch me? When is she going to find out? When is this going to end?

When I finally confessed, Fran took it very hard. I don't think I've ever seen her in such agony. I never thought I was capable of hurting anyone that badly. It was as if I had cut out her heart. I never realized what I had created. I never realized how an affair can devastate a wife and destroy a family.

I went to the WESOM meetings with her at first, but not for myself. I didn't think I needed the help, but she did. I thought this group could help her deal with what she was going through. But I was the one who really needed the help. I didn't even know it.

I couldn't lie or bullshit at WESOM. That was *real clear, real fast*. My whole life I had gotten away with lying, but not at those meetings. You can't, because every man there who has ever had an affair is just as big a liar as you are and one liar can spot another liar a mile away. At WESOM my old way of life wouldn't cut it. These guys had no hesitancy in calling me on things.

Going to WESOM not only changed my life, it saved my life. I was a drunk, a liar, and a cheat. I screwed up my whole life. I'm not very proud of it, but I did. I felt bad about the way I had treated Fran and the things I had done to her and the kids. I'd never been religious. I guess you could say I was a hypocrite. I had learned all about the Twelve Steps of A.A., but I just made a mockery of them. I never really put them into practice. I wasn't the type of guy to turn my will over to anyone. I didn't think I needed to.

When I started going to the WESOM meetings I listened to the other people, and I think I finally realized just how screwed up I was. There were times when I was so depressed I would fantasize about ending it all. That seemed to be the only way to end all the stuff going on inside me. When I started going to WESOM, I realized I could turn my life around if I wanted to. *But I had to want to.*

I had a lot to live for; I wanted to save my marriage and repair the damage I had inflicted on my wife and my family. In this program you have to open up and be honest with yourself and your wife. I finally had to take a good look at myself and I didn't like what I saw.

I knew I had to dump all the emotional crap I had inside me. All the other people in the group had been through the same thing, and had survived, so maybe there was hope for me. For the first time in my life I stopped lying. I made a real effort to turn my life around.

Even after we started going to the meetings, we continued going to therapy, but we'd come out of the therapy sessions feeling worse than when we went in. At WESOM we would come home from the meeting feeling hopeful. For the first time in my life I was being honest with Fran. I told her things I'd never even discussed with her before.

It was difficult for me to work the Steps, but I kept trying. I figured if all these other guys could do it and make it work to turn their lives and their marriages around, so could I. I wanted to be a better person and a better husband. It wasn't until I found WESOM that I finally knew I could be.

I finally told Fran *everything* about my affair. It was very difficult. But, like Liz says, "What you sow, you reap." I created the problem, now I had to deal with the shock waves. I had never been a humble person, but I became humble when I realized just how much I had hurt my wife and my children. The pain is so deep, and I feel such shame it's difficult even to talk about.

My children are deeply scarred, not just because of the affair but because of my drinking. I wish I could take back all those years I lost; I wish I could go back and make it up to them, but I can't. It's too late, they're all grown now. The time has passed. But what I'm trying to do now is make amends by showing them an improvement in my behavior.

At WESOM, for the first time I found other guys I could relate to. We're all liars and cheats. It's the same story, just different players and circumstances. By making a conscious effort to improve myself and actually working the Steps, I became spiritual for the first time in my life. I learned to tell the truth. You have to at WESOM or you'll never get any better, and neither will your marriage.

I would be nothing without Fran. She put up with a lot of crap for many, many years, but I think the final straw was my affair. I don't ever want to hurt her like that again. I love Fran now, more than ever before, and I think I've finally come to appreciate just what a wonderful person she is.

We're still working on our marriage. I think Fran loves me, but she doesn't trust me. I don't know if she'll ever be able to trust me again, but I'm trying to prove to her I am trustworthy.

You know, you hear about people "seeing the light." When I went to WESOM I *finally* saw the light, and it saved my life. People think a leopard can't change its spots, but I'm here to tell you, this leopard did. I'm not very proud of the person I was, but I'm trying to be proud of the person I'm learning to be. It's not easy.

For the first time in my life I feel as if I have a real chance at happiness. WESOM gave me that chance. Fran still says she doesn't know if our marriage will work out, but I do. I'm going to *make it work*. I'll do whatever is necessary to make sure it does. I've never wanted anything more. It took me a long time to get my life together. Now that I'm finally getting it together, I don't want to lose the most important person in the world to me, my wife.

Fran and I are very involved in WESOM. We haven't missed a meeting since this whole thing began. We've even been able to help another couple who had the same type of problem. They're coming to the meetings now, too. What's nice about the group is that everyone has gone through the same experiences, felt the same thing. Not everyone is at the same stage of recovery, though. There are some couples who are a few steps ahead of you, and some a few steps behind. The ones who are ahead of us hold out their hands and help us along, and the ones behind us, we hold out our hands to them to help them along. Everyone helps the others. We're all in this together, plugging along, trying to make our marriages work. So I'll keep trying. Hopefully Fran will keep trying, too. Maybe someday we'll have the kind of marriage we both want. We're not there yet, but slowly, day by day, we're making progress. The important thing is that Fran and I both want our marriage to work out. With the grace of God and WESOM, it will.

D ENNY AND L UCY

Denny and Lucy have been married for twenty-five years. They have three grown children, two girls and a boy. Four years ago, shortly after Denny turned forty-five, Lucy began noticing a change in his behavior. The couple was having financial difficulty, and Lucy attributed her husband's depression to midlife crisis.

L UCY ' S S TORY

One day Denny came home and announced he didn't want to be married anymore. He left that night, and the next day filed for divorce. I didn't have any idea at the time that he was seeing another woman. It really hadn't occurred to me. Denny was not the type of man you would expect to have an affair.

When he left so suddenly and unexpectedly I was shocked, but I didn't fall apart. I would not run after him or badger him. I refused to lower myself to chase after something that belonged to me. If he wanted a divorce, fine, I'd give him a divorce.

I met with my attorney and made arrangements to go through with the divorce. I knew Denny was emotionally ill; it was the only explanation for his bizarre behavior. It was as if his body had been taken over by some demonic force.

About this time I started hearing rumors that Denny was having an affair with a friend of his sister who had recently been divorced. This woman lived in the apartment upstairs from his sister, and people saw them together.

One night Denny called and asked me to go to dinner with him to talk. I assumed he wanted to talk about the divorce. I was very concerned about the financial arrangements. I wanted to make sure he agreed to pay at least half of the mortgage payment. That's all I wanted from him. We went to dinner and had a long talk. Denny said he didn't want a divorce. He wanted to come home. I asked him if he was seeing the other woman and he said no. He claimed his sister's friend was newly divorced and feeling down. Denny said she had been a friend of the family for so long she was like a sister to him.

I didn't know what to do. I really didn't want to let him come home because I still didn't know why he had left. We dated for about a week. Then I agreed to let him come home. He was home one night and then he told me it wasn't going to work. Denny left again.

He was gone for a few months this time. The kids and I adjusted but everything was really kind of a mess. It's very hard to have any kind of security when your life is up in the air.

This went on for almost four years. He kept moving in and out, still claiming he didn't know what he wanted, and that he wasn't involved with another woman.

He wasn't involved with one woman; he was involved with two. He *did* have an affair with his sister's friend. Had I known that for certain, I never would have let him come home the first time. I don't rate second place with anyone, especially my own husband.

The longest Denny was home during this period was a year and a half. The kids and I were always wary and on guard when he came home because we never knew if he would just up and leave us again. It was an extremely difficult period for the kids and me.

During one of Denny's moves back home he became friendly with the woman across the street. I, too, had been friendly with her, but once Denny moved back home, she suddenly stopped talking to me. It didn't take long for me to put two and two together. Denny was having an affair with her, too, although he continued to categorically deny it. He insisted I was imagining things and that I was going crazy. I was beginning to believe him. I really did feel as if I were the one going crazy. He was *making* me crazy.

One day Denny went to a football game and didn't come home for ten days. I finally called his parents to find out if he was there. He was. Denny's parents have always protected him. They tried to protect him even during all this craziness. They placed the blame squarely on my shoulders and tried to bad-mouth me to the rest of the family. They totally turned on me. It hurt very much because Denny and I had been married so long. I had been very close to his parents over the years, and I really didn't think I deserved to be treated like this. I hadn't done anything. It was their son who was acting like a lunatic.

I knew he was having an affair with the woman across the street. I didn't care how much he denied it or tried to tell me I was imagining things or going crazy. One night I got up and heard him on the basement phone. I knew he was talking to a woman just by his tone of voice, and what he was saying. I caught Denny red-handed on the phone with this woman and he stood there and lied *right to my face*. He made all kinds of lame excuses and kept insisting I had heard wrong and was misinterpreting everything. *Denny convinced me I was imagining things and going crazy.*

I couldn't take any more. That night I got dressed and left the house. I didn't go back for three days. I called the kids and told them where I was so they wouldn't worry. I just had to get away from Denny and his lies. I was so confused. He actually had me wondering if I was just imagining all these things or if I really was crazy. Denny's actions and behavior caused me to truly doubt my own sanity.

One of my neighbors is a police officer. I walked down to his house one day to see if he knew a private investigator I could hire. I had to know if Denny was really having an affair or if I was losing my mind.

It turned out that this couple had had problems with adultery in their marriage, too. They told me about WESOM and I went. The only reason I went was to find out if I *was* crazy. I sat there and told Liz everything that had happened.

She leaned over to me and said, "Lucy, you are not crazy, and you are not imagining things. Your husband *is* having an affair. That's why he's acting so crazy."

Hearing someone tell me I wasn't going crazy was such a tremendous relief I could have cried. I *hadn't* imagined all of this, as Denny kept insisting. He really *was* having an affair. The knowledge hurt deeply, but it was such a tremendous relief. *I wasn't going crazy.*

Going to WESOM was probably the best thing that ever happened to me. The people at WESOM were concerned about my marriage, but they were more concerned about *me*. My emotional health was totally shattered. It felt good to know someone cared about me. I felt ashamed and worthless because of what was happening in my life. My husband had actually driven me to the point where I believed I was losing my mind. Do you have any idea how frightening that is?

I really believe God directed me to WESOM. Although the Bible says, "When you marry two shall be as one," I knew when I started attending the meetings it was okay for me to live and go on with my life without this man if that's what I chose to do. God and I were a majority on this. I don't think I totally collapsed through all of this because I had such a strong faith in God. I've always been very religious and very spiritual, and it's the only thing that kept me going during those four awful years.

I kept attending the WESOM meetings. I learned how to cope with my situation by practicing the Twelve Steps. I finally reached the point where I knew I couldn't take this anymore. I was so sick of the whole situation that if someone had called me and told me Denny had been killed, I think I would have said: "Praise God." It would have been a relief.

Denny had filed for divorce twice, then changed his mind. I finally decided we should go through with it. I felt it was best. But Denny's attorney kept being evasive. Finally Denny called one day to talk to me. I kept hanging up on him. I had no desire to speak to him. He'd said all the things I ever cared to hear. But he kept calling and calling. He finally asked the kids if he could talk to me, but they had absolutely no use for their father.

The holidays were approaching and I didn't want to see Denny or talk to him. I didn't want our holidays ruined. For the first time in over four years I was feeling peaceful and I didn't want Denny to spoil things.

He came over Christmas Day to see the kids, even though they didn't want to see him. He left a letter for me, which I never opened. I just put it in the drawer and forgot about it.

That Christmas was probably the nicest holiday the kids and I had ever had. It was very peaceful, and we enjoyed it immensely. Denny kept calling, but I still refused to talk to him. I was finished with him, and I wanted him to know it.

One night the phone rang at midnight. The kids were in bed and I grabbed the receiver before it could wake them. It was Denny. He begged me not to hang up on him. He asked if I had read his letter. I told him no, but I would. I didn't want to talk to him so I hung up.

I went and got the letter and sat down and read it. Denny said he was very sorry for everything he had done. He said he didn't want a divorce, that he loved me and the kids and he wanted to come home. It really was a very sad letter, but it had absolutely no effect on me. I felt nothing. I read it, then put it back in the drawer. I didn't call Denny or accept his calls.

He finally got hold of the kids and asked if I had read the letter. They confirmed that I had. Very late one night the phone rang again. It was Denny. Once again he begged me not to hang up. He asked me if I would please give him a half hour of my life so he could talk to me. He promised that if I gave him the time he would never bother me again. I agreed.

I only agreed to see him because I wanted to be sure he would give me the house in the divorce petition. I was concerned because Denny had stopped making the mortgage payments. I wanted to be sure the kids and I were going to keep the house.

Denny sat and talked and I listened. We were in a restaurant, and he told me a lot, but he still held back. He admitted he had had an affair with his sister's friend. He also admitted he had had an affair with the woman across the street. His parents had known about it all along; in fact, they'd had the woman across the street over for dinner!

Denny told me a lot that night, but he was still holding back. I told him he had hurt me as much as he could, and that by telling me the truth he would finally release me. I was pretty angry and upset. I guess I made a bit of a scene in the restaurant, but I didn't care. I was so furious at him for what he had done to me and the kids.

He told me he didn't know what had happened to him, but he didn't want a divorce, he wanted to come home.

I refused, of course. I wasn't about to let him come home, not at that point anyway. I still kept going to WESOM because I needed the support of the other members. Dick and Liz both felt that Denny was ready to change his behavior. They felt he had finally come to his senses. I spent a great deal of time talking to Dick and Liz. They gave me a lot of guidance. I was very, very angry and I had a hard time dealing with all that anger. But Dick and Liz helped me.

Denny kept calling me, begging to let him come home. He swore he had changed, and he swore his affair with the other woman was over. He was very repentant for everything he had done, but I still wasn't sure. He had literally made me crazy for almost four years. Overnight the man I had been married to had turned into a stranger. By this point, I really didn't know who Denny was. I did know he was miserable, though.

After about a month of him begging to come home, I finally agreed to let him. I was willing to try, as long as he attended the WESOM meetings with me. He agreed.

My kids were absolutely livid that I let their father come home. Then they really thought I *was* crazy. My kids have been deeply scarred because of this. Their relationship with their father has been damaged and I don't think it can ever be repaired. When Denny first came home, my son stuck his fist in his father's face and said: "If you ever hurt my mother again, I'll kill you."

It was very hard for Denny to cope with the aftermath of his actions. He's never had to face anything in his life. His parents had always protected him from everything, including himself. Denny never had to face the consequences of anything he did—until now.

If he wanted to save our marriage, then he was going to have to grow up. He finally told me the whole truth—about everything. But as Liz always says: "No sin is to be covered. Every sin to be forgiven must be confessed."

The first year after Denny came home was a nightmare. I had flashbacks that were unbearable. I couldn't forgive him, I couldn't forget, and I couldn't justify taking him back. Liz Brzeczek was very inspirational in helping me deal with all of those negative feelings. She told me I had to get all of those feelings out in the open so that Denny and I could work them through. He kept going to the meetings with me, and I began to see a change in him, too. I don't think he ever realized just how much damage he had done to all of us until he started going to the WESOM meetings. I knew that my marriage could not be restored until I was healed. If the marriage is restored but the partners are not healed, the marriage will not work.

Denny's been home almost two years now. He *has* changed. He's really trying. I do believe he loves me. He just went nuts for four years. I still think it was midlife craziness. Whatever it was, thank God it's over.

Our marriage is working now, but we're both giving one hundred percent in an effort to make it work. Denny constantly reassures me of his love and his sorrow over what happened. I love him, but I don't know if I respect or trust him—yet. Liz assures me that all those feelings will eventually come back. We've made so much progress, I'm beginning to believe her.

I know one thing: I would *never* let it happen again. My life is too valuable to be treated like that. But I sincerely doubt it would ever happen again.

A lot of people were hurt over this. What my in-laws did to me was very difficult for me to handle. I knew that I had to talk to them and heal our relationship. I had to get rid of all the negative feelings I harbored toward them. I had to work Step Eight in order to find some peace for myself. One afternoon I went over and talked to Denny's mother. She admitted that what she had done was wrong and she apologized. She was very upset with Denny for what he had done, but because he was her son, she felt she had to take his side. I can understand that.

My relationship with my in-laws is healed, but their relationship with my children is completely and totally destroyed. The children have absolutely no use for their grandparents because of how they treated me during this whole affair. I can understand how the kids feel. I'm not happy about it but I can't force them to mend the relationship. Only they can do that. They're adults and make their own decisions. But I do feel sad about it.

My life is peaceful and happy now. Denny and I have a very good relationship. There has been some good to come out of all this. Before his affair, I loved him so much, I used to pray I'd die before he did because I didn't know if I could go on without him. Now, I still love him, but I know I can go on without him and make myself happy. I think I'm a much better and stronger person now. But so is Denny. He's changed and grown. He really listens to me now, and he's much more sensitive to my needs and desires. Through WESOM he learned how to be a better person and a better husband.

Our marriage isn't completely healed, but we're getting there. As long as we both keep trying, I can't help but be hopeful. I don't know what the future will bring, but whatever it is, I know I'll be able to handle it.

I have seen miracles happen at WESOM; marriages that appeared to have been shattered beyond repair have been repaired and saved. Other people have been able to heal themselves and go on with their lives, and then heal their marriages, and even have *happier* marriages.

I truly believe Liz Brzeczek had a special calling. There was a reason for all of Liz's pain, and that reason was WESOM. She has helped so very many, and in turn, those of us she has helped have been able to go on and help others. Without Liz Brzeczek I wouldn't have a marriage. Without Liz there wouldn't be a WESOM.

They say "God wounds the deepest the ones he intends to use the most." I believe God wounded Liz so deeply because He had a special purpose in mind for her. *I truly believe Liz Brzeczek was chosen.* Her own personal experiences and pain have been a healing tool for helping so many others. Liz has touched so many lives and so many marriages. She is loved by many, and is truly an inspiration to all of us because of her personal courage and her deep compassion. Liz Brzeczek is a truly remarkable woman.

E LLEN AND F RANK

Ellen is forty years old and has been married to Frank for thirteen years. They met in high school and dated for almost eleven years before they married. They have two children, ages nine and eleven.

E LLEN'S S TORY

My husband's family background was very troubled. His mother essentially committed suicide as a result of his father's adultery. After many, many years of marriage, my father-in-law left my mother-in-law for another woman. My mother-in-law went into such a deep depression over this that she gave up her will to live.

Shortly after my mother-in-law's death, my father-in-law became critically ill. His mistress insisted he marry her, or she would leave him alone to die, the same way he had left my mother-in-law. He married this woman just a few weeks before his death and she inherited everything.

My husband, Frank, had a difficult time after his mother's death. He never talked about it, but I knew he was having problems coming to terms with what had happened between his parents and to his mother. He never once confronted his father about what he had done, and I think it really bothered Frank. He turned all that anger on me, and our marriage began to suffer. Frank became very cold toward me. He started having trouble at work, and our entire life seemed up for grabs. We were always fighting and arguing. I tried to get him to open up and talk to me, but he refused. He claimed that nothing was wrong.

When his mother died, she left him a tavern. He kept his regular day job and worked at the tavern at night. One evening I called the tavern and was told he wasn't there. I got worried and went down there. I found him with another woman. From her clothes and her behavior, I thought she was a neighborhood prostitute.

Frank was furious that I had come down to check on him and insisted I go home. He didn't want a scene, and he didn't want me to embarrass him. He just wanted me to evaporate. When he came home that night, he never said a word about what had happened.

After this incident I took my children and started seeing a counselor. Frank wouldn't go, but I knew I had to. I was going mad. Frank was drinking very heavily, and our marriage was going right down the tubes.

About two weeks after the incident at the tavern, Frank came home one night, sat me and the kids down, and told us he was leaving us. He didn't want to be part of our life anymore and he didn't want us to be part of his. You can imagine how my children took this. Even though Frank left us, I never imagined he was emotionally involved with someone. But he was.

The woman I had thought was a prostitute was my husband's mistress. She had four small children and lived in a tiny apartment. My husband left his own wife and children to be with her and her children.

What Frank did totally destroyed me. Perhaps part of it was the way he did it. Before he left, he told me it was my fault that he was having an affair. He claimed I was worthless and not a good wife. He insisted I had never encouraged him or supported his ideas or opinions. He claimed I was fat, ugly, and a terrible lover, and that no other man would ever want or love me again.

His words, his actions, and his affair—I can't tell you the anguish I felt. Each word was like a knife stabbing my heart. I seriously contemplated suicide.

I couldn't understand how Frank could say those things, or leave everything and everyone in the world who loved him. How could he just walk away and give up everything?

When this happened, I was totally incapable of doing even the slightest little thing for myself. I was so emotionally shattered I couldn't even function on a day-to-day basis. I went into what I call my "robotic stage." I functioned, but if you ask me how I got through those days, or what I did, I couldn't tell you, because I don't know. I don't remember.

I saw something about Dick and Liz in the paper and went to a WESOM meeting. I knew I had to do something to help myself. I was still seeing the psychologist, but he would just say: "Take care of yourself." Those were empty words. He couldn't understand that at that point I was totally incapable of taking care of myself. I desperately needed help and support on a daily basis.

I truly believe God directed me to WESOM. If it weren't for the group, I think I would have tried to commit suicide. I just wanted to die to end the pain because I couldn't bear it any longer.

I was in very bad shape when I went to my first meeting. Dick took me aside and talked to me for a long time. Up until then, I never realized that my husband might be in pain, too. Dick confirmed my suspicions that my husband was emotionally ill and needed professional help. No man behaves like my husband was behaving if he's in full control of himself.

I can't tell you what going to the group did for me. The foundation of my whole life had collapsed. The group slowly helped me to build it back up again. I had to do it brick by brick. I was like an infant. I couldn't do a thing for myself. My life was dependent on all external stimuli. I received immediate major support from the group that allowed me to keep functioning. Without their support, I don't know what I would have done.

I found people in the group who understood exactly what I was going through. My husband took so much away from me; he even took away my humanity. But the group gave it back. I didn't even know who I was or what I was, but through the meetings I slowly learned all over again.

I kept attending the meetings every week, but during the week I spent a lot of time on the phone with the members, including Liz. It helped to know there was someone I could call when it got really rough. The phone became my lifeline. The people at WESOM were always there for me, and I finally felt as if I wasn't totally alone in this. It was very hard for me. But just knowing there was another human being I could call, someone who would understand exactly what I was feeling, made all the difference in the world.

Frank continued to see the children every week. They adore him in spite of what he has done. But my children are deeply scarred by this. They are terrified of losing their father's love, so they never question him or make him accountable for what he's done. When I took them to counseling, they adamantly refused to talk about their father. The kids are keeping everything buried inside and that's not good for them.

Any kind of stress is very difficult for the children. When their father drops them off after a visit, they stand by the window and watch and wave long after he's gone. Each time it's like an emotional rape. They go to their rooms close their doors and cry. Their emotions are totally confused. If they have to endure any kind of stress, they lash out at me, because they know if they lash out at their father they'll lose him totally. He'll walk out of their lives, and I don't think the kids could bear that.

During the first six months I'll admit I wasn't there emotionally for the kids. I think they suffered because of it. But I wasn't there emotionally for myself. I couldn't be. It was a horror for all of us.

A few months ago the kids came home after a visit with their father and they were both unusually quiet. I didn't want to press them because I know how emotionally unstable they are right now. A few days later something minor happened. They both started screaming. The three of us had a big fight, and we all ended up crying. The kids finally admitted that when they had been with their father over the weekend he had taken them to his mistress's house and introduced them to her and her children.

My kids were afraid to tell me, and afraid not to tell me. This kind of pressure is too much for these kids. They are only nine and eleven, and they are not equipped to deal with all the emotional and psychological garbage. When my husband introduced the kids to his mistress, it was like he stuck a sword in their chests and told them to sit there with it. My heart breaks for them, but I can't control their father or his behavior. I wish I could.

My husband stopped paying our bills and I had to go back to work full-time, but it gave me something to keep my mind occupied. A lot of people at work didn't know what was going on in my life, and I didn't tell anyone. There is a great deal of shame when your husband is involved with another woman. There are so many emotions you have to deal with, you would have to be superhuman to be able to handle it all.

Thank God I had Dick, Liz, and WESOM. They got me through the roughest days and nights. I felt as if I had people who truly cared about me. I was still having a hard time coping, but knowing they were there helped a lot.

My life and my marriage were in limbo. I didn't want to divorce Frank because I felt he was truly emotionally ill. But something happened that really forced my hand. One day my daughter said to me: "Mom, what do you care what Daddy does as long as he pays our bills?" I was shocked that she would even say such a thing. I realized my husband's behavior was totally corrupting the morals and values of our children. I knew then I had to divorce him. It was time to let go. I had no other choice.

I decided to file for divorce. My attorney called and told me the papers were ready and I should come down to his office to sign them. When he handed me the papers I couldn't read them because tears blurred my vision. I had the pen in my hand, but I just couldn't sign the papers.

I suddenly felt a cold chill. I felt a hand on my shoulder, and I heard my late mother-in-law's voice whispering in my ear: *"I had to die to emancipate myself from the pain your father-in-law inflicted on me. All you have to do is sign those papers."*

I signed the papers that day. As far as I know my husband is still living with his mistress. I really don't know. Now, I'm just concerned with getting through each day, one day at a time. As for the children, they need intensive therapy. This has been a terribly traumatic experience for them. They're so young, and so confused. I found a counselor who specializes in young children and they'll start therapy soon. I'm hoping it will help heal them emotionally.

As for me, I'm still attending WESOM every week. Day by day I'm growing stronger. I have much more confidence in myself now. I've learned to be my own best friend. I've also learned to like myself. I'm trying very hard to be the best human being I can be. I'm also trying to be the best mother I can be. These kids didn't ask to be born, nor did they ask for all this pain. They shouldn't have to suffer because of their father.

Going to WESOM has almost been a rebirth for me. I feel as if I've cleansed myself. The meetings give me the energy to go on day by day. As for the future, I only know I can take it one day at a time. But for now, that's enough. It's a lot better than it was. I've learned that the only thing I can count on is myself. Some of the wounds are slowly healing. But it hasn't been easy. I live my life by the Twelve Steps of WESOM, and it's given me new hope.

At one time I loved Frank very much, but now it's almost like the man I knew and loved is brain-dead. I know he's ill and I hope he will get help.

I know now I'm going to make it. I'm going to survive. For a long, long time I didn't think I would. But with the grace of God and the strength and support I've received from WESOM, *I know I will survive.*

Ellen's divorce from Frank will be final in a few months. She still continues to attend WESOM meetings every week, and her children have now begun therapy.

All of the stories told have been cases of *male* infidelity, with the exception of Larry, whose first wife was unfaithful and whose first marriage ended in divorce. At the present time there have been no couples in WESOM where it has been the wife who has been unfaithful, although Liz has talked to numerous couples in this situation.

When a wife has an affair, her husband is reluctant to discuss it or even admit it to anyone. That is not to say that men hurt any less when they are the offended spouses; only that they are much more inclined to keep their feelings to themselves. In instances where a wife has been unfaithful, most marriages end in divorce. This again is not because a husband is unwilling to be forgiving, but more because it's difficult for men to ask for help in dealing with their wives' infidelity.

Men and women who are the offended parties appear to view adultery through different eyes. For a man, the most painful part of infidelity is the physical act, the knowledge that his wife has made love with another man.

For a woman, the most painful part is the emotional betrayal, not the physical act. While men tend to be devastated more by the physical aspects of an affair, a woman has a tendency to be more devastated by the emotional betrayal.

When a wife has an affair, she is generally not looking for sex, but for something emotional that's missing in her marriage: romance, intimacy, or perhaps tenderness. The physical act is usually secondary.

When a husband has an affair, generally it's the physical aspect that is enticing at first, then the emotional aspect comes into play.

Chapter Sixteen

Hell Hath No Fury

WESOM blossomed and so did Liz. She continued to receive calls and letters from distraught individuals and couples who had heard either about her and Dick or about WESOM. She faithfully answered each inquiry and followed up with anyone who contacted her. Week by week WESOM grew. Liz and Dick finally began to see something positive come out of their experience.

They also discovered an unexpected bonus. Dick and Liz found that WESOM was actually helping their own marriage.

"We received as much as we gave," Liz said. "Our marriage still wasn't perfect. But I wasn't looking for perfection, just progress. Until we actually started WESOM, Dick never really practiced the Twelve Steps. Once he saw other people living their lives by the Steps, he realized they *did* work. When Dick finally accepted the premise, our marriage really improved. I saw a tremendous difference in him and his attitude toward life and toward me. I also began to see an inner peace in Dick that I don't think I'd ever seen before. He really was a different person, a person I loved very much."

The Brzeczeks finally seemed to have their life back on the right track. Dick and Liz had made real progress in their marriage. Each day brought them closer than before. The past was forgiven and they were grateful to have a second chance with each other. Their children were healing, too. The kids had finally accepted and forgiven their father. Once again the Brzeczeks were a family. The future looked brighter than it had for years.

But the black cloud that had been hovering over Dick and Liz erupted one March afternoon shortly after they founded WESOM. Dick was driving home from court when his secretary called him on his car phone.

"My secretary was pretty upset. There was a contingent of press outside my office: reporters, cameramen, television crews. I guess they were waiting for me. My secretary had no idea what was going on, and neither did I. I'd been out of the public eye for almost a year, so I couldn't imagine why I rated such publicity. I called my attorney from the car, and he informed me that I'd been indicted that morning by the grand jury on twenty-three counts of theft and official misconduct pertaining to my handling of the police contingency fund while I was police superintendent. The total amount of money involved was twelve hundred and thirty-one dollars. The state had one star witness against me—Diane, my former mistress."

During Dick's tenure as police superintendent he was in direct control of a budget of over $400 million. While he was superintendent, Dick's travel expenses were handled in one of two ways: if he traveled on police business, the department paid all of his expenses. If Dick traveled to teach a seminar or appear on a television show, his expenses would be paid by the firm or station that had requested his appearance. Generally they did not pay in advance, so the police department would issue a check to Dick to cover his expenses. Then Dick, in turn, would reimburse the department once he had received payment.

During the course of the investigation into Dick's handling of the police contingency fund, the state's attorney's office found two checks totaling $1,231 that could not be reconciled. Part of that—$931—was for expenses related to a trip Dick took to San Diego in August 1982. The balance of $301 was for a trip to Minneapolis in December 1982.

As soon as Dick learned of the indictment, his first thought was of Liz. She was working at home, and he wanted to call and tell her before she heard it on the news.

"I called Liz from the car," Dick remembered. "She was pretty upset. I told her about the press in front of the office, but she insisted on coming down to be with me."

When Dick arrived at his office, he was mobbed by reporters, but he refused to issue a statement. Liz arrived a few moments later.

"It was a horrible scene," she recalled. "I literally had to push my way through all these people to get to the door. The reporters were yelling questions and shoving microphones in my face. I couldn't believe it. I finally got into the office, slammed the door shut, and fell into Dick's arms."

Dick and Liz went into the back of the office so they could have some privacy away from the eyes of the press. They just held each other, unable to believe what had happened. Liz was very concerned about Dick and how he would react to the indictment.

"I knew something like this could send him back into a tailspin, and my first concern was him," Liz said. "But Dick seemed to be handling it fine. *I* was the one who was really upset. I couldn't believe this was happening. It was like the nightmare was starting all over again. I couldn't believe they had indicted Dick.

"My husband is not a crook. For the state's attorney's office to indict him on the strength of Diane's testimony made me absolutely livid. I couldn't believe it. This woman had shattered our lives once, and now, through the government, she was about to do it again."

Dick seemed to take the indictment in stride. "I wasn't really upset about it, because I knew I was innocent. I never touched a penny of the police department's money, *not a penny*. I knew the state didn't have a case, particularly if Diane was their star witness."

Dick and Liz weren't the only ones who were shocked by the indictment. Dick and Liz's children and family were stunned.

Kevin, the Brzeczeks' youngest son, remembers how he felt:

"It was horrible. Our lives had just returned to normal and then this happened. All the stuff about my dad and the affair was in all of the papers again. It was very difficult for me. I was beginning to think it would never, ever end. Every time we thought things were back to normal, something else happened.

"I was a senior in high school when my father was indicted. It was the same old stuff all over again. I could just imagine what people were saying. I'll admit at first I was kind of angry at my dad. If he hadn't had an affair, none of this would have happened in the first place. But I kept my feelings inside me until one day I sat down and talked to my father. I was really afraid he was going to go to jail. We had just mended our family and now we had something else hanging over us. After I expressed my fears to my dad, he told me not to worry because he *wasn't* going to be found guilty. He assured me he wouldn't lose his law license, nor would he have to go to prison. We talked for a long time, and my dad made me feel much better about everything. Our relationship had healed enough so that I felt very comfortable talking to him about my feelings. We were finally beginning to be close again."

Joe and Rita were equally upset. "In my opinion, the only reason Dick was indicted was to teach him a lesson," Joe said. "He'd had the audacity to run against Richie Daley and now they were going to make him pay. I think they were scared and wanted to make sure Dick would never again be a political threat. This was a good way to ensure that he wouldn't be."

The Brzeczeks' families weren't the only ones who were upset by the indictment. Judges, lawyers, and other law enforcement officials came to Dick's defense, openly expressing outrage at the indictment.

Because of Dick's past political position and reputation, his indictment made news around the country, but particularly in Chicago, where the press had a field day rehashing the whole story of Dick's dramatic fall from grace and the reasons for it.

"The whole mess about Dick's affair was dragged out in the open again," Liz remembered. "The media printed every single juicy tidbit, from his hospitalization to the loss of the election to my divorce action, and of course all the information they had about Diane. The fact that she was testifying against Dick for the state just added to the luridness of the situation.

"It was a nightmare that only served to open up a lot of old wounds. The week the indictment came down I went to the WESOM meeting and just talked and cried. I had to get all of these feelings out. It was like the nightmare was starting all over again. I was so grateful for the group; the last time my world had collapsed I had no one to talk to, no place to express my feelings. Now, I did. I was now leaning on the group for emotional support. The indictment blew away all the security I had worked so hard to achieve. It wasn't just my marriage that was in jeopardy this time, but my husband and my family as well. Dick could go to prison for something like this!

"I just kept thinking: 'How could this happen again?' We had worked so hard to put our lives and our marriage back together. I just couldn't believe it was happening. It just didn't seem fair, not to me, not to Dick, and not to the kids.

"The support Dick and I received from everyone in the group was incredible. They just rallied around us. I don't know what we would have done without them. They were a tower of strength for us during this whole miserable mess."

Dr. Fawcett had read about Dick's problems and immediately called Liz.

"I was deeply concerned about Dick's emotional health because of his current problems," Dr. Fawcett said. "I asked Liz to please bring Dick in to see me. When they arrived, I was more than a bit surprised at Dick's reaction. He was totally calm about the whole thing. In fact, he was reassuring *me* that there was nothing to worry about. He said he was going to beat this thing and then go on with his life. From his confident demeanor, I couldn't help but believe him. He really didn't seem in the least bit disturbed about the whole thing.

"Dick went on to ask if it was all right if he went off his medication. I told him quite bluntly that due to the current crisis he was facing, I didn't think this was the proper time for him to discontinue his medication. Dick finally agreed, a bit reluctantly. Before Dick and Liz left my office, I had Liz promise me that if Dick suffered any emotional problems whatsoever, she was to call me immediately."

Dick seemed to be handling the crisis very well. "I knew I was innocent," he explained. "I never had a moment's doubt that I would be found not guilty. I may have cheated on my wife, but that was my only crime. I just tried to go about my business and ignore the whole thing. I had learned my lesson. For the first time in a long time I had finally found some peace, and I wasn't about to let anyone or anything disrupt me or my emotional health. I'd worked too hard to get it back to let anything destroy it."

Two weeks after Dick was indicted, he was arraigned before the chief judge of the criminal court. He was booked and fingerprinted. He also had to pose for a mug shot. Dick's bond was set at five thousand dollars, but he was released on his own recognizance. However, Dick did have to give his attorney a retainer of fifteen thousand dollars. It was money the couple could ill afford to spend.

"Our savings were depleted," Dick recalled. "I was making good money, but every penny went back into trying to build up my practice and pay off all our medical expenses. I didn't know how we were going to pay all the legal expenses I would incur trying to mount a proper defense, but I was certain we'd manage. Liz and I hadn't come this far only to be beaten back down again. As long as I had my health and my family, I was certain everything would turn out all right."

Liz went with Dick to the arraignment. Bill Hanhardt and Dick's brother-in-law Joe sat with her in court. Liz recalled: "I had to sit behind a Plexiglas partition while I watched Dick being led away through a side door. I never expected them to treat him like a criminal, but they did. I started crying. After all we had been through, I couldn't believe this was happening to us again. The press covered Dick's arraignment, and I think I was more upset about the mass media coverage than Dick. Reporters mobbed us going in and coming out, asking all kinds of questions about Diane, our marriage, and the indictment. They kept shoving cameras and microphones in our faces. It was horrible.

"It took about forty-five minutes for the arraignment. Then Dick was released and we left. We all went to breakfast, and then I went back to Dick's office. We had decided to carry on as normally as possible. In fact, Dick had to return to court that afternoon on a case he was representing. It was kind of ironic.

"Although Dick seemed to be taking the whole thing in stride, I was very worried about him. He appeared very calm and totally unruffled by the whole thing. The trial date was almost a year away and I knew it was going to be a very long year for all of us.

"Even though Dick kept assuring me that he would be found not guilty, I was still worried. If he *was* found guilty, he would lose his law license and probably end up going to jail. I couldn't bear the thought, not after what we'd just gone through. I couldn't bear the thought of losing Dick again."

Dick and his attorney immediately set about preparing his defense. They hired a private investigator who specialized in financial investigations. Dick's attorney repeatedly tried to have Diane's attorney produce her for a deposition, but her attorney repeatedly put them off.

"Finally, a couple of months before the trial, Diane's attorney advised us she would be in Chicago for a two-hour layover," Dick remembered. "My attorney went out to the airport to interview her. He spent two to three hours interviewing Diane. After talking with her at length about the case, he assured me that everything was going to be fine. She told him she was quite concerned about me, Liz, and the children as well as the indictment. My attorney assured me we would have no problems with her testimony in court."

But there *were* problems. When Dick's attorney interviewed Diane, he did not take a court reporter, an investigator, or any witnesses with him to corroborate her story. It proved to be just one of many problems in the case.

Dick and Liz somehow managed to get through the year until the trial. They tried to go on with their lives as normally as possible. Despite the rash of new publicity, Liz handled herself well in public. She held her head high and carried on with her life despite the lurid details rehashed over and over in the press. Dick continued building his practice and Liz continued building WESOM. They took Liz's parents to Las Vegas for their golden wedding anniversary, and then Dick and Liz spent the Christmas holidays at their condominium in Cancún, Mexico.

The couple continued to attend WESOM meetings every week and continued practicing the Twelve Steps. Dick and Liz were happy now and determined that nothing would ever tear them apart again. Dick and Liz trusted in God and were determined to follow His lead.

As the date of the trial drew closer, Dick's attorney expressed concern about Liz appearing in court. He felt that because of Diane's testimony and the sensational nature of the trial, Liz might break down in court and perhaps hinder their case. Dick's attorney suggested that Liz take a trip during the trial. But Liz had absolutely no intention of being anywhere but by her husband's side.

"I had stood by Dick through thick and thin, and I wasn't about to abandon him now," Liz said. "It was very important to me that people realize we were united, that we had weathered all of this adversity and still managed to repair our marriage. This woman ruined our lives once, and I wasn't about to let her do it again. The last time, her presence tore Dick and me apart. But this time, it just brought us closer together."

Liz had no doubt that she would be able to keep a handle on her emotions during the trial. But four days *before* the trial, Liz fell apart.

"I don't know if it was a delayed reaction, or just the stress of the whole thing, but I woke up one morning and started crying. I just couldn't stop. I was hysterical to the point that I feared I was having a breakdown. For four days and nights I just lay in bed and cried. The enormity of the situation finally hit me. I was just beside myself. I prayed a lot during that time. I couldn't understand why God was doing this to us again.

"I had so much on my mind, I couldn't even think straight. I was deeply concerned about the attorney representing Dick. I thought he had lulled Dick into a false sense of security about the trial, and about Diane's testimony. I also had some concern that Diane was going to get on the stand and publicly reveal all the lurid details of her affair with Dick. I didn't know if I would be able to stand that."

For four days and nights Liz couldn't stop crying. But on the morning of the first day of the trial, Liz woke up totally calm. "I felt such a deep inner peace. All my fear had subsided, and I just knew everything was going to be all right." Ironically, the trial lasted four days. Liz felt God had given her those four days *before* the trial to fall apart, so that she could be calm and serene during the four days *of* the trial.

Dick was brought to trial amid a blaze of publicity; his story had all the ingredients necessary to keep it in the public eye: sex, politics, scandal, and corruption.

When the trial began, Dick's attorney was the only one allowed to sit at the defense table. Liz had to sit behind Dick, but she wasn't alone. Bill Hanhardt, Russ DiTusa, Don De Franza, and Dick's sister Rita and her husband, Joe, as well as many members of WESOM, sat nearby.

"I was glad the members came. It gave me a great deal of strength during a very stressful time. There were a lot of female reporters in the courtroom who watched me very carefully during Diane's testimony. Every time she would answer a question, it was as if all eyes turned to me to see my reaction. I never lost my cool or showed any emotion the whole time Diane testified. I knew I had to be strong in order to support Dick, but he was a tower of strength for me. It was important to me to show the world that Dick had my entire love and support."

The state called their first two witnesses, both employees of the police department's financial division. Both witnesses had admitted altering official police department financial records. They had been given immunity from prosecution in order to testify against Dick.

After their testimony, a police department investigator was called. Then it was Diane's turn. When she arrived, the state ushered her in and out the back door in order to avoid the reporters. No pictures were allowed to be taken of her, nor were interviews permitted. The prosecutors asked for a recess in order to confer with Diane before she testified. They talked to her for several hours before Diane finally took the stand.

Once on the stand, Diane alleged that Dick had no official business on the dates in question or at the places in question, and that the sole purpose of those trips was to see her. Her testimony on the stand was in direct contrast to statements she had made to a police investigator, and totally opposite of what Dick's attorney said she had told him.

When Dick's attorney cross-examined her, he could not submit into evidence any of Diane's statements made to him during their initial interview because he had questioned her alone, with no court reporter or other witnesses, and had no one to corroborate what she had said at that time. Dick's attorney could not take the stand himself to enter into evidence her original statements to him because a lawyer cannot serve as an attorney and a witness in the same case at the same time.

When the trial broke for lunch, reporters mobbed Liz as she left the courtroom, wanting to get her reaction to Diane's testimony. She remained calm, and simply assured them of Dick's innocence.

Inside, Liz was seething at the way Dick's attorney had handled Diane. In her opinion, he was very gentle in his cross-examination and had never really tried to pin Diane down on replies that Dick and Liz knew weren't truthful.

When the trial ended for the day, Dick and Liz went home. By now Dick too was seething inside. "I was absolutely furious," he said. "She sat there and lied right on the stand. She told the court that I never used her car and I never rented a car. So how did I get around when I was in Minneapolis?

"It took me about twelve hours to finally calm down that night. I called my attorney at midnight because I was so furious with him because of the way he had handled Diane. He was behaving like he was *her* attorney, not mine."

After Diane's testimony, the state rested its case.

Diane had impeached herself under oath by admitting to the court that the initial statements she had made to the state's attorney's office when she was originally questioned had inaccuracies in them. (These statements were made three weeks after Dick broke off his affair with Diane.) She also admitted that she had been confused and in "quite an emotional state of mind" at the time she had given her statement. The morning of the trial, when she had been ushered into a room by the state's attorney's office, she also admitted to reviewing the notes that had been taken during her initial interview with the state's attorney's office.

Dick's attorney called only one witness in his defense: the police department investigator who was an adverse witness, but nevertheless testified, and helped prove Dick's innocence. On Wednesday afternoon Dick's attorney rested his defense. Dick never had to take the stand.

That Wednesday evening, Dick and Liz went to the WESOM meeting.

"It was our place to go," Liz said. "We needed to be there. We had no idea what was going to happen the next morning when the judge issued his decision. We needed the strength and love of the members. They had supported us tremendously during the entire year of this ordeal; they had been with us every step of the way. It seemed only right that we spend that evening with them."

The next morning, May 14, 1987, Judge Robert V. Boharic found Dick Brzeczek not guilty on all counts.

The courtroom erupted as Dick and Liz fell into each other's arms in relief. Reporters swarmed around them as they tried to push their way out of the courtroom.

It had been just seven short years since Dick's appointment as police superintendent. But to Dick and Liz Brzeczek it seemed like a lifetime. Finally, their long nightmare was truly over.

Chapter Seventeen

Dick's Story: Part 6

I guess I shouldn't have been surprised when I was indicted, but I was. In order to understand, you have to know a little about Chicago politics and the police department and how they work.

During my years with the department, before I became superintendent I served under four different acting or permanent superintendents, including O. W. Wilson, the California criminologist who was brought in to clean up the department and its rather blemished reputation. Wilson did clean up the department—for a while. After Wilson departed, though, the superintendent of police was once again thought of as just a puppet of whoever was mayor.

When I was appointed superintendent, one of the first things I told Jane Byrne was that I was going to run the department my way and on my own, or I wouldn't accept the position. She agreed.

After I resigned, Mayor Harold Washington appointed Fred Rice as the new superintendent. Rice's allegiance to Washington was obvious. (Fred Rice retired as superintendent in 1987. But shortly after he retired he publicly admitted that during his testimony in another trial in connection with a lawsuit involving the Chicago Police Department he had given false testimony in a deposition. But no action or indictment was ever sought against him.)

Considering *my* prior relationship with Washington, I should have expected the investigation by Rice and the police department and the subsequent indictment by the state's attorney's office.

There are some very interesting facts about my indictment that were never really brought out. First, after the police department took its case to the United States Attorney's Office, they declined to prosecute or indict me based on the evidence. Then, the department took its evidence to the first assistant state's attorney, who also refused to prosecute or indict. That should have been the end of it, but it wasn't.

Shortly after this happened, the first assistant state's attorney resigned and Mike Angarola was appointed. Angarola decided to reopen my case and indict me based on Diane's statements to the grand jury—statements that she made on February 5, 1985, three weeks after I had broken off our relationship. I'd hardly say she was an impartial witness.

Another thing I thought was quite unusual: on one of the dates in question on the indictment, the day I was supposed to have been in Minneapolis, the Minneapolis airport was shut down because of a snow storm.

During the fourteen months between my indictment and my trial, we tried to mount a proper defense, but we kept running into roadblocks with the state's attorney's office. At one point, we appeared before the judge in his chambers because the state refused to turn over the twenty-seven cartons of personal financial records they had subpoenaed. We needed those documents for our defense.

The judge had some pretty harsh words for the state at that time. He wasn't very happy about the state's tactics and the way things were proceeding. The judge accused the state of dragging its feet, and of non-compliance with his order. He had ordered the state to turn the financial materials over to my attorney, but they did not comply with his order. In chambers the judge went on to say that "there is a *real question of selective prosecution, vendetta, et cetera*' regarding the state's case against Mr. Brzeczek."[1]

Regarding some newspaper clippings, the judge also stated that "there's a very clear pattern of disclosure to the press on the part of the Chicago Police Department and/or the state's attorney's office. There's no way in the world that that material could have been—the defense sure didn't put it in the paper during the '84 election, where Brzeczek was running against Richard Daley. That's for sure. We know that didn't happen.

"It's clear from that, that during 1984—either the state or the Chicago Police Department was plainly trying to destroy the political career of Mr. Brzeczek, plainly. There's no question about it. Just go through those . . . newspapers and use common sense. They were collecting them at the time. So I admonish both sides. I want you to sit down, gentlemen, and draft a protective order concerning the materials, and I also want compliance with the subpoena to the extent that I have ordered it.

"Now, it has not been complied with. It has not been complied with, and I'm prepared to take drastic—and I repeat the word, drastic steps on this case if I don't think that this subpoena has been complied with and there's been a violation of due process. If I conclude that, gentlemen, I'll tell you the third time. I'm prepared to take drastic steps concerning the prosecution."

The judge went on to state: "I don't know how strongly I can emphasize this: that I don't appreciate being trifled with by the Chicago Police Department or by the prosecution or by anyone else in this matter. We're talking here about a former superintendent that you charged with a felony case; a person who is an attorney, a person whose whole life is at stake here, a person you might ask me to send to the penitentiary, and if I can't get out of the prosecution and/or the police department simple compliance with a subpoena, there will be drastic steps that will be taken by this court.

"You tell those people at the Chicago Police Department, and in the mayor's office, and anybody else that's involved in this, that I'm not playing games with respect to this case, and there might be somebody going to jail if I think they're obstructing the subpoenas of this court. I'm putting it in the simplest terms that I can, and I think there has been dragging of the feet and nondisclosure here. That's apparent."

It was clear that the state was trying to hide exculpatory evidence, but the state wasn't the only problem we had trying to mount a proper defense. Diane had hired an attorney in Chicago to represent her. We tried repeatedly to get him to produce her so we could interview her, but he kept stalling. Finally, two months before the trial, my attorney went out to the airport and took a statement from her—a statement that would no way have led to my indictment.

Although my attorneys assured me we would have no problems with the case, Liz was still very worried. I know it had to be hard on her, having to come face to face with my mistress in front of a courtroom full of people and reporters, but she handled herself wonderfully. I don't think I was ever prouder of her.

Diane did what I expected; what she testified to in court was totally different from what my attorney said she told him, and was different from her initial statements to the investigators. The day she testified I was absolutely furious. My lawyer should have taken a court reporter with him to the airport so her statements to him could have been introduced into evidence. But he didn't. Diane impeached herself on the stand, anyway.

A lot of people, myself included, think Richie Daley indicted me just to make sure I would never be a political threat to him again. What he didn't know was that I had no intention of ever entering the political arena again. All he proved by bringing me to trial was that I had cheated on my wife. The state spent almost four million dollars investigating me and prosecuting me just to prove I had cheated on my wife. Seems like a waste of money, considering that they didn't tell my wife, or the world, anything they didn't already know. My own legal fees were over thirty-five thousand dollars.

Looking back at my whole situation now, you can see how having an affair can have far-reaching implications that can last for a long time. You can never anticipate how something's going to turn out; I never imagined when I began my affair with Diane that one day she would be testifying against me in a case that could not only have had me disbarred but sent to prison.

The day I was acquitted was probably the second happiest day of my life; the first was when Liz agreed to give our marriage another chance. I allowed myself a few moments of absolute fury to blast Richie Daley in the media. I couldn't help it; I was livid. What the hell did he prove? Nothing, except that I had been unfaithful. Hell, he didn't need a trial to do that.

When the trial was finally over, I felt like I was free for the first time in years. Liz and I no longer had any part of our past clouding our future. We could finally go forward without any threats hanging over us and build our life together.

A lot of people are probably wondering why on earth I would ever openly admit everything that happened to me. Why not? I did it, I admit it, and now it's time to go forward. One of the first things I did after the trial was call Dr. Fawcett. He agreed to let me go off all medication. I think that's when I knew I was finally well. This thing had been one hell of a long nightmare for both Liz and me.

I made a mistake that hurt a lot of people I love, but I think I've paid for it. Am I sorry for what happened? Absolutely. Would I do it again? Never in a million years. Not many people can screw up as badly as I did and get a second chance, but I did.

I've learned a lot from this experience. I learned I'm not invincible, and I don't always have to be in control. I also learned that Liz has a strength I never thought she had. She also has a deep faith, not just in me but in herself and in God. Without her, we wouldn't have a marriage or a future today, nor would there be a WESOM.

I was lucky, very lucky. Not only did my wife forgive me, but my kids did too. I'm probably closer to my kids now than I ever was before. Although this experience tore us apart, when we came together again it was with a new appreciation for one another. I'm very proud of all my children; they all turned out wonderful despite the problems they had to deal with. I'm also very proud of my wife.

Liz and I are totally devoted to WESOM. Adultery is a societal disease. It's estimated that one out of two marriages are touched by adultery. That's a high percentage. We know there are other marriages and other people who are hurting. Maybe we can use our pain, and our experience, to help someone else. I've caused so much pain for so many people. Maybe this is my way of erasing some.

With God's help, Liz and I intend to see to it that as long as there are people hurting from adultery, there will be a WESOM.

Chapter Eighteen

Second Time Around

Dick's trial and subsequent acquittal had been picked up by a national cable news show; the fact that his former mistress testified against him made headlines around the country.

After they left court, Dick and Liz agreed to grant an interview to a local television station. Although the station was interested in the couple's reaction to the trial and Dick's subsequent acquittal, they were more interested in how Dick and Liz had repaired their marriage, particularly under the glare of public speculation and humiliation they had had to endure.

The couple openly discussed Dick's affair and the harm it had done to their lives and Dick's career. They also went on to explain *how* they had repaired their marriage and then had gone on to form WESOM. It was really the first time a politician had ever openly discussed a very personal tragedy.

After the interview aired, Liz was overwhelmed with letters and calls requesting information about WESOM. Her story was so unusual, she began receiving numerous requests to appear on television shows to tell her story and the story of WESOM.

The story about WESOM was picked up by the national wire services and there was a tremendous amount of interest in the couple and their unique support group.

One of the networks contacted Liz with a request that she appear on a special they were preparing about adultery and political wives. Liz agreed to appear. When the show aired, Liz was featured along with stories on Lee Hart and Jackie Kennedy.

Liz began to receive calls from women all over the country.

"One woman called me from Texas. When I told her that the only chapter of WESOM was in Chicago, she said she was coming in for the meeting. She drove up and attended the meeting. I talked to her at length and tried to help her as much as possible during the short time we had together. She was very impressed with the group and promised to go home and start a WESOM chapter in Texas.

"I guess that says a lot about what a person goes through during this type of crisis and how little help is really available. Do you know how much pain a person has to be in to drive nearly across the country to have someone to talk to about her problem? She was just one of hundreds of women I talked to."

There was suddenly a great deal of national interest in WESOM. Dick and Liz received a request to appear on *Donahue*. They agreed, if only to give more information about WESOM.

"The audience was very hostile, particularly the women," Liz recalled. "One woman got up and said that if Dick were her husband she would have shot him. You know, I would have said that at one time, too. But unless you're put in the situation, you really don't know how you're going to react. No one chooses to become the offended party; it just happens, and you have to deal with it in the way that's best for you. For me, staying married to Dick was the best thing.

"It's easy to get divorced, but it's tough to stay married after something as devastating as adultery. I chose to stay married because in spite of everything I loved Dick. I felt it was the right thing for *me*.

"To say you wouldn't do this, or wouldn't do that, is really unfair. You're not given choices in this life as to what you'll accept and what you won't. You have to deal with the cards you're dealt however you can. When you're faced with a situation, you have to meet it the best way you know how. It's easy to say you wouldn't take your spouse back, but until it happens to you, you don't really know how you'll react.

"If someone had told me I would have to live through this, I would have told them they were crazy. But then, you don't know your own strength until it's tested.

"I know there are a lot of people who would *never* take their spouses back after an affair. *But there are a lot more who would.* I know, because I've listened to their stories and read their letters. I wanted those people to know there was a place to go for help and support to get over the emotionally damaging effects of adultery. WESOM was the place to heal the wounds and the marriages.

"I think it's better to have two people who love each other together, and perhaps working through some tough times after an affair, than to see two people who love each other split up. What do you have then? They're both in pain, and the family is broken up.

"But every couple has to do what's right for *them*. For those who wanted to stay married and try to work through their grief and the pain in order to heal themselves and their marriages, WESOM was the place where they could learn how to do both. I just wanted people to know that there was finally help available from people who had already gone through it."

Despite being alternately lauded and lampooned by the audience, Liz held her ground. It was a sign of her new strength, and her growth not only as a woman but as a person.

The original chapter of WESOM that Dick and Liz founded grew so much that Dick's office could no longer accommodate all the members. Liz rented space in a church in order to accommodate all the people who needed the group. A dollar a week (voluntary) was collected for coffee and soft drinks, and the balance was put in WESOM's treasury. The Brzeczeks have never made money from WESOM and in fact spent their own funds in order to get the group off the ground.

The group changed in other ways. They now used two books as guides for the meeting: *The 12 Steps for Everyone*, by Grateful Members[1], and *A Day at a Time*[2], published by CompCare Publications.

Two additional chapters of WESOM are now in the planning stages.

Today, Dick and Liz are committed to WESOM and to helping other couples and individuals endure and survive the emotional pain of adultery. More important, they are totally committed to each other.

Dick's practice is growing, and he now has several attorneys working for him. The only effect the trial had on his practice was to increase the number of clients he represents.

After living in Chicago all their lives, the Brzeczeks have just moved to an exclusive North Shore suburb in Lake County, away from Chicago and Cook County politics.

Liz is still working for Dick as his office manager, but a great deal of her time is spent with people from WESOM. It's not unusual for her to receive a call in the middle of the night and spend hours on the phone counseling someone. For her, it's a labor of love.

The Brzeczek children, Natalie, Mark, Kevin, and Holly, are now young adults. Natalie, who at one time thought she would never marry because of her parents' problems, met a young man while vacationing in

Mexico, and in June 1988 she became Mrs. Michael Loria. Having graduated from college as a business major, Natalie now has an executive position.

Mark and his father have totally repaired their relationship. Today, they are closer than ever. Mark is currently enrolled in college and plans to marry after he graduates.

Kevin, the Brzeczeks' youngest son, is also away at college and plans to become an attorney.

Holly just turned eighteen and is ready to start college. The Brzeczeks' youngest child, who at one time lay griefstricken across pictures of her mother and father, has little memory of those horrible years.

All four children seem to have recovered totally from the trauma that tore apart their family. To see the children with their father, to see the obvious love and devotion between them, you would never know that at one time this was a family torn in two.

Rita and her husband, Joe, are still happily married and very close to Dick and Liz. Rita continues to idolize her brother, perhaps now more than ever.

Dick's mother recovered fully from her heart attack. She still attends Mass every morning to light a candle and give thanks for restoring her son to sanity and to his family. Dick's parents will soon be celebrating fifty years of marriage.

Liz's parents also recently celebrated their golden wedding anniversary. They are as close to Dick now as ever before. To them, he is their son. They are incredibly proud of Liz for having the courage to go against tremendous odds in order to save her marriage.

Dick and Liz are currently making plans to celebrate their twenty-fifth wedding anniversary. They travel several months a year, depending on Dick's schedule.

Dick is finally at peace with himself and the world around him. He has had no further problems with depression or with alcohol. Dick had his day in the spotlight and is quite happy now to remain in the background. All he wants is to be left alone to enjoy the rest of his life with the most important person in his life—his wife.

"I never realized how much Liz meant to me until I almost lost her. I intend to spend the rest of my life making Liz as happy as she's made me."

Dick claims he will never again run for public office or enter the political arena, but there are those who feel he has too much to offer not to contribute and become involved in some capacity. Despite his personal tragedy, Dick still enjoys a reputation as a brilliant legal mind and continues to be in demand as a lecturer and teacher at numerous seminars and universities across the country.

As for Liz, she's truly come into her own. The experience she went through taught her to be strong and independent. She is not the same woman Dick married, and they both happily admit it.

"The difference now," she said with a smile, "is that I don't need Dick. But I *want* him. What could be better? He's a different person, as I am. Dick is no longer arrogant, nor does he have that air of superiority I found so intimidating. Dick is warm and caring. I love the new Dick Brzeczek. Every day I'm grateful for the second chance God gave us.

"That morning in church, when I thought God had deserted me, I felt so alone. But now I know that by questioning my faith, God was giving me the strength for all that was to come. I have never lost the inner peace and joy I felt that morning in church and I don't think I ever will.

"For so long I didn't understand why God had given me such pain to endure, such a heavy burden to carry. I didn't understand what I had done to warrant this; but it wasn't something I had done, *but something I had yet to do. You see, WESOM wasn't my idea, it was God's.*"

APPENDIX

Reference Notes

Chapter 2

1 **The Twelve Steps of Alcoholics Anonymous***

1. We admitted we were powerless over alcohol—that our lives had become unmanageable.
2. Came to believe that a Power greater than ourselves could restore us to sanity.
3. Made a decision to turn our will and our lives over to the care of God *as we understood Him.*
4. Made a searching and fearless moral inventory of ourselves.
5. Admitted to God, to ourselves, and to another human being the exact nature of our wrongs.
6. Were entirely ready to have God remove all these defects of character.
7. Humbly asked Him to remove our shortcomings.
8. Made a list of all persons we had harmed, and became willing to make amends to them all.
9. Made direct amends to such people whenever possible, except when to do so would injure them or others.
10. Continued to take personal inventory and when we were wrong promptly admitted it.
11. Sought through prayer and meditation to improve our conscious contact with God *as we understood Him,* praying only for knowledge of His will for us and the power to carry that out.
12. Having had a spiritual awakening as a result of these steps, we tried to carry this message to alcoholics, and to practice these principles in all our affairs.

*The Twelve Steps are taken from *Alcoholics Anonymous*, third edition (1976), pp. 59–60. Published by Alcoholics Anonymous World Services, Inc. Reprinted with permission.

Chapter 7

1 *Love Must Be Tough—New Hope for Families in Crisis*, by Dr. James C. Dobson. Published by Word Books, Waco, Texas, 1983. Letter on pp. 67–68. Reprinted with permission.

Chapter 8

1 *Depressive and Manic Depressive Association,* 222 South Riverside Plaza, Suite 2812, Chicago, IL 60606. 312–993–0066. The national office of DMDA is also located in Chicago: The National Depressive and Manic Depressive Association, P. O. Box 3395, Merchandise Mart, Chicago, IL 60654. 312-939-2442.

Chapter 17

1 *State of Illinois, County of Cook, S. S.,* in the Circuit Court of Cook County, County Department—Criminal Division: The People of the State of Illinois vs. Richard Brzeczek Criminal Indictment No. 86-3438, Charge: Theft.

Report of proceedings ("in camera") of the hearing before the Honorable Robert V. Boharic, on the 13th day of February 1987.

Chapter 18

1 *The Twelve Steps for Everyone . . . Who Really Wants Them,* by Grateful Members, published by CompCare Publications, 1975.

2 *A Day at a Time,* published by CompCare Publications, 1976.

Recommended Reading

The Twelve Steps for Everyone . . . Who Really Wants Them
by Grateful Members
CompCare Publications
2415 Annapolis Lane, Suite 140
Minneapolis, Minnesota
55441
1-800-328-3330

A Day at a Time
CompCare Publications
2415 Annapolis Lane, Suite 140
Minneapolis, Minnesota
55441
1-800-328-3330

Love Must Be Tough
by Dr. James C. Dobson
Word Books, Incorporated
Waco, Texas

Insights for Today:
The Wisdom of the Proverbs
arranged by F. LaGard Smith
Harvest House Publishers
Eugene, Oregon 97402

Forgive and Forget—Healing the Hurts We Don't Deserve
by Lewis B. Smedes
Pocket Books
1230 Avenue of the Americas
New York, New York
10020

Back from Betrayal—Recovering from His Affairs
by Dr. Jennifer P. Schneider, M.D.
A Harper/Hazelden Book
Harper & Row Publishers
San Francisco, California

How to Break Your Addiction to a Person
by Howard M. Halpern, Ph.D.
Bantam Books,
666 Fifth Avenue
New York, New York
10103

Up from Depression
by Leonard Cammer, M.D.
Pocket Books
1230 Avenue of the Americas
New York, New York
10020

Out of the Shadows—Understanding Sexual Addiction
by Patrick J. Carnes, Ph.D.
CompCare Publications
2415 Annapolis Lane
Minneapolis, Minnesota
55441

Self-Help Groups

WESOM, Inc.
Post Office Box #46312
Chicago, Illinois 60646
312-792-7034*

*This is a computerized answering service. Please leave a message and your telephone number, and your call will be returned.

Alcoholics Anonymous World Services, Inc.
General Services Office
468 Park Avenue
New York, New York 10016
1-800-252-6465*

Al-Anon Family Group Headquarters, Inc.
P. O. Box 862, Midtown Station
New York, New York 10018-0862
1-800-252-6465*

* This is a toll-free, twenty-four-hour hotline.

National Association for Children of Alcoholics
31706 Pacific Coast Highway
Laguna Beach, California 92677
714-499-3889

Depressive and Manic Depressive Association
Chicago Chapter
222 South Riverside Place
Suite 2812
Chicago, Illinois 60606
312-993-0066

The National Depressive and Manic Depressive Association National
Headquarters
P.O. box 3395
Merchandise Mart
Chicago, Illinois 60654
312-939-2442